THE
DAHLGREN
AFFAIR

Wake Island: The Heroic Gallant Fight

Hero of Bataan: The Story of General Jonathan M. Wainwright

The Last Battle Station: The Story of the USS Houston

The Maverick War: Chennault and the Flying Tigers

The Doolittle Raid

*Month of the Freezing Moon:
The Sand Creek Massacre, November 1864*

Over the Earth I Come: The Great Sioux Uprising of 1862

*Glory Enough for All: The Battle of the Crater:
A Novel of the Civil War*

*Quantrill's War: The Life and Times of
William Clarke Quantrill, 1837–1865*

THE DAHLGREN AFFAIR

Terror and Conspiracy in the Civil War

DUANE SCHULTZ

W. W. NORTON & COMPANY
New York · London

Copyright © 1998 by Duane Schultz

Printed in the United States of America

First Edition

For information about permission to reproduce selections from this book, write to
Permissions, W. W. Norton & Company, Inc., 500 Fifth Avenue, New York, NY 10110.

The text of this book is composed in Adobe Caslon
with the display set in Copperplate Gothic
Desktop composition by Gina Webster
Manufacturing by the Haddon Craftsmen, Inc.
Book Design by BTD/Mary A. Wirth

LIBRARY OF CONGRESS CATALOGING-IN-PUBLICATION DATA
Schultz, Duane P.
The Dahlgren Affair : terror and conspiracy in the Civil War / by Duane Schultz
p. cm.
Includes bibliographical references and index.
ISBN 0-393-04662-1
1. Kilpatrick-Dahlgren Raid, Va., 1864. I. Title
E476.27.S38   1998
973.7'36—dc21   98-11245
CIP

W. W. Norton & Company, Inc., 500 Fifth Avenue, New York, N.Y. 10110
http://www.wwnorton.com

W. W. Norton & Company Ltd., 10 Coptic Street, London CW1A 1PU

1 2 3 4 5 6 7 8 9 0

To Sydney Ellen
who continues to make everything better—
including this book

The war had changed, and something hard and cruel and vicious was coming to the surface, and [Dahlgren's] raid was a dark ominous symbol of it, with bitterness and hatred visible behind it and growing out of it.

—BRUCE CATTON

The blood boils with indignation in the veins of every officer and man as they read the account of [Dahlgren's] barbarous and inhuman plot.

—ROBERT E. LEE

C o n t e n t s

Acknowledgments   11

1. MANY ARE DEAD AND GONE   15
2. IT IS A PERILOUS TIME   24
3. IT IS A GREAT PLAN   33
4. THE TIME TO STRIKE   48
5. WHOLESALE MISERY AND DEATH   57
6. THE CHANCES ARE PRETTY HAZARDOUS   68
7. THE PALACE OF PLEASURE   83
8. HOW LITTLE WE KNOW WHO WILL GO NEXT   91
9. DON'T KNOW YET WHERE WE ARE TO GO   101
10. A DARKNESS THAT COULD BE FELT   108
11. WE ARE GOING ON   117
12. THE CHASE WAS A NIGHTMARE   127
13. RETURN THEIR FIRE!   136
14. LIKE A PARCEL OF OLD WOMEN   144
15. ULRIC THE HUN   152

16. AN EXPRESSION OF AGONY   171

17. A PRETTY UGLY PIECE OF BUSINESS   180

18. FULL AND BITTER TEARS   190

19. ON THE EVE OF GREAT EVENTS   202

20. A VERY RISKY VENTURE   213

21. BITTER, BITTER DEFEAT   224

22. DESPERATE MEASURES: WHO WROTE THE DAHLGREN

    PAPERS?   239

23. THE DAHLGREN AFFAIR: AFTERMATH   258

    Chapter Notes   273

    Bibliography   283

    Index   289

Acknowledgments

It is a pleasure to acknowledge the assistance of the dedicated librarians, archivists, and photo researchers with whom I was fortunate to work. I am grateful to the reference and interlibrary loan staffs at the Clearwater, Florida, Public Library, especially Candace McDaniel, for cheerfully filling my requests, many of which were for materials long out of print. Also helpful were the staffs of the Prints and Photographs Division of the Library of Congress, the Still Picture Branch of the National Archives, and Archival Research International of Washington, D.C. In addition, I wish to thank Teresa Roane of The Valentine: The Museum of the Life and History of Richmond; Lisa Carter, the audiovisual archivist at the Margaret I. King Library of the University of Kentucky; Sharon Bidwell, the reference librarian for the *Courier-Journal* of Louisville, Kentucky; and Trace Kirkwood and James Holmberg of The Filson Club Historical Society, Louisville, Kentucky. Finally, I would like to record my gratitude to Starling Lawrence, the editor-in-chief of W. W. Norton & Company, for sharing his ideas and challenging me to consider most carefully the issues raised by the Dahlgren affair.

THE
DAHLGREN
AFFAIR

MANY ARE DEAD
AND GONE

January 1864: The country divided began its third cruel year of civil war. In the freezing months of an awful winter, two great armies—the Army of the Potomac and the Army of Northern Virginia, under George Meade and Robert E. Lee—faced each other warily on opposite banks of Virginia's Rapidan River. It was a time of restoring and repairing, equipping and recruiting, but mostly, as for all armies in all wars, it was a time of waiting. In a few months, spring would come, and with it the inevitable round of renewed campaigns and clashes for what everyone knew surely would be, *had to be*, the final year of war.

It was quiet in the camps along the Rapidan. The concerns of the soldiers were, as always, private, personal, and narrow: keeping dry and warm that winter, keeping alive the rest of the year. And by 1864, staying alive and surviving the war seemed less and less likely. Young veteran soldiers of Vicksburg, Gettysburg, Fredericksburg, and all those other towns suddenly become dreaded household words would shake their heads wearily, their eyes staring, their faces bearing the vacant gaze of their stricken generation, stamping their feet to keep warm while waiting for springtime.

A Union lieutenant captured the mood in his diary on the first day of the new year.

> Who would have dreamed in '61 that those of us who started out to finish the war in the course of three month's service, would still be in the fields three years afterwards, with the task still unaccomplished? . . .
>
> Over one half of our original number has died of wounds, of disease, of fatigue and exposure, or perhaps resigned, unable to stand the constant shock of arms. This old state of Virginia has become a vast cemetery, in which thousands of once bright and ambitious men belonging to the army of the Potomac now lie scattered in its shady nooks or somber woods, unmarked except by their bleaching bones and the accumulation of various parts of their accoutrements, which still lay rusting and rotting about them. Amongst the survivors, the excitement and enthusiasm of early days has long since passed away.

The soldiers didn't sing so much anymore, not in North or South. Seldom heard were the rousing songs of victory—"Cheer, Boys, Cheer" or "Battle Cry of Freedom." Most of the voices had fallen silent back in '62 and '63. For the men who reached the winter of 1864, the songs were of weariness and death. The popular new ballad "Tenting Tonight," written by a New Hampshire boy, caught the forlorn spirit: "We are tired of war on the old camp ground. Many are dead and gone. . . ."

In the parlors of northern homes, other tunes were hummed by tearful mothers, wives, and sweethearts, songs with melancholy titles that told of the sorrows of a war gone on too long, songs telling of too much pain and too much dying. "When This Cruel War Is Over," "Bear This Gently to My Mother," "Tell Me, Is My Father Coming Back?," "The Vacant Chair."

Equally sad laments echoed in the parlors of southern homes. Most people realized it was the beginning of the end for the Confederacy; most knew their cause was doomed. Mary Chesnut, the wife of a southern senator, pleaded in her diary on the first day of the new year: "God help my country."

The Confederacy had been drained of almost everything needed to wage war: horses, ammunition, weapons, food, medicine, iron, rolling stock. Most of Lee's soldiers camped at the Rapidan shivered without blankets, coats, or shoes to protect them from the freezing temperatures, the ice and snow. They had little to eat, usually no more to fill their bellies each day than a few ounces of rancid fatback and meal, and, if they were lucky, a cup of ersatz coffee brewed from ground, roasted acorns.

Horses went hungry, too, reduced to gnawing the bark from trees. "Unless there is a change," General Lee wrote to the Secretary of War, "I fear the army cannot be kept together."

In fact, Lee's army was not holding together very well that winter. Desertions were running dangerously high as men simply gave up and went home. They saw no point to it anymore, to the cold, the hunger, the killing. By spring, Lee would be left with no more than sixty-five thousand troops to carry on the war. Worse, the Union had all but stopped exchanging prisoners on a one-to-one basis. The North could afford to lose the services of the thousands of its men held in Confederate prison camps, but the Confederacy could not. In northern prison camps the Union held as many rebel troops as could now be counted in all the armies of the South.

Southern manpower had been exhausted. As Ulysses S. Grant noted, the South was reduced to robbing the cradle and the grave, taking conscripts as young as seventeen and as old as fifty. Even then, recruiters had a hard time filling their quotas. Many conscription officers were shot at and chased away when they visited homes and farms seeking men for the army. Prospects seemed dismal, and even the most optimistic of Confederate leaders had become discouraged.

The idea of suing for peace, a treasonous notion only a year before, was being discussed openly in southern newspapers, particularly in Georgia and North Carolina. Some politicians, including Alexander Stephens, the Confederate vice-president, were openly sympathetic to the idea of a negotiated peace. But Jefferson Davis would not consider it and so the war continued, despite growing resentment against his decision.

Never especially popular, Davis was becoming the target of

increasingly bitter attacks, most notably when he pressured the Confederate congress in February to suspend the writ of *habeas corpus*. Many people believed Davis had gone too far, clothing himself in dictatorial powers. Citizens had been dragged from their homes in the middle of the night, under arrest for criticizing the government, and held in jail without benefit of trial. Journalists clamored for Davis's impeachment. Prominent voices throughout the South maligned him with contempt, calling him an "imbecile President," a "miserable, stupid, one-eyed, dyspeptic, arrogant tyrant."

They saw clearly, much more so than Davis could yet bring himself to admit, that the South could lose the war that year. The Confederacy and its people were being ground to pieces. Little but continued death and destruction, and inevitable defeat, remained.

Those bitterly cold months of the winter of 1864 were desperate for the Confederacy, a time clearly calling for desperate measures. And so it happened that a desperate and devious measure was conceived and set in motion to save the Confederate States of America.

In the North, the situation was not much better. Although not faced with the equipment and food shortages that plagued the Confederacy, the North had a manpower problem and, more significantly, a morale problem. The Union was no longer united in support of the war. Serious opposition was mounting, particularly in the northwest states: Ohio, Iowa, Indiana, Illinois, and Michigan. Thousands of antiwar dissidents joined groups and societies that collectively came to be known as Copperheads. That label, a deliberate reference to the poisonous snake, had been bestowed by their antagonists, those who desired to continue the war.

The Copperheads themselves quickly adopted the name, proudly wearing lapel badges displaying the Goddess of Liberty as depicted on the Copperhead penny. Copperhead groups encompassed the radical wing of the Democratic party (the so-called Peace Democrats) and included, among others, the Knights of the Golden Circle, the Sons of Liberty, and the Order of the American Knights.

Replete with secret symbols and handshakes, passwords and rites of entry, these societies were more than political clubs. Not content to rail against the war, they opted for action, openly enlisting troops for the Confederacy, burning government buildings and military warehouses, torching stores, ransacking the homes of Union soldiers and supporters, and bootlegging guns to Missouri for southern guerrillas.

By the winter of 1864, with victory not yet in sight for the North and even Republican loyalists weary of the fighting, the Peace Democrats had grown more violent and extremist, prepared to consider operations on a grander scale. In the halls of the Capitol in Washington, in newspaper articles, and in rallies in the streets, the Copperheads attempted to enlist the support of the people, calling for new leadership, and, most disturbing to President Abraham Lincoln, for recognition of Confederate independence. Had the president sent thousands to die in vain? Would the heightened emotions of a political campaign render permanent this division of the nation? Had the carnage been for nothing?

Volunteering for the army had come to a virtual standstill. Huge numbers of men were approaching the end of their three-year enlistment. In a risky move for an election year, Lincoln issued a draft call for five hundred thousand men. Just the year before, New York City had seen bloody rioting against the draft. Protest groups had sprung up. Underground societies were formed actively and openly to discourage enlistments, to foment resistance against the draft. Their numbers flourished, their members brazenly threatening violence against the government. Would Union troops again be called on to fire on their own people to enforce the latest draft call and restore order?

Horace Greeley, the influential editor of the *New York Tribune*, wrote directly to the president to echo the thoughts of his readers. "Our bleeding, bankrupt, almost dying country longs for peace—shudders at the prospect of fresh conscriptions, of further wholesale devastations, and of new rivers of human blood."

Lincoln took harsh measures against what he viewed as treasonous thoughts and deeds. The writ of *habeas corpus* was suspended, and people were locked away in military prisons for urging resistance to the war. Secret agents of the government stalked and listened, ready to arrest on the slightest suspicion. To criticize the government was to court imprisonment.

This was what happened to Clement Vallandigham, the chief spokesman for the antiwar Copperhead movement. This former congressman from Ohio was arrested by soldiers who broke down the door of his home in the middle of the night and dragged him away at gunpoint. Put on trial as a civilian before a military tribunal, Vallandigham was found guilty of antiwar activities and sentenced to a prison term. His family was not told where he was.

It was illegal, of course. All the man had done was exercise his First Amendment right to speak out against the war. But he was only one of hundreds locked away during this time, many without formally being charged. Protests erupted throughout the North against Vallandigham's arrest, but Lincoln would not be swayed. "Must I shoot a simple-minded soldier boy who deserts," he asked, "while I must not touch the hair of a wily agitator who induced him to desert?"

Vallandigham was eventually released from prison and exiled to the South, but the damage was done. The president's image was now that of a tyrant, a dictator, denying American citizens their basic rights of free speech and a speedy and open trial in civilian court.

Another problem for the Lincoln administration that winter was the highly publicized plight of up to twelve thousand northern soldiers being held in Richmond's prisons. Reports of starvation, disease, and death appeared daily in the newspapers. Banner headlines alerted Northerners to the horrors—men going nearly two weeks without meat, five hundred deaths in a single month, the twelve thousand soldiers packed in quarters designed for three thousand.

Parents of captives, newspaper editors, politicians, all raised cries of protest against the inhumane treatment of their men and brought their protests in person and in letters directly to the desk of the president. After all, *he* was responsible for the conduct of the war. Strident demands were issued: Lincoln had to do something about the prisoners in Richmond—and do it soon.

To the president of the United States, the times seemed as hopeless as they were for the president of the Confederacy. It was possible Lincoln could lose the war that year, not on the battlefield but in the ballot box, unless he answered his critics and took some action to free the prisoners. And so in Washington, as in Richmond, the winter of 1864 was a desperate time calling for desperate measures.

While the people of North and South grew increasingly angry and bitter, and their armies watched and waited for spring and a resumption of the fighting, a series of events—isolated, unrelated, and little known—occurred in Richmond, in Washington, and along the Rapidan River. Each incident by itself was no more than a speck, all but invisible, on the huge canvas of the war. But together they would form a picture so contrary to the war as it had been fought, understood, and romanticized that it would shake each nation to its core.

Near Winchester, Virginia, on the bank of Opequan Creek, a twenty-one-year-old Union lieutenant deserted to the Confederacy. Paroled under the oath of allegiance to the Confederate States of America, the deserter moved in with the family of the man to whom he had surrendered and soon became like a surrogate son to the man's mother.

A few things puzzled the family, however. The young man refused to share a room. At parties, he always declined to dance, nor would he accept a challenge to run a foot race. But those quirks were overlooked in view of the Yankee's considerable charm and wit. One day he obtained an official pass to visit Richmond to inspect the city's fortifications. He never returned. The family next saw him two months later, when authorities in Richmond put his corpse on public display.

A twenty-three-year-old Confederate captain, fresh from engineering the escape from a Yankee prison of the celebrated General John Hunt Morgan, presented a bold plan to Jefferson Davis. It was an audacious, almost desperate plan, befitting its designer, considered one of the most dangerous men in the Confederacy.

The proposal involved striking at the heart of the enemy by arranging to release the Confederate soldiers being held in northern prisons. The soldiers and their Copperhead supporters would spread terror and revolution throughout the North by setting ablaze New York, Chicago, and other major cities, and by assassinating political leaders. This was not the first time such an idea had been offered to

Davis, but circumstances had changed. Now Davis listened with more interest and told the young captain to wait in readiness; he would take the plan under advisement.

In Richmond's fashionable Church Hill neighborhood, not far from the Confederate White House, a forty-six-year-old woman was engaged in the dangerous game of espionage. In her old family mansion, secret passageways and hidden rooms had been built to hide couriers heading for the Union lines. Neighbors called her Crazy Bet, but her strange, seemingly demented behavior was only a ruse that enabled her to avoid arousing the suspicion of the Confederacy's intelligence agents.

The courier she sent north in January had memorized the latest information she had acquired on Richmond's defenses. And she had one more piece of news. Crazy Bet had learned that the city's Union prisoners would soon be moved south to someplace in Georgia, a new prison camp called Andersonville.

Beneath Richmond's Libby Prison, a group of fifteen captives led by a thirty-three-year-old Union colonel from Pennsylvania toiled for forty-two nights using knives, spoons, and their bare hands to scratch their way through the earth to a point beyond the prison walls. When their sixty-five-foot tunnel was completed in February, one hundred nine Union officers crawled away from Libby Prison, eager to relate their first-hand accounts of the horrible conditions.

In a large frame house near Brandy Station, close by the Rapidan River, an ambitious twenty-eight-year-old Union brigadier general, notorious for his immoralities, had worked out a scheme to release the Union prisoners being held in Richmond. He had dreams of becoming president of the United States after the war; the promotion to major general, which his successful raid on Richmond's prisons would surely bring, would be an important step along the way. Through his considerable political connections, he bypassed his superiors in the army chain of command and made certain that Abraham Lincoln himself knew of his plan to free the prisoners.

The bizarre clash of these seemingly independent incidents would bring death, of course, which is standard in war, along with charges and countercharges, righteous indignation, and fury. The ultimate result would be a new kind of war involving terror and conspiracy. The *Richmond Examiner* would write, when the affair was over, that the conflict had become "a war of extermination, of indiscriminate slaughter and plunder on the part of our enemies." Both sides would call for reprisals; they would soon be forthcoming.

All from a few sheets of paper, the Dahlgren papers, found on a muddy trail. More than a century later, Bruce Catton, the prominent Civil War historian, offered the following judgment. Because of the Dahlgren papers, he wrote, "in both North and South there was fury, and the propagandists righteously sowed the wind, and the war between the sections, which once seemed almost like a kind of tournament, had at last hardened into the pattern of total war."

IT IS A
PERILOUS TIME

January and February of 1864 were unusually cold in northern Virginia. In Richmond, the first thing the residents did each morning was break the ice in their wash basins. Even in opulent Ballard House, where the visiting generals Jeb Stuart and John Hunt Morgan had suites, ink froze in the inkwells and the gas lamps would not work because of the intense cold. No one could remember so frigid a winter.

While the officers shivered in Richmond, the private soldiers on picket duty in the field nearly froze. And for those who became careless and fell asleep during the night, death was the result. Private Thaddeus Walker was too conscientious to fall asleep on guard duty or to let his mind wander too far. But on one night in mid-January he would have given everything he owned—which wasn't all that much—to be resting in his own warm, quilt-topped bed, back in his family's house on the outskirts of Richmond.

Walker stood guard in a thick clump of trees and bushes on the Opequan Creek's southern bank, near Winchester, north and west of the main armies that were camped along the Rapidan River. The first light of dawn was beginning to streak the sky—his relief would soon appear—when he heard someone call to him from the underbrush, only a short, heart-stopping distance away.

Although Walker had worn the Confederate uniform for a full two years, he was only seventeen, and at that moment he was badly frightened. He had never met the enemy in combat, never been shot at, never "seen the elephant," as old soldiers described their first time in action. Young Walker had spent most of his service in the president's guard in Richmond, reasonably safe, sheltered, and well fed.

Standing as straight and determined as he could, rifle at the ready, Walker concentrated on the spot where the voice was coming from. Suddenly the bushes shook, then parted, and a man emerged and started toward him. He wore a mixed uniform of blue and gray and appeared to be about twenty-three years old. His hands were high in the air, and he waved a white flag over his head. Walker raised his rifle the way he had been taught, took careful aim, and swallowed hard to keep the fear out of his voice. Ordering the stranger to halt ten feet away, Walker demanded to know who he was and what he wanted.

The man declared that he was Thomas Murray, a lieutenant in a Union cavalry outfit and that he wanted to desert to the Confederate States of America. He was tired of the war, tired of risking his life for slaves, tired of all the killing. He told Walker he wanted to go to Richmond and help the South end the war.

When Walker's relief arrived, he led his prisoner back to the headquarters of the Second Maryland Cavalry, where Murray was questioned briefly by a major who did not seem very interested in him. The major knew Walker was about to go on leave and had to pass through Staunton on the way home, so he suggested that Walker escort Murray to the provost marshal there. Let *him* decide what to do about the deserter.

Walker and his prisoner shared a meager breakfast of rancid bacon, corn pone, and coffee brewed from acorns. Walker assured the lieutenant that this was a good meal compared with some he had eaten. The two men boarded an army stagecoach, and by the time they reached Staunton several hours later, Walker was enthralled by the charming and congenial Yankee. Indeed, Walker hardly thought of him as a prisoner, but rather as an old friend. Thomas Murray was obviously well read and well educated and had proved to be much more pleasant company than Walker's fellow soldiers, many of whom could not read or write.

Walker took Murray to the provost marshal and listened while Murray repeated his story of his disaffection with the war and his plan to go to Richmond. The provost marshal granted Murray an immediate parole and made him swear an oath of allegiance to the Confederacy. That done, and the proper papers signed, Murray was free.

Walker and Murray stayed in Staunton long enough to shop for new clothes, then boarded the train for Richmond. Reluctant to part with his new friend, young Walker invited Murray to his parents' home on Topopotomoy Creek, near Old Church, about sixteen miles from the capital city. They arrived at the old Virginia farmhouse the following day, where the former Yankee officer was warmly greeted by the Walker family.

In little time, Thomas Murray enchanted them all—Walker's father, mother, and three younger brothers. He was quickly added to the guest list for local parties and dances, where his polished manners and brilliant conversation ensured his popularity.

A few things puzzled Thad Walker. Why did Murray refuse to share his bedroom when otherwise he was so companionable? Why wouldn't he accept the challenge to a foot race? All young men enjoyed the sport. And why did he decline to dance with the willing belles? Pretty girls teased him, trying to wangle an invitation, but Murray would have none of it. Still, these little foibles were easy to overlook in view of Murray's charm and wit.

Not everyone was so enthralled. A woman on a neighboring farm sent Walker a note after meeting Murray at a party. She wanted Walker to know that she did not trust the Yankee and warned him not to be deceived. Walker dismissed her misgivings as foolish talk, not to be taken seriously. There was no reason not to trust Thomas Murray— no reason at all.

During his stay with the Walkers, Murray twice visited Richmond, insisting to a disappointed Thad Walker that he had to go alone. On his first trip, Murray called on the Confederacy's provost marshal, the hated General John Henry Winder, who was responsible for security and intelligence operations.

The sixty-one-year-old Winder, a scion of a prominent Maryland family and a West Point graduate, had near-dictatorial powers over the city. He was known to drink heavily, take bribes, and act with unreserved cruelty toward anyone not from his home state. His agents, rogues and cutthroats, spread terror among friend and foe as they pursued spies and deserters, enforced curfews, and seized profiteers. In the overly diligent performance of their duties, they intimidated and arrested many innocent citizens.

High public officials had accused Winder of selling passes for one hundred dollars, no questions asked. And when Murray left Winder's office, he had obtained just such a pass, enabling him to visit otherwise secure areas in Richmond and the vicinity, including military posts and defensive fortifications. Winder had opened the city to a Yankee deserter.

When Murray returned from Richmond and told Thad Walker what he had seen of Richmond's defenses, the young man was startled. Obviously, Murray had made good use of his time. He had rented a horse and ridden around the city's perimeter, stopping to chat with the soldiers on patrol or on guard duty whenever he had the chance. In the bars of the fashionable Ballard House and the Spottswood Hotel, he talked with officers, tobacco planters, contractors, even a southern senator. People were surprisingly and easily forthcoming with this charming fellow.

Murray had quickly learned how poorly Richmond was defended. Few regular troops were stationed in town or even nearby, only some field artillery batteries and a small cavalry outfit. The main defense consisted of some three thousand local militiamen—factory hands, clerks, retirees, war cripples, and anyone else who could carry a gun.

Impressive fortifications in the form of trenches and breastworks ringed the city and were particularly strong on the northern side, but only a handful of soldiers were available to man them. The nearest regular troops were two brigades of Wade Hampton's cavalry, sixty miles away near Fredericksburg. Together the brigades numbered only

719 men with horses fit for duty. The capital was clearly vulnerable to a surprise attack.

Murray was deeply shocked by how much Richmond had changed in the few years since he had been there before the war. Then, the city's population was fewer than forty thousand, but by 1864, it had swollen to one hundred forty thousand, altering its character and charm. Richmond was no longer the symbol of the gracious southern way of life. It seethed and roiled with every kind of vice and corruption.

Inflation was rampant, food and clothing were scarce—the ideal combination for a flourishing black market. Favoritism and bribery characterized much of the financing, equipping, and managing of the war. The streets were unsafe; murders, robberies, and assaults were commonplace. To combat the raging crime wave, Winder's police had become brutally oppressive.

Evidence of the war was widespread. It could be seen in the growing numbers of buildings and homes requisitioned for hospitals, in the cemeteries spreading over the neighboring hillsides, in the long lines of wounded arriving by train and ambulance and on foot. Daily casualty lists appeared in the newspapers. Tired, dispirited soldiers marched the streets. No one among the residents would forget the day when the remnants of Pickett's division passed through after Gettysburg.

Amid Richmond's crime, corruption, prostitution, and gambling, rumors raced like fire through a dry forest on a windy day. The story that Jefferson Davis had committed suicide spread with such force and speed that it was telegraphed throughout the North only a few days later. Every ship that slipped through the Union blockade carried reports of the Confederacy's long-awaited recognition by France and England. The poor, so it was said, did the fighting, while the rich, safe at home, reaped huge profits from their deals. Bitterness ran deep, not only among the lower classes but also among those whose incomes were once considered comfortable.

People on modest salaries, such as government clerks who earned one hundred twenty-five dollars a month, found it difficult to subsist. The cost of feeding a family had increased tenfold over the last four years, but wages had not kept pace. War Department clerk John B. Jones lamented the high cost of survival in his diary.

> Beef was held at $2.50 per pound in market to-day—and I got none. . . . An old pair of boots with large holes in them, sold to-day for $7.00—it cost $125 to foot a pair of boots. Flour sold to-day at $200 per barrel; butter $8 per pound; and meat from $2 to $4. This cannot continue long without a remedy. I have not tasted coffee or tea for more than a year.

Jones had lost twenty pounds on this meager diet, and he was not alone. Nor was Richmond the only place suffering these hardships. Such conditions were common throughout the Confederate states. In Salisbury, North Carolina, soldiers' wives rioted over the staggering food prices. In Raleigh, the state capital, the local newspapers challenged the government in Richmond to make peace with the Union at any price, even surrender. The alternative was starvation.

Residents of Richmond recalled the bread riots of the previous April. For several days, there had been no bread to be found, not even the so-called secession bread, an awful mixture of rice and flour. At Eastertime, on April 2, several hundred angry women marched on the governor's mansion, armed with knives, axes, and hammers, demanding either bread or blood. When nobody emerged from the governor's house to talk to them, they headed for the grocery stores on nearby Cary Street, where the protest quickly became a riot. The women broke store windows and began looting, carrying away food, clothing, jewelry, and anything else they fancied from the shops but could no longer afford. "As fast as they got what they wanted they walked off with it," wrote a soldier who witnessed the scene. "It was the most horrible sight I ever saw."

Jefferson Davis, who lived just a few blocks away, heard the commotion and knew he had to take action. Standards were breaking down, first in North Carolina, now in Virginia. If he did not put a stop to such lawless behavior among the populace, it could spread throughout the South. Anarchy would rule. Why, only the previous night someone had broken into Davis's stables and stolen one of his favorite horses.

Davis quickly walked the few blocks to the Cary Street shopping district and found the city's mayor, Joseph Mayo, and a phalanx of armed policemen confronting the rioters. Mayo told the women that if they did not disperse within five minutes, he would order his men to open fire. The women stood their ground, shouting for bread.

Jefferson Davis climbed atop a wagon and waved his arms, trying to calm the protesters, pleading with them for quiet. Eventually, people recognized him and stopped yelling, waiting and watching him expectantly. In a quiet, firm voice, wrote a biographer, Davis "chided them for crying that they were after bread, when he saw in their hands jewelry and fabrics. However just their cause, they would disgrace it and their city by becoming mere plunderers. He promised that food would be given them if only they would disperse."

No one moved. The women stood silent, implacable, staring at the president. Davis took out his pocket watch and repeated the mayor's threat: If they did not leave in five minutes, the police would be ordered to shoot. "We do not desire to injure anyone," Davis told them, "but this lawlessness must stop." Slowly, the protesters dispersed, but if not for Davis's intervention and his promise of food, the Confederacy might have begun to collapse from within.

Jefferson Davis may have saved the Confederacy that day, but he worried about the repercussions. If news of the bread riot became known, it might touch off similar demonstrations elsewhere. He ordered the secretary of war to censor any telegraph messages dealing with the incident. He also requested that editors of the Richmond newspapers suppress the story, but they refused.

Many journalists believed Davis was going too far in trying to manage the news. This incident, coupled with his suspension of *habeas corpus*, led to public concern about his assumption of too much authority, even dictatorial powers. John Jones wrote in his diary his worry that the president would soon institute martial law. But Jones closed his diary entry with a comment that revealed his most pressing concern: He had no meat for dinner the next day. Freedom was all well and good, but it didn't fill your belly or feed your children. Of what concern were civil rights to those without bread?

Not all of Richmond's citizens were suffering such deprivations. For the wealthy and well connected, the winter social season, with its entertainments and formal dinners, continued relatively unchanged.

There were glamorous balls, afternoon teas, lavish receptions. One Christmas menu featured oyster soup, mutton, ham, boned turkey, wild duck, partridge, and plum pudding. Sauternes and burgundy were served with the meal, sherry and Madeira after.

The aristocratic Mary Chesnut gave a supper that January, serving her guests "wild turkey, wild ducks, partridges, oysters, and a bowl of apple toddy." When she attended a ladies' luncheon at the Confederate White House, given by First Lady Varina Davis, she recorded in her diary the "Gumbo, ducks and olives, suprême de volaille, chicken in jelly, oysters, lettuce salad, chocolate jelly cake, claret soup, champagne, &c, &c, &c."

All the rage among those who could still afford to eat well were "starvation parties." Friends were invited for music and dancing, but no food or drink were served. Thus, while many people in the South could barely feed their children, others found it chic to entertain without food; this so-called sacrifice allowed them to feel they were doing their bit for the war effort.

In some quarters of Richmond, even the rats and mice were starving. Cats and dogs were fast disappearing, too, some eaten by their owners. "My daughter's cat is staggering today for want of animal food," War Department clerk Jones wrote. "Sometimes I fancy I stagger myself."

Yet the winter of 1864 had its moments of glory. The gallant generals were in town. Sam Hood, adored by half the women of society, hobbled about on crutches. Every gathering seemed filled with cripples; soon there would be a generation of them. The magnificent Jeb Stuart was there, described by one Richmond beauty as "gilt-edged and with stars." Causing the greatest sensation was the raider John Hunt Morgan, fresh from his sensational jail break in Ohio. Before the year was out, Stuart and Morgan, the dash and valor of the Southern cause, would both be gone.

Thomas Murray, the Yankee deserter staying with the Walker family, saw the suffering and the glory, the misery and the glamour, on his two visits to Richmond. He shared with the Walkers his dismay at the deplorable state of the Confederacy's proud old city. What he witnessed persuaded him that the war had to end soon, for the good of both North and South, and he concluded that he had to do something to bring it about.

He had walked past Libby Prison, a former warehouse that now housed several thousand Union officers, and he had ridden to the banks of the James River to look across to Belle Isle, where some eight thousand enlisted men were imprisoned. He had shuddered and reaffirmed his personal vow that he would never allow himself to be captured.

Murray knew from the Richmond newspapers that the Belle Isle prisoners had gone eleven days without meat. Authorities feared the desperate men would stage a mass prison break and that the local inhabitants would join them, for they had no meat either. And if the people rioted, the police might not be willing to fire on them—on their friends and neighbors. Or if they did, the army might desert to come home and protect their families. "It is a perilous time," wrote John Jones in his diary.

Thomas Murray took to riding alone to the nearby town of Old Church, telling the Walkers he was going out to collect mail. The Walkers could not recall seeing any letters, though Murray claimed to have heard from his mother in Bel Air, Maryland. Following one of these rides, he was stricken with chills and a high fever. Confined to bed, he was nursed by Mrs. Walker as attentively as if he were her own son. He told her he felt fortunate in having two mothers. When he rallied a bit, he insisted on returning to the post office at Old Church. Thad Walker, concerned for his friend's fragile health, begged to accompany him, but Murray would not allow it. For the first time, harsh words passed between them.

Walker's anger soon gave way to sorrow, because Murray never returned. Although some family members would see Thomas Murray not many weeks later, Thaddeus Walker would not. He mourned the loss of the man he had loved as a brother, and even many years later recalled Murray with fondness.

Less than a week after Murray's disappearance, while Thad was still home on leave, a Yankee raiding party swept through the area, burning barns and running off livestock. Every farm in the area was devastated, except that of the Walkers.

C h a p t e r   3

IT IS A
GREAT PLAN

Another young man traveled to Richmond that winter to try to change history. Thomas Henry Hines, a twenty-three-year-old captain with General John Hunt Morgan's Kentucky raiders, had already made history as a secret agent, planning and executing raids throughout Kentucky, Indiana, and Ohio. By meeting and plotting with leaders of the Copperheads—the dissident Yankees acting to end the war—Hines had spent nearly as much time operating behind enemy lines in the North as he had in the South.

Hines was leading a charmed life of espionage, sabotage, and conspiracy. Union intelligence agents considered him the most important Confederate agent in their midst. But no matter how hard they tried, they had a difficult time running him to ground. And when, finally, they did succeed in capturing him, they could not keep him long.

He did not appear particularly menacing. It was said he bore an uncanny resemblance to that handsome actor, John Wilkes Booth. At five feet, nine inches, Hines was slender and weighed no more than 140 pounds. He had long black curly hair, a bushy mustache, and dark, slanting eyebrows. A friend described him as "modest, courteous and imperturbable, with a voice as soft as that of a refined woman." Hines appreciated fine horses, good music, and beautiful women, though there was only one woman he truly loved.

On the day after war began, Tom Hines organized a fifteen-man cavalry troop in Lexington, Kentucky. Not surprisingly, he was elected captain. He resigned from the faculty of the Masonic University, where he had been a classical scholar, and led his troop off to war. The unit served for a time as the scouts for General Albert Sidney Johnson's army and began learning their trade on bridge-burning missions and other raids behind enemy lines.

In January 1862, following the Confederate retreat from Kentucky into Tennessee, Hines quit the army on the grounds that he had enlisted to fight only in Kentucky. He stayed out of action until May, when he enlisted as a private in John Hunt Morgan's raiders.

Quickly promoted to captain in this outfit, Hines continued his undercover missions, slipping back and forth across the border into his beloved Kentucky. Sometimes he led troopers of Morgan's cavalry in guerrilla operations, destroying trains, burning bridges, tearing up railroad tracks, and stealing horses. On other occasions, Hines crossed the border alone, knowing he would be strung up as a spy if he was caught dressed in civilian clothes.

Often, Hines was able to make his way to the town of Brown's Lock, not far from Bowling Green, to spend a few hours, even a few minutes, with Miss Nancy Sproule, his childhood sweetheart. Brown's Lock was occupied by Yankee troops who knew Nancy Sproule was Tom Hines's special friend. Enlisting the aid of local spies and informers, the soldiers waited for Hines to show up. He was too nimble, however; they never succeeded in capturing him at the Sproule house. Nor could they catch him at his parents' house in Lexington, not even after they jailed his father or set informers to work when his mother fell ill, knowing Hines would try to see her. Several times reports reached Union headquarters that Hines was at his mother's bedside, but the man had friends everywhere. They warned him in time, and he was able to make his escape through a rear window.

Hines's journeys into Kentucky always had a hidden purpose. Often, he met secretly with Copperhead leaders and with others who professed dissatisfaction with the war's progress. He knew that the presence of so many dissidents behind Union lines could be useful to the Confederacy, so he cultivated these contacts, encouraging the men to take active measures against the North. Hines's goal was to meld these groups into a fighting force that would bring the war directly to the hated Yankees, not only in Kentucky, but in Ohio and Indiana as well.

In the summer of 1863, the Federals caught Tom Hines. He had joined a raid into Ohio and Indiana led by John Hunt Morgan. It was not Hines's fault that the plan went terribly wrong. Morgan and several hundred of his men were captured.

They were interned at a prisoner-of-war camp on Johnson's Island in Lake Erie, until Union military authorities decided that Morgan, Hines, and sixty-nine other officers should be treated as the criminals and thieves Union leaders believed them to be. Because the men had, on their aborted raid, seized considerable money and property, it was decreed that they be housed in a Columbus, Ohio, penitentiary with other criminals.

Some of Morgan's troopers remaining on Johnson's Island organized a memorable sendoff for the officers by taking revenge on the camp commander. The men, whose food rations were always inadequate, coveted the colonel's dog. On the day before Morgan, Hines, and the other officers were scheduled to be taken away, the dog disappeared. A poem was left in its place. Although ungrammatical, the message made its point.

> Dear Col.
> For want of bread
> Your dog is dead
> For want of meat
> Your dog is eat.

Conditions at the Columbus prison were harsh. The Confederate officers found the experience humiliating and degrading. The worst shame was when their long hair and beards were cut, making them look like ordinary convicts. Clearly, no honorable Confederate officer could tolerate such conditions. And so, thanks to the efforts of Tom Hines, they escaped. At least that was the story they all later told.

It began one day in November when Hines, brooding over what he considered rude treatment by the warden, a man named Merion, read about the escape of one Jean Valjean in *Les Misérables*, the new book that was all the rage. Thus inspired, Hines organized his fellow prisoners into tunnel-digging details, using a broken penknife and some cutlery stolen from the prison kitchen. Hines served as lookout, sitting on his cot reading Gibbon's *Decline and Fall of the Roman Empire*. The project took twenty days. When Hines, Morgan, and five other officers were ready to slip through the tunnel to freedom, Hines pinned a note to the straw-filled dummy he left on his bed.

> Castle Merion, Cell No. 20
> Commencement November 4, 1863,
> conclusion November 24, 1863.
> Number of hours for labor per day, five; tools, two small knives.
> *La Patience est amère mais son fruit est doux.* [Patience is sour but its fruit is sweet.] By order of my six honorable Confederates,
> T. H. Hines
> Captain, C. S. A.

Some historians later cast doubt on that version of the escape, arguing that the men bribed their way out. The tunnel story was devised, they say, to protect the identities of those who supplied the money and those who accepted the bribes.

Whatever the truth, Hines emerged as the indisputable hero of the escape. The tale enhanced his already considerable reputation in the South for boldness and courage, and it strengthened the credibility of the plan he would soon present to Jefferson Davis. Surely the man who had masterminded the sensational escape of the great raider John Hunt Morgan from a heavily guarded Yankee prison was a man to be listened to.

And if that story did not add sufficient luster to Hines's name, the truth about how he later saved Morgan's life made him a legend. While they were making their way south toward Confederate lines, first by train to Cincinnati, then by horseback and on foot, Hines allowed himself to be captured by a local militia patrol so Morgan could get away. Hines's sentence was immediate death by hanging.

His captors bound his hands behind his back, hoisted him onto his horse, and fashioned a noose from a length of stout rope. The loop was slipped over Hines's neck and he was asked if he had any last words. Most assuredly he did, a great many of them, and he used them so persuasively that he talked the soldiers out of hanging him.

Two days later, Hines escaped from the home guard's camp, only to be captured by a different Yankee patrol. He started talking fast as another noose was prepared. His words made the soldiers hesitate, and that was all Hines needed. He dug his spurs into his horse, making it rear violently, hooves flailing, sending his captors scurrying out of the way. In an instant, Thomas Henry Hines was gone; he would never be captured again.

In January, 1864, Tom Hines rode to Richmond, intending to tell Jefferson Davis about his plan to end the war—not through costly battles in the southern states but in the cities of the North instead. The plan would not involve Confederate troops but would use the Copperheads to instigate revolution from within. Hines's tactics included arson, terrorism, treachery, conspiracy, and assassination.

The idea of spreading social unrest throughout the North was not original with Hines. Early in the war, others had proposed similar operations. In 1862, some Confederate leaders recognized that dissension already existed in the Union, that a wedge was growing which, if properly applied, could split the North asunder.

They knew that from the onset of the war there had never been total unity of purpose in *all* of the United States. In the border states, for example—Delaware, Maryland, Kentucky, and Missouri, with their plantation system and slaves—Federal troops had been needed to keep them nominally within the Union fold. Yet those same states furnished whole regiments of soldiers to the South. Kentucky and

Missouri, though occupied by Union troops, formed governments that were formally admitted to the Confederacy.

In the powerful eastern states, dissidents found strong support among the immigrant population, particularly the Irish. Insecure in their newly adopted nation, these people feared that if the black slaves were freed, they would come North and compete for unskilled jobs. In Cincinnati, when Negro workers were brought in to replace striking Irish dock workers, the fired men rampaged through black neighborhoods. In Brooklyn, an Irish mob set fire to a tobacco warehouse where black women and children had jobs formerly held by Irish workers.

Of all the states remaining in the Union, the strongest support for the southern cause came from the northwest, particularly from Ohio, Indiana, and Illinois. It was among these people—southern in sympathy, hostile toward eastern and New England business interests, and conservative in their politics and personal lives—that organized antiwar sentiment flourished.

In many ways, it was an old, familiar story: conservative versus liberal, farmers versus big-city interests, and blatant racism. Those forces fueled the fires of opposition to the Union cause, providing an opportunity Hines hoped to exploit.

The most intense criticism of the war was coming from the Democratic party. Although divided into three factions—two pledged to winning the war, and the third, the so-called Peace Democrats, committed to a peaceful settlement with the South—the Democratic politicians joined in criticizing the way President Lincoln was conducting the war. Calling it "the Republican's War," or "Mister Lincoln's War," they charged that the president had refused to settle the war peaceably. Arguing that the union of states was based on consent, they concluded that forcing the South to remain in the Union against its will would bring about despotism.

Democrats also accused Republicans of establishing a military dictatorship. Indeed, many Americans, not only Democrats, were disturbed and offended by the censorship, the pressure on newspaper editors, the suspension of the writ of *habeas corpus*, and the arrest and military trial of civilian dissenters.

A number of newspaper editors had been fired or prosecuted by military commissions for publishing articles critical of the military's conduct of the war and for advising resistance against the draft. A Missouri state congressman was arrested for denouncing the president. As many as three hundred northern newspapers had articles suppressed, and estimates of arbitrary arrests for publicly opposing the war ran as high as thirty-eight thousand.

The greatest erosion of individual liberty was considered to be the military draft. The provision that allowed a man to purchase a substitute to serve for him was seen by many as undemocratic. Thus, there was ample reason for the frequently voiced charge that this was a rich man's war—and that the poor were doing the fighting and dying.

However, another issue was even more emotionally explosive than the draft, an issue that was exploited successfully by the Democratic opposition to the war. This was the Negro question. When people could sincerely proclaim that the war was being fought to preserve the Union, then the conflict enjoyed popular support, particularly in the eastern states. That sentiment changed with the Emancipation Proclamation of 1862. Suddenly, the purpose of the war was to free the slaves.

Many people in the northwestern states were not willing to die for the Negro cause, nor did they want black people living next door. In 1862, Illinois voters approved a state referendum by a one-hundred-thousand-vote majority, barring the entry of freed slaves into the state. In addition, more than a dozen northern cities saw antiblack riots.

These feelings against the reason for the war and the Lincoln administration led, inevitably, to the formation of the secret societies that came to be known collectively as the Copperheads. Captain Hines knew all about the Sons of Liberty, the Order of the American Knights, and the other Copperhead sects. In fact, he knew more about them than the federal Secret Service agents who had been tracking them for two years. Hines had been hidden in their homes. He knew the leaders and their families. He had worked with them to plan his and General Morgan's raids into the northwestern states.

Hines knew that the membership of all the Copperhead organizations together was now great enough—and angry enough—to conduct a major operation, one of such terrifying dimensions that it would force the Union to shift troops away from the fighting in the South. Whole divisions would have to be sent north to quell the uprising that the Copperheads, if properly led, could foment. Their action could paralyze the Union war effort, demoralize the people, and delay prosecution of the war—perhaps even end it.

As Hines neared Richmond in the first week of January 1864, he was determined to be the man to provide the leadership for a conspiracy of revolt in the states of the Northwest.

This was Hines's first visit to Richmond since the war began. He was disturbed not only by the living conditions in the capital city but also by the dissatisfaction with the war and the talk of peace. Having spent the war in the border states and the Northwest, where enthusiasm for the southern cause remained high, Hines was ill prepared for pessimism and defeatist views. It seemed to him that a plague had descended on Richmond, blighting everyone's lives, particularly that of Jefferson Davis, president of the Confederacy.

Hines was also unprepared for Davis's physical appearance. Gaunt and emaciated with a ghostly pallor and eyes dulled by the continued responsibilities and pressures of leading a nation in its third year of a terrible war, Davis looked old beyond his fifty-six years. He was nearly blind in his left eye and had lost his erect, soldierly bearing. He was plagued by almost constant pain, his health so greatly eroded that on many days he did not even go to his office. The doctors feared for his life.

His manner and temperament had hardened as well. Always difficult, prone to fits of temper and easily offended, he was now more irascible than ever. It was said that when he had been a U.S. senator, he had been involved in more threatened duels than any other man there. Although he no longer challenged his critics to duels, Davis had assumed an air of arrogance and haughtiness. And as the war dragged on, and the vitriolic personal attacks against him increased, he succumbed to defiance, belligerence, and even offensive behavior. It seemed somehow fitting that he kept a paperweight on his desk that looked like a lump of coal; it was really a bomb.

Coal bombs had been developed to be placed in Union coal piles behind the lines; when tossed into a fire with the coal, they would explode. The bomb on Davis's desk had probably been defused, but the president himself had not.

His temperament and health were made worse by his style of leadership. Davis felt the need to direct every detail of even the smallest bureau of his government; no issue was ever too small for his attention. "He passed his good right eye over seemingly every document—passes and transfers, promotions and assignments, complaints of every description, and even minor civil matters."

Even on Christmas Eve, Davis was hard at work in his cramped eighteen-by-twenty-four-foot office, its two tables smothered by papers, the walls hidden by maps, busying himself with promotions of mid-level officers. He was drowning himself in details.

He was sorely vexed at home as well. The executive mansion provided no refuge, no haven, from his tidal wave of troubles. One trusted slave—a personal servant for twenty years—ran off to the Yankees. Another fled after stealing a large sum of money from the house. A fire was deliberately set in the basement of the Confederate White House, presumably by some of Davis's slaves. Others were felled by the smallpox epidemic.

The Davis family, not being overly wealthy, experienced the shortages and inflated prices that had dimmed the lives of so many other Richmond residents. However, the Davises were expected to host lavish, formal receptions and dinners that cost more than they could afford. In the first month of the new year, Davis had to sell two slaves, bringing in $1,612. Two months later, he sold three horses for $7,330. The first lady, Varina, sold her carriage and team for $12,000; sympathetic friends bought them back and restored them to her. But these sums did not last long or buy much, so high was the rate of inflation. When they were not entertaining officially, the Davis family ate no better than the ordinary people of the city.

"Meals at the Executive Mansion took on an austere character," wrote Davis's biographer, "with breakfast often little more than hot ersatz coffee, some corn cakes or pones, bread, and a small dish of fat bacon fried crisp." Overall, Davis's "indifference to food increased as the war went on. Even little luxuries like a gift of real butter rarely tempted him, and often he simply forgot to eat entirely."

Davis knew he faced the prospect of a crushing defeat for the dying Confederacy. And in his office now was yet another person—this young captain from Kentucky—with yet another plan to win the war. He had long ago lost count of those who had schemed for an audience with him. Some were dedicated patriots, some foolish and naive, others blatantly unscrupulous, all offering a magic potion, a miraculous weapon, a decisive battle. Nothing had worked, and he was reluctant to hear another plan, but General John Hunt Morgan had been so persuasive that Davis agreed, as a favor, to see Captain Hines.

On the basis of what Morgan had told of Hines's character and exploits, the president was prepared to be impressed. But when the earnest young man sat down in the chair across from Davis's desk and quickly displayed his considerable charm, intelligence, wit, and gracious manners, Davis found himself studying the man and his plan more closely than he had intended. Davis was aware of the dissension in the North, of the activities of the Peace Democrats and Copperheads, primarily on the basis of second- or even third-hand intelligence reports. However, hearing Hines describe so passionately his personal dealings with Copperhead leaders, the virulent antiwar sentiments in the Northwest, and his ideas for turning those sentiments to the advantage of the Confederacy, Davis's attention became fully engaged.

Hines was proposing a series of raids and acts of sabotage to be carried out over a broad area, though concentrated in the Northwest, where Copperhead sentiment was strongest. He expected to create nothing less than a full-scale revolution. Working from bases in Canada, he would need only about a score of Confederate agents to organize the Copperheads into effective military units. The dissident Northerners were already well armed, with caches of weapons in readily accessible places, including a warehouse in the heart of New York City.

Armed bands of Copperheads led by Confederate agents, Hines explained, would first execute a series of surprise raids on northern prison camps to release thousands of southern troops. Supplied with arms, these freed men would foment chaos as they made their way south to rejoin the rebel armies.

At the same time, other units would set fires in hotels, warehouses, and shops in New York, Chicago, and other major cities. Rebel groups would attack banks and treasury buildings to steal vast sums of money for the Confederates' dwindling coffers. These planned operations ranged from the Northwest to the Maine coast. But the ultimate acts of terror called for the assassination of northern political leaders.

So persuasive was Hines and so detailed his plan that Jefferson Davis canceled his afternoon appointments to continue questioning Captain Hines, probing for oversights and omissions, weaknesses and errors. He found none. Hines's most telling argument was the effect such terror and destruction would have on Union troops stationed in the faraway states of the South.

Hines painted a graphic picture of the panic among the Union soldiers. Hearing that their home towns were in flames, their houses looted and destroyed, their families in danger, the Federals would desert in great numbers, rushing north to protect their loved ones. Men from areas not affected directly would fear their homes would be next, and the entire Union army would become demoralized. Any units still intact would have to be withdrawn from the front and sent home to restore order.

The conspiracy couldn't fail, Hines insisted. The Copperheads were armed and angry, eager to bring down the Lincoln administration and end the war. The cities of the North and the prison camps housing rebel soldiers were only lightly defended. Bring the war to their doorstep, Hines urged, and the people of the Union would clamor for peace.

And it was urgent to bring war to their doorstep before the coming election. Then Lincoln surely would lose. A victory for the Peace Democrats, Davis knew, would mean a negotiated settlement, a chance for the South to keep its independence.

Davis was clearly impressed with Hines and his plan for decisive operations in the Northwest, but this was not the first time such an idea had been presented to him. In 1862, Captain Emile Longuemare of Missouri had outlined a similar scheme. As Longuemare later described the meeting, Davis had jumped to his feet and begun pacing the room in his excitement.

"It is a great plan," Davis said. "In the west you have men, in the east only mannikins. You show me that this Conspiracy is engineered and led by good men. I want military men, men that are connected with West Point. Give me some, even if only one or two, and I will then have confidence in it."

However, Davis chose John Hunt Morgan (who was not a West Point graduate) to implement Longuemare's plan by invading Indiana. This major thrust deep into northern territory was expected to be the catalyst for a general uprising of the Copperhead groups. That was the idea—and it might have worked, except that Davis had picked the wrong man to lead the invasion, and the timing could not have been worse.

The operation got off to a good start. Morgan led three thousand men north in mid-June 1863, and by early July had reached Indiana, which lay open to conquest. The citizens were terrified, yet the governor's call for able-bodied men to defend the state produced only eleven hundred untrained recruits. There was little to stop Morgan's foray but the undisciplined actions of his own men.

Looting the homes and farms of both loyal Unionists and Copperheads, the Southerners failed to distinguish between friend and foe, quickly turning the former into the latter. Often, they deliberately sought out Copperhead property, figuring that if the dissidents supported the southern cause with their rhetoric, they should be eager to meet Southerners' demands for money and goods on the spot.

Morgan himself took seven hundred fifty dollars from one county's treasury and elsewhere was paid two thousand dollars for sparing a flour mill from the torch. His failure to maintain discipline haunted the expedition, eventually dooming it. Still, he forged ahead, mile after mile, day after tiring day. His column was strung out for miles, horses laden with loot, men asleep in their saddles, increasingly demoralized, pursued by the home-guard militia. No one came to their aid. Local Copperheads and Peace Democrats were unwilling to help men who were stealing from them. Deep inside Union territory, Morgan's raiders were on their own.

And so they headed back home through Ohio the way they had come, unaware that the Confederacy was then suffering its darkest week: the disastrous defeats at Gettysburg and Vicksburg, only three days apart. While loyal Northerners were wild with jubilation, the Copperheads fell silent, stunned by the major Union victories after so many losses. After all, what was the point of protesting against the government, now that it was obvious the war was all but won?

In Richmond, General Josiah Gorgas, the Confederacy's ordnance chief, recorded in his diary his thoughts on the impact of the Union victories. "Yesterday, we rode on the pinnacle of success—today absolute ruin seems to be our portion. The Confederacy totters to its destruction."

And in East Liverpool, Ohio, on July 25, John Hunt Morgan, Thomas Henry Hines, and many others of Morgan's raiders surrendered. The officers were led to jail to have their heads shaved, and the hopes of the Northwest conspiracy were drowned out by the joyous pealing of church bells celebrating imminent victory.

Seven months later the war still raged, and the casualty lists were growing longer. Copperheads and Peace Democrats were again talking of revolution against Lincoln's government. In the South, the prospect of defeat seemed ever more real, the criticisms against Davis's leadership more vociferous. And so, during that awful winter of 1864 when Davis learned of Hines's plan for a new Northwest conspiracy, to be led by secret agents instead of an invading army, he grasped at the hope the young captain was offering. Hines and his men would organize and lead the dissident groups, but the Copperheads themselves would do the fighting.

The federal election had been on Davis's mind for some time. He knew that the northern peace parties, though gaining strength, might not be victorious. Unless . . . Unless the horrors of the war that had ravaged the southern states of Virginia, Tennessee, and Mississippi were loosed on the prosperous, peaceful cities of the North. If the

Northerners felt the burden, not just in newspaper stories or letters from the front or even casualty lists, but bearing down on them with rifle and firebrand in the night, they would soon be more than weary of war; they would act to end it.

Davis sent Captain Hines to see his trusted colleagues, Secretary of War James A. Seddon and Secretary of State Judah P. Benjamin. Like Davis, Seddon was thin, weary, and chronically ill, his unkempt hair turning gray. Benjamin, a man of great intellect and affability, well educated and well read, was a round-faced sixty-year-old who looked no more than forty. Neither he nor Seddon was averse to clandestine warfare and the use of spies and saboteurs; indeed, each man ran a personal intelligence service for his own government department.

Both saw the usefulness of Hines's plan. They liked his tactics, his familiarity with conditions in the Northwest, and his personal contacts with the Copperhead leaders. If put into operation, the program would be the responsibility of Seddon's War Department. Over the next few weeks, he held more than a dozen meetings with Hines to refine the details.

Together, Davis, Seddon, and Benjamin concluded that the plot could well be the South's salvation. They knew that Robert E. Lee, military genius though he had proven himself to be, could only do so much with the limited supply of men and materiel left to him. At best, Lee was only delaying the inevitable.

General Lee had recognized the inevitability of defeat on the battlefield as early as June of 1863, a month before Gettysburg, when he urged Jefferson Davis to take advantage of the Peace Democrat movement in the North. "We should," Lee argued, "neglect no honorable means of dividing and weakening our enemies, that they may feel some of the difficulties experienced by ourselves. It seems to me that the most effectual mode of accomplishing this object . . . is to give all the encouragement we can, consistently with truth, to the rising peace party of the North."

And yet Davis, Seddon, and Benjamin hesitated to order the Hines plan into operation, not because they doubted its feasibility, but rather out of a concern for its effect on public opinion. How would Southerners react when they learned that their government was responsible for a covert campaign of terror and death, waged against civilians in their homes? This was a different kind of warfare, shockingly different. The people might not support it. Had not Lee himself written that the government should use any *honorable* means to ensure victory? Would not he, and many others, see this attempt as dishonorable?

Morgan's earlier discredited foray to incite revolution in the North at least had the appearance of a daring cavalry raid, a straightforward military operation. If it had succeeded, if the Copperheads had risen against their government, that action could have been considered a fortuitous side effect of a raid into a territory already seething with dissatisfaction. Killing civilians and burning northern cities would have been viewed as a natural outgrowth of that discontent.

But this new plan—if it succeeded and if the roles of Hines and his agents operating behind the lines became known—might well be considered underhanded and deceitful, dishonorable and ungentlemanly, a type of warfare Yankees might wage but to which civilized people would not stoop.

Then, too, there was the unanswerable question of how England and France would respond. The Confederate government had been diligently seeking recognition from those nations since the war began. Confederate diplomatic missions in London and Paris were actively at work. What would happen if the South took the war beyond the battlefield to the civilian populace?

And so Jefferson Davis waited, unable to decide whether the conspiracy, for all its probability of success, was worth the risk of outraging public opinion at home and abroad. Hines was informed that his plan was under consideration. He was ordered to hold himself in readiness and leave word with Secretary Seddon as to where he could be reached.

THE TIME TO STRIKE

Elizabeth Van Lew shuffled along the Richmond streets and up to the gates of Libby Prison, walking like a demented old woman, her head and neck twisted to one side, seemingly permanently deformed. She mumbled incoherently to herself and sometimes hummed tunes only she knew. Her old black clothes and bonnet were tattered and her hair unkempt, as if she had been fighting a strong wind.

No wonder her neighbors and the prison guards at Libby called her Crazy Bet behind her back. No wonder they laughed and made fun of her. That was just what she wanted them to do. Then they would never suspect that this deranged hag was the most successful Union spy in Richmond.

In 1864, Elizabeth Van Lew was forty-six years old and unmarried, referred to in polite society as an "old maid." But to her, this was another mark of her eccentricity at a time when, to most other women, marriage was the goal, focus, and definition of life.

It was not that she had been ineligible or undesirable when she was younger. Far from it. She had been an attractive, refined, and cultured member of Richmond's aristocracy. And she was wealthy, too.

The four-story Van Lew mansion, in which she had been born and reared and in which she would live all her life, stood on Church Hill, the city's most prominent vantage point. It was across the street from St. John's Church, in which Patrick Henry had uttered his immortal words, pleading for liberty or death.

The house was a showplace:

> For years the great of America and some from the Continent visited the house to admire the chandeliered parlors with their walls covered with brocaded silk, mantels of imported marble, the sixteen foot hallway, the terraced gardens lined with boxwood.

Jenny Lind, the world-famous Swedish soprano known as the Swedish Nightingale, stayed at the house in 1850, during her tour of the United States. Other notable visitors included John Marshall, the chief justice of the Supreme Court, and the writer Edgar Allan Poe. It was said that Poe used to recite his poems in the parlor.

Young Elizabeth had been a quiet child, serious and introspective, possessed of an unbending sense of right and wrong. She developed strong, unyielding principles and later described herself as "uncompromising, ready to resent what seemed wrong . . . This has made my life sad and serious."

What she was most uncompromising, resentful, and earnest about was slavery, the practice of which lay at the heart of the society in which her family was so prominent. To belong to Virginia society and oppose the institution of slavery put Elizabeth Van Lew at odds with virtually everyone around her. People began to think of her as different, deviant, surely odd. It may explain why she never married. "Southern swains did not queue up to court a girl with such strong convictions." And such wrong convictions!

Of course, everyone knew where she got such wicked ideas about slavery—and about everything else. Her father had come to Richmond from Long Island, New York, in 1816, and her mother was from Philadelphia, so they were not true Southerners. And Elizabeth had been sent to school in Philadelphia, where she had become indoctrinated with that nasty abolitionist virus, for which there was no cure.

When she returned to Richmond from the North, she did not hide her sentiments. After her father died, Elizabeth and her mother decided to free their nine household slaves, an action that was considered scandalous. Worse, the Van Lews provided transport for the slaves who wanted to go north and paid for their schooling. The other servants chose to stay with the women, becoming part of Elizabeth's spy network.

When war began, Elizabeth's loyalty was put to the test. A delegation of ladies called at the house, asking her and Mrs. Van Lew to aid the war effort by sewing shirts, flags, and banners for the gallant southern troops who were preparing to march off to war.

They refused, of course, as the ladies must have known they would, and the thinly veiled hatred against them became open, bold, and ugly. But it did not frighten the Van Lews, so convinced were they of the rightness of their position. "We had threats of being driven away," Elizabeth wrote, "threats of fire, and threats of death. Some wished all Union people could be driven into the streets and slaughtered. Some proposed the hanging of all persons of Northern birth, no matter how long they had been in the South." And the war had only just begun.

Nobody recruited Elizabeth Van Lew to become a spy, to put her family, her home, and her life at risk by gathering intelligence information in Richmond and sending it to Union authorities. Nor did she join an intelligence organization already in place. She started working on her own and eventually established a highly efficient network. Not one member ever betrayed her or got caught.

Her adventures started when Union captives were brought to Libby Prison after the first Battle of Bull Run. When stories leaked out about the mistreatment of the officers penned up in this old warehouse, she resolved to do whatever she could to help them. One day, she marched down the hill from her home to the warehouse to confront the prison commandant, David Todd, a lieutenant in the new Confederate army and Abraham Lincoln's brother-in-law. Despite the family connection, Todd's allegiance was clearly to the South. He had no sympathy for the prisoners in his charge and certainly none for Elizabeth Van Lew, who declared that she intended to help them. He refused to allow her to enter the prison, not while he was in charge.

Undeterred, Elizabeth called on an old acquaintance, the Confederacy's secretary of the treasury, Christopher Memminger, and asked him to permit her to visit the Yankee prisoners. Absolutely not, he replied. The idea was preposterous for a woman of her standing. They were not of her class and not worthy of her concern.

She reminded the devout, German-born Memminger of a talk he had once given on the importance of Christian charity. When she quoted his own words, about how charity must be granted even to the unworthy, he relented. He wrote a note in support of her unorthodox mission to aid the enemy and sent her to the provost marshal, General Winder.

Elizabeth confided to a friend that she was sure she could wheedle anything she wanted out of Winder by appealing to his overwhelming vanity. She was right. She left Winder's office with a pass granting her complete freedom to visit the prisoners and to bring them books, food, and whatever else she thought they required for their comfort.

She spent enormous sums of money on food, medicines, blankets, clothing, and furniture for the Union officers confined to Libby Prison. She persuaded Confederate authorities to transfer the ill prisoners to civilian hospitals. As she became a regular visitor to the prison, she easily learned how to ingratiate herself with those in charge.

When she discovered Lieutenant Todd had a weakness for buttermilk and gingerbread, she made sure he had a steady supply of both. When Todd was replaced by Captain George Gibbs, she graciously offered the Gibbs family the hospitality of her home until they could find suitable living quarters. Neither Todd nor Gibbs could deny her anything.

But others in Richmond were not so gracious or forgiving. Many prominent families watched in mounting fury as Elizabeth and her mother carried their bundles of goods to the prisoners. Soon they were the subject of angry newspaper editorials.

Two ladies, mother and daughter, living on Church Hill, have lately attracted public notice by their assiduous attention to the Yankee prisoners. . . . Whilst every true woman in this community has been busy making articles for our troops, or administering to our sick, these two women have been spending their opulent means in aiding and giving comfort to the miscreants who have invaded our sacred soil, bent on rapine and murder. . . . The course of these two females, in providing them with delicacies, bringing them books, stationery and paper, cannot but be regarded as an evidence of sympathy amounting to an endorsement of the cause and conduct of these Northern vandals.

Everyone knew who the two ladies were. They made no effort to hide their activities or the items they were bringing into the prison. But they made every effort to hide what they were bringing out.

In gratitude, the Union officers fashioned small gifts for the Van Lews. Some carved rings and other objects out of bone and horn buttons. Others, particularly those newly arrived, offered valuable military information, telling of the Confederate troop movements they had observed while being transported to Richmond. From casual conversations with prison guards, the Van Lews learned of regiments and divisions being shifted from one location to another and where shipments of rations and materiel were being sent.

As the amount of information they were receiving mounted, Elizabeth became increasingly determined to transmit it to Union authorities. But how? At first, she wrote letters to government authorities in Washington, D.C., sending them through the private couriers who had organized a regular mail service between the two capitals. But by November of 1863, she was able to implement a more formal, secure channel. A German physician then living in Richmond decided to travel to the coast to return to Europe. Elizabeth knew him well enough to entrust him with an important mission, to deliver a letter to General Ben Butler at Fortress Monroe, Virginia, offering her services as a spy. Along with the letter, she sent the general a bouquet of flowers.

Butler replied in mid-December with an innocuous letter reporting family events and local gossip. The courier who delivered the letter told Elizabeth that Butler's real message, written in invisible ink, could be detected by applying acid and heat to the paper:

> My dear Miss,
> The doctor who came through and spoke to me of the bouquet said that you will be willing to aid the Union cause by furnishing me with information if I would devise a means. You can write

through Flag of Truce, directed to James Ap. Jones, Norfolk, the letter being written as this is, and with the means furnished by the messenger who brings this. I cannot refrain from saying to you, although personally unknown, how much I am rejoiced to hear of the strong feeling for the Union which exists in your own breast and among some of the ladies of Richmond.

Her return letters to General Butler were written in a colorless liquid that only became visible when milk was applied to the paper. She developed a cipher system, a five-by-six matrix with both letters and numbers in the various cells. She signed her letters "Mrs. Babcock." (When Elizabeth Van Lew died in 1900, the key to her cipher was found in the back of her watch, where it had remained hidden all those years.)

With a line of communication established, Elizabeth systematically undertook the task of recruiting a network of spies to increase her supply of information. She enlisted the assistance of a number of Union sympathizers, including housewives, merchants, farmers, a railroad manager, and a supplier of goods to the Confederate army. She also successfully recruited one of General Winder's detectives, a few War Department clerks, and a prominent businessman who had once run for mayor.

Elizabeth even placed a spy in the Confederate White House. Mary Elizabeth Bowser was one of Elizabeth's freed slaves who had been sent north to receive an education. She willingly returned to Richmond when Miss Van Lew contacted her, even though the war was well under way. Elizabeth arranged for Mary Bowser to obtain a job on the White House staff, working as a nanny for the Davis children and as a waitress in the dining room. Mary overheard a great deal of useful information at dinner parties and she conscientiously passed it on.

Next, Elizabeth arranged her own courier system to send her messages north. The family also owned a farm not far outside of town and she acquired a pass for her servants to travel between the farm and the house in town. The farm was only the first link; eventually she had five safe houses between Richmond and General Butler's lines to the east.

The Van Lew servants carried messages in baskets with false bottoms and inside hollowed-out eggs. They knew the risks—they could be jailed or hanged for their activities—but all willingly played their parts.

Elizabeth also smuggled letters into and out of Libby Prison, usually in the double bottom of a plate warmer. Once she overheard one guard tell another that he intended to examine the warmer the next time she brought it. Forewarned, on her next visit she removed the cover and handed the warmer to the guard. He took hold of the bottom, let out a yell, and dropped it. She had filled it with boiling water. He never tried to check it again.

She outwitted the Confederates in other ways. As the war ground on, more and more horses belonging to private citizens were confiscated by the army. Warned by a contact in the War Department that soldiers were coming for her horse, Elizabeth hid it in the smokehouse. Tipped off again several days later, she led the horse into the house and up the stairs, where she had covered the library floor with straw. A dutiful animal, the horse made no noise when the soldiers arrived. They left empty-handed.

Escaped Union soldiers were welcome to hide in the Van Lew home, in rooms she converted into secret asylums. One had blankets tacked over the windows and a gas heater for warmth. Another could be reached only through a door concealed behind a book case. Many years after the war, Elizabeth's niece recalled seeing her aunt "glide toward the attic with a plate of food, and tiptoed after her. As the niece peered around a corner, the spinster touched a panel. It slid back, and a bearded man reached out hungrily for the food. Years afterward the girl found the concealed chamber beneath the slope of the rear roof."

Suspicion and hostility toward the Van Lews intensified. "I always went to bed at night with anything dangerous on paper beside me, so as to be able to destroy it in a moment," Elizabeth wrote. "The threats, the scowls, the frowns of an infuriated community—who can write of them? I have had brave men shake their fingers in my face and say terrible things." Few people believed any longer that she was a harmless spinster.

She knew that some of General Winder's detectives were shadowing her. "I have turned to speak to a friend and found a detective at my elbow. Strange faces could be seen peeping around the columns and pillars of the back portico." A Richmond grand jury issued warrants for Elizabeth and her mother for dealing in Union greenbacks, but the charge could not be proved.

Attempts were made to entrap Elizabeth. A stranger sidled up to her on the street, whispering that he was going through the lines that night. Elizabeth said nothing. She was too clever to respond to such a blatant invitation to carry a message north. The following day, she chanced upon the man again; he was wearing a Confederate uniform.

Written death threats were slipped beneath the door of the Richmond house, but nothing would deter her from her self-appointed task of helping the Union win the war. So efficient was her operation that when Ulysses S. Grant established his headquarters near Petersburg, twenty-two miles south of Richmond, he received flowers for his breakfast table that Elizabeth had picked the day before from her own garden. With the flowers, of course, came intelligence. Grant later told her: "You have sent me the most valuable information received from Richmond during the war."

Among the letters Elizabeth Van Lew routed north during the winter of 1864 was one that contained vital information about the Union prisoners being held in Richmond and about the capital city's defenses. On January 30, she gave it to a trusted seventeen-year-old servant who hid in her house for a week while he memorized the strength and locations of Confederate troop concentrations around Richmond and her recommendations on the best approach for an attacking force to take. In case he lost the letter, the information would still get through.

The courier reached General Butler on February 4 with the letter in his hand and Elizabeth's well-drilled suggestions clear in his memory. "It is intended to remove to Georgia very soon all the Federal prisoners," she had written. And as the young man recited his list of troop dispositions, he offered a comment made by another of Elizabeth's operatives, a shipping agent named Charles Palmer. "He said to say that Richmond could be taken easier now than at any other time since the war began."

Butler recognized the significance of that news. If there was any chance of saving the Union prisoners in Richmond, it had to be undertaken soon. He forwarded Elizabeth Van Lew's message to Secretary of War Stanton in Washington, with the admonition: "Now or never is the time to strike."

Chapter 5

WHOLESALE MISERY
AND DEATH

Colonel Thomas Ellwood Rose, 77th Pennsylvania Volunteer Infantry, was a large, imposing man, thirty-three years old, with a thick black beard. He had been captured at Chickamauga on September 20, 1863, and spent the next ten days traveling on foot and by train the eight hundred miles to Richmond. As Rose and the other officers herded along with him neared a ramshackle three-story warehouse, he noticed the sign reading "Libby and Son. Ship Chandlers and Grocers."

He had heard of Libby Prison, chilling stories of cold and filth, vermin and disease, of men starving to death for want of the most basic sustenance. Rose vowed he would not let himself end the war there. He was going to escape, and the sooner the better.

His experiences over the next several days strengthened his resolve. The Libby warehouse was huge, about 140 by 105 feet, and the three floors were divided into nine rooms, each approximately 100 feet long, 45 feet wide, and 7 feet high, to house more than fifteen hundred Union officers.

There were no beds and few chairs, nowhere to sit except for a half-dozen camp stools and some hard-bottomed chairs, gifts from a

Miss Van Lew. At one end of each room stood a row of dirty tin washbasins and a wooden trough to be used as a bathtub. Although windows lined the walls from ground to rooftop, not one contained a pane of glass. There was nothing to keep out the cold of that bitter winter of 1864, nothing to stop the winds howling through day and night.

It was impossible for the men to get warm. The Confederate captors provided no stoves or fireplaces, no coal or wood to burn. Few of the prisoners possessed blankets, and the men huddled against one another at night, drawing on the body heat of their comrades to keep from freezing. Others paced the floor, thinking the movement would keep them warm. But usually all they succeeded in doing was stumbling over the men sleeping on the floor, keeping everyone awake.

And they had so little food! The Confederates had enough trouble feeding their own people. There was nothing to spare for the enemy. The usual daily fare was a piece of cold, clammy bread baked from unsifted cornmeal. Only rarely were the men given beef, rice, or real corn bread. Sometimes there was vegetable soup, but few men had cups or plates to contain it. The more resourceful ate out of their shoes.

Fleas, lice, and bedbugs were common. The rats were so large that they could not be intimidated, and they crawled freely over the men day and night, spreading disease. The sick were taken to a small ground-floor room that passed for a hospital, where prisoner-doctors did what little they could. The casualty rate soared. The dead were laid in crude boxes and carted by wagon to unmarked graves.

Most of the guards were cruel, openly contemptuous of their captives. Depending on their mood, the guards might take aim and fire at a prisoner who was just looking out a window. The maltreatment and disease, and the boredom of days and nights with nothing to do, combined to make Libby Prison a hell. Many prisoners went insane. All reason gone, with nothing to live for and no resources to make it through another day, some would deliberately stand before an open window to invite a quick bullet in the chest. Death came as a welcome release.

But for all the horrors of their incarceration, Colonel Rose of

Pennsylvania and his fellow officers knew that the enlisted men a few miles away on Belle Isle were enduring worse conditions. Despite its name, "pretty island," there was nothing pretty about it. It was a flat, barren spot in the James River; not a single tree grew in its sandy soil. A three-foot-wide ditch encircled the prison compound, the dirt from the ditch heaped on the rim. The ditch formed the dead-line. Any prisoner who dared cross it was instantly shot down.

Far too many men were jammed in too small a space, sometimes up to ten thousand confined in less than six acres. One-third that number would have seemed crowded. There were not enough tents; most prisoners lived day and night in the open, with nothing to burn for warmth. Lice swarmed over the bare ground in such numbers that the dirt appeared to be in motion.

Open latrines had been dug at intervals, but the men were not allowed to use them after dark, lest anyone try to cross the dead-line. Men were forced to relieve themselves where they stood. Often, they were packed so tightly that there was no way to remove the excrement during the day. They had to learn to live with it.

The men on Belle Isle had less food than the officers in Libby. They went many days without meat, and the rations they did receive were moldy and rife with bugs. Sergeant John Ransom, Ninth Michigan Cavalry, kept a diary. On January 26, he described the meal of the day: bean soup.

> Beans are very wormy and mushy. Hard work finding a bean without two or three bugs in it. . . . Six pails full for each squad— about a pint per man, and not over a pint of beans in each bucket.

Also in January, some prisoners stole the commandant's dog. "Seems pretty rough when a man will eat a dog," Sergeant Ransom wrote, "but such is the case."

The men preyed on one another, stealing food, a scrap of blanket, a pair of shoes, anything that might keep them alive a day longer. "A good deal of fighting going on among us," Sergeant Ransom recorded on January 28. "A discontented set of beings; just like so many hungry wolves penned up together."

The fate of these men was the same as that of the officers. The vermin, cold, and starvation meant that disease ran rampant. Diarrhea and dysentery were common; in a single month, two hundred sixty-five enlisted men died of chronic diarrhea. Dozens of others, admitted too late to Richmond hospitals, succumbed each month to typhoid fever and pneumonia or simply wasted away.

The men began to believe that the only way they would ever leave Belle Isle was in a pine box. Then in late January, word spread that they would be moved deeper into the Confederacy, to Georgia. At least the climate would be warmer, and maybe the food would be better, and maybe conditions would offer more space. But some men realized that the move would make any possibility of escape or rescue more difficult. If Union forces were planning to liberate them, they had better do it soon.

Colonel Rose was not interested in waiting for anyone to rescue him. He was determined to leave Libby Prison on his own. Risking a glance outside, Rose had noticed workers lowering themselves into a ditch to repair the sewer line that ran alongside a canal. If the prisoners could dig a tunnel to reach the sewer line, that could become their escape route.

Rose organized a group of fifteen men to undertake the dangerous job of tunneling their way out. They started digging in an unused basement storage room so overrun with rats that the men dubbed it "rat hell." To reach it, they first had to hack through the brick and masonry of an unused ground-floor fireplace.

Night after night, they scraped away at the hard-packed earth. Their tools included a table knife, an auger, a chisel, a couple of spoons, and their own bare hands. Two men worked at a time. One would crawl into the lengthening tunnel, carrying his tools and dragging a spittoon on a string for the excess dirt. The second man remained at the hole's entrance, fanning air into it with his hat. He also had a string attached to the spittoon, and when it was full, he would drag it back to the entryway and mix the dirt with the rubbish and straw on the floor of rat hell. The men in the work parties had to fight off the rats constantly, but that situation did offer a singular advantage. Because of the rats, the guards avoided the basement.

Every morning before dawn, the men in the work detail dragged themselves out of the basement, replaced the bricks in the fireplace, and spent most of the day asleep. And that was their routine, night after back-breaking night. Claw at the earth, breathe the foul rancid air, ignore the rats crawling over your legs while you're jammed into the crawl space, and pray the tunnel doesn't collapse and bury you alive—because there's no wood to shore up the ceiling.

Then a new obstacle presented itself: a wall of wooden pilings, a foot thick, driven into the ground. The men lost track of how many nights it took to whittle away at the hard wood with their penknives. But once they broke through, Colonel Rose found that they were beneath the sewer that they intended to be their avenue of escape.

Raw sewage began seeping into the tunnel, threatening it with collapse. The stench was overpowering, causing the men to gag and vomit. One man fainted. His partner had to drag him from the tunnel feet first.

They were left with no alternative but to fill in the tunnel, to restore the dirt they so laboriously had removed, in order to keep the sewer line from breaking through and flooding the basement. But Colonel Rose refused to be thwarted, and he immediately started work on a tunnel in the opposite direction.

This time he planned to dig under a street—praying the heavy paving blocks and passing wagons would not collapse the tunnel—and come up inside a carriage house on the far side. Only a few feet in they struck a stone wall. It turned out to be three feet thick. Toiling around the clock, the men worked in shifts nineteen days and nights to break through the wall.

Beyond it lay a new concern. How close were they to the carriage house? Had they dug too far or were they still inside the prison walls? Rose knew there was only one way to find out. Someone had to walk off the actual distance.

The carriage house was used as a storeroom for boxes and goods sent to the prisoners by their families in the North. On the pretext of searching for his belongings, a captain was taken under guard to the building. Moving as slowly as he dared, he paced off the distance.

By the captain's reckoning, Rose's men began to angle the tunnel upward on their fortieth day of digging. As they were about to break through to the surface, they heard the voices of Confederate guards overhead. The prisoners were still several feet short of the safety of the carriage house.

The Union officers filled in the shaft so a guard would not accidentally fall into it, and continued to dig forward until they were certain they were beneath the building. By then, Rose was so obsessed with gaining his freedom that he dug for twenty-four hours straight. Grimy and exhausted, he pulled himself up through the hole to enjoy a few breaths of fresh air before slipping back down and covering the tunnel entrance with a wooden plank.

The following night, February 8, 1864, the one hundred nine men who had chosen to attempt the escape were alerted. They were told to gather all the food they could carry and to wear whatever civilian clothing they could find. Colonel Rose led them through the sixty-five-foot tunnel into the carriage house. The men remaining behind watched from the prison windows as the escapees boldly walked out through the carriage house gate. The streets surrounding the prison were well lighted by gas lamps. Sentries were stationed every thirty feet. But none of Rose's men was spotted as they slipped away in the darkness.

Elizabeth Van Lew could not sleep. She felt overcome by a sense of foreboding, a nervous feeling that something was about to happen. She knew about the tunnel and was prepared to shelter as many of the escapees as possible. She had arranged for extra cots and mattresses and had blanketed the parlor windows. And she had made sure the prisoners knew how to reach her house.

Although she had been kept apprised of the progress of the escape plan, she did not know when the break would occur. The prisoners did not know either, until Colonel Rose broke ground on February 7. There was no time to get word to her before the men fled the following night. To her everlasting regret, February 8 was one of the rare occasions when Elizabeth Van Lew was not at home. She had gone to visit her thirty-nine-year-old brother, who was leaving the country to avoid conscription in the Confederate army.

Several of Rose's escapees came to her door, begging to be hidden, but the servants, who knew nothing of the breakout, refused to allow them in. Others took shelter across the street, in the darkness of St. John's Church. When they saw that the Van Lew house would not provide sanctuary, they decided to head out of the city and try to make their way to Union lines.

The next morning at Libby Prison, pandemonium broke out among the guards when one hundred nine officers did not answer their names at roll call. General Winder arrived to examine the warehouse. He concluded that the guards on night duty had been bribed. He could not conceive of any other way such a large number of captives could have escaped. He ordered the guards arrested and their quarters searched for the piles of greenbacks he was certain would be there. But no money was found. A few days later, when the entrance to the tunnel was discovered, the guards were released.

Of the one hundred nine escaped prisoners, forty-eight reached the safety of Union forces. Two others drowned and the rest were recaptured. Colonel Rose—without whose imagination, daring, and persistence the break would not have occurred—was retaken when he was within sight of Union lines. He and the other captives were returned to Libby Prison and confined for thirty-eight days in basement dungeons that were awash at high tide with up to two feet of icy, brackish water. It was reported that when Rose was finally released, his "hair, beard, and clothing were covered with mold from the dampness."

But thanks to his courage, forty-eight Union officers went free, able to describe to the people of the Union in detail the terrible conditions under which their loved ones were forced to live in the prisons of the Confederate States of America.

Many Northerners already had an idea that Richmond's prisons were awful. Letters had been smuggled out, most through Miss Van Lew's network. A few men had escaped, and some who were extremely ill or badly wounded had been repatriated, all with horrifying tales to tell.

No one was more concerned about these conditions than the president of the United States. Certainly, no one was more anguished or felt more helpless at his inability to relieve the soldiers' plight. Not a morning passed—after his usual sleepless night and meager breakfast of coffee and an egg—that Lincoln was not besieged by scores of people, even before he reached his office. They waited for him, these so-called morning vultures, as he walked slowly down the long second-floor hallway from his bedroom in the White House's southwest corner to his office in the southeast corner.

The president's home was open to the public. An elderly doorkeeper was supposed to screen visitors, but he was ill prepared to deal with the hordes who wanted to wander about at all hours. The first floor, with the exception of the dining room, and most of the second floor were accessible to all. Outside the privacy of their own small living quarters, the Lincolns frequently found themselves confronting strangers.

This situation was disconcerting to Mrs. Lincoln and to those concerned with the president's safety. As the death threats against Lincoln increased in number, their sense of alarm grew apace. By the winter of 1864, with the war dragging on, the casualty lists lengthening, and the tales about the Union prisoners in Richmond becoming more vivid, a great many letters arrived at the White House warning of plots to kidnap or kill the president.

Lincoln ordered his secretaries to throw the letters away—he did not want to see them—and he tried to appear nonchalant about his safety, although it may have been a feeling of fatalism, or perhaps realism. He recognized that if anyone seriously intended to harm him, no security system could prevent it. In addition, he genuinely desired to keep the White House open. It was, after all, the people's house. "It never would do," he said, "for a President to have guards with drawn sabers at his door, as if he fancied he were, or were trying to be, or were assuming to be, an emperor."

So Lincoln continued to permit himself to be accosted every morning on his slow, rambling walk to his office. Many of the beseechers had slept overnight in the hallway for the chance to have a word, a moment of his attention, sometimes grabbing his arm until the gaunt, tired man had to struggle to pull himself free. By the time he had walked the full length of the red pile carpeting to his office door, he had heard a litany of weeping and threats, moans and prayers, and, as always, demands.

It was a taxing way to begin a day, just one more reason why the president looked so ill, ground down by pressures and responsibilities. His black suit hung loosely on his underweight body, the circles under his drawn eyes were heavy, the skin sallow. Libby Custer, newly married to George Armstrong Custer, described him as the "gloomiest, most painfully careworn looking man I ever saw." The president's close friend Admiral John A. Dahlgren wrote in his diary on February 6: "I observe that the President never tells a joke now."

Increasingly among the early morning voices were pleas about the prisoners: "Libby . . . Belle Isle . . . My son . . . My father . . . Won't you help?"

Once Lincoln was in his office, the official round of appointments brought legislators, businessmen, and other prominent citizens to echo the faceless voices in the corridor. "You must do something about the prisoners. My constituents are threatening to support a peace candidate." "He's our last son. One fell at Bull Run and the other at Fredericksburg." "Here's his picture, Mr. President. You can see he's only a boy."

Journalists added to the frenzy of outrage at the treatment of the Union prisoners. The *New York Times* of November 28, 1863, headlined a story written by surgeons recently released from Belle Isle:

FIFTY VICTIMS EVERY DAY; DISEASE, STARVATION AND DEATH; SICK DENIED HOSPITAL TREATMENT; SHOCKING PICTURES OF DESTITUTION AND ABJECT WRETCHEDNESS.

The doctors wrote that the death rate among the prisoners was at least fifty a day, fifteen hundred a month. Some 10 percent of the prisoners were judged to be seriously ill, doomed to die for lack of proper medicines, food, and clean water. The report went on:

The first demand of the poor creatures from [Belle Isle] was always for something to eat. Self-respect gone, hope and ambition gone, half clad, and covered with vermin and filth, many of them too often beyond all reach of medical skill. In one instance, the ambulance brought sixteen to the hospital, and during the night seven of them died. Again, eighteen were brought in, and eleven of them died in 24 hours. At another time fourteen were admitted, and in a single day ten of them died. Judging from what we have ourselves seen and do know, we do not hesitate to say that under a treatment of systematic abuse, neglect and semi-starvation, the number who are becoming permanently broken down in their constitutions must be reckoned by thousands.

We are horrified when we picture the wholesale misery and death that will come with the biting frosts of Winter. . . . We leave it for others to say what is demanded by this state of things.

Clearly, only one thing was demanded: the freeing of the prisoners.

An attempt to rescue the prisoners was made in early February. Acting on information provided by Elizabeth Van Lew, General Ben Butler dispatched a force of six thousand cavalry toward Richmond, led by Brigadier General Isaac Wistar. The men rode to within twelve miles of the city, where they planned to ford the Chickahominy River at a point that had been unguarded for two months. But that day it was heavily defended, and the cavalry was forced to retreat. A Union deserter had forewarned the Confederates, supplying information about when and where Wistar's force would attack. The mission was a failure.

Lincoln, who had approved Butler's expedition—which included a plan to capture Jefferson Davis at his home—was greatly upset at the outcome of General Wistar's raid. The pressure from the press and the public for action was unrelenting.

Perhaps his disappointment helps explain a change in his character that people close to him observed that winter. A biographer wrote: "In these grim months, a streak of ruthless determination, not hitherto noticeable, began to appear in Lincoln's character." Increasingly frustrated and impatient, he "betrayed his sense that the war had gone on too long, with too much loss of blood and treasure, and that it was time to force it to a close." His personal desperation was calling for desperate measures.

Lincoln knew the Confederates were building a new prison in Georgia, and that it was only a matter of time before they moved the prisoners south. Once they were there, it would be more difficult to free them, and an attempt to do so probably would not be possible until the Confederacy was broken.

According to Elizabeth Van Lew, Richmond was still only lightly defended. If a cavalry unit, operating with speed, secrecy, and nerve, could slip into the city and release the prisoners, that success would provide a tremendous morale boost to the North. In more practical terms, it could also save Lincoln's presidency.

Lincoln had heard about another idea, mentioned to him by a senator. That brash, young cavalry general nobody liked—Kilpatrick— had boasted that he could fight his way into Richmond and set the prisoners free. Perhaps his plan was worth considering.

On February 11, Lincoln received the first fragmentary word that a large number of Union officers had tunneled their way out of Libby Prison. He knew that when they reached Washington, they would bring fresh accounts of prison horrors for the newspapers to headline. And these men had freed themselves by their own initiative. People would ask, If they can do it, why can't the government get them all out? Another raid would have to be launched. There was no more time to dawdle. At 9:25 that night, Lincoln sent a telegram to Brigadier General Hugh Judson Kilpatrick, ordering him to report to Washington immediately.

Chapter 6

THE CHANCES ARE
PRETTY HAZARDOUS

At Brandy Station, sixty miles from Washington, D.C., General Kilpatrick, commanding the Third Division, Cavalry Corps, of the Army of the Potomac, received the president's telegram with his characteristic bravado and unrestrained excitement. Kilpatrick had made sure his plan for a raid on Richmond was well known in Washington's most influential circles, just as he had made sure *he* was well known.

At twenty-eight, Kilpatrick was young for a brigadier general, and he intended to be a young major general as well. After that? Well, the war would not last forever. It was common knowledge among Kilpatrick's friends that he planned to become a senator from his home state of New Jersey and later president of the United States.

Kilpatrick was also a figure of considerable controversy. He had been nicknamed Kill-Cavalry because of the daring but usually reckless way he led his troops in battle. Colonel James Kidd of the Sixth Michigan wrote the following about Kilpatrick:

> He had begun to be a terror to foes, and there was a well-grounded fear that he might become a menace to friends as well. He was brave

to rashness, capricious, ambitious, reckless in rushing into scrapes, and generally full of expedients in getting out, though, at times he seemed to lose his head entirely. He was prodigal of human life [and] many lives were sacrificed by him for no good purpose whatever.

Others complained about Kilpatrick's "Pyrrhic victories when rallying his men to escape from situations in which he should never had led them," and "the needless sacrifice of his men to accommodate [his] personal dreams of glory."

Restless, cocky, and aggressive, Kilpatrick stood five feet, seven inches tall, with a wiry build and a weight of about one hundred forty pounds. With dark eyes, a long thin jaw, and thick sandy sideburns to his chin, his appearance certainly made an impression on people, though not always a positive one. One of General Meade's staff officers said it was hard to look at Kilpatrick without laughing.

A nineteen-year-old U.S. senator's son remembered Kilpatrick as "a little man, with loud, swaggering voice, full of fun and profanity, florid face, square, prognathous jaw, firm, large mouth, prominent Roman nose, quick, deep-set, piercing, fearless gray eyes, full, square forehead, large round head, large ears, dark, thin, and short hair."

In contrast to most of the army's officers, Kilpatrick neither drank nor played cards, but his reputation with the ladies was infamous. "Stories about his multifarious affairs with women of both races circulated throughout the camp. The soldiers snickered about the two black women who cooked for him."

They also snickered about a comely, dark-eyed, teen-age girl named Annie Jones. The soldiers called her "Gen'l Kill's Aide," and it was common knowledge she was his mistress. He didn't bother trying to hide the fact, giving Annie a horse, a major's jacket and cap, and a pass to go sight-seeing throughout the camp. There was quite a flap in Union headquarters when she bragged about making similar amorous visits to the camp of Jeb Stuart.

She also bestowed her favors on George Custer. When the scandal reached a peak and General Meade ordered a provost marshal to investigate Annie Jones's presence in the cavalry camp, both Custer and Kilpatrick professed innocence, each trying to place Annie in the bed of the other. The episode was allowed to die gracefully, and neither man received official censure, but Kilpatrick "could not escape the embarrassment and ridicule that followed." However, even this outcome did nothing to change his future behavior.

Kilpatrick had influential friends in Washington, but many in the Army of the Potomac were wary and distrustful of him, and sometimes disgusted. Earlier in the war, Kilpatrick's report of a raid had come under suspicion. Colonel Charles Wainwright wrote:

> It sounds like a big thing for the cavalry, but the fact that Kilpatrick makes the report leads to some doubt of its accuracy; that general's reports being great in "the most glorious charges ever made," "sabring right and left," and such stuff. They tell me at headquarters that General Meade required a reiteration of the report, before he was willing to send it up.

Throughout the war, the veracity of Kilpatrick's battle reports would be questioned. He "consistently demonstrated an aversion to the unpleasant truth. Repeated evasions, misrepresentations and distortions of the actual situation made the general appear even more preposterous and susceptible to grave accusations."

An aide of Meade's noted that many people said Kilpatrick was a "frothy braggart, without brains and not overstocked with desire to fall on the field; and that he gets all his reputation by newspapers and political influence."

Thus, few in the Army of the Potomac had much use for Kilpatrick. It was only after he was forced out because of his actions during the Dahlgren raid, that he found a vocal supporter, someone who appreciated his brashness and daring. That was when Sherman offered him a vital role in his march to the sea. "I know Kilpatrick is a hell of a damn fool," Sherman said, "but I want just that sort of man to command my cavalry on this expedition."

On that march through Georgia and South Carolina, Kilpatrick would tell his men:

> In after years, when travellers passing through South Carolina shall see chimney stacks without houses, and the country deso-

late, and shall ask, "Who did this?" some Yankee will answer, "Kilpatrick's cavalry."

To a generation of Southerners, he became known as "that savage, little rooster of a man who commanded Sherman's horse. The mark of 'Kill' lay on Georgia and South Carolina—smoking ruins, desolate fields, gutted granaries."

Kilpatrick had never wanted to be anything but a soldier. As a boy growing up on his parents' prosperous farm in Deckertown, New Jersey, he devoured books about military heroes. There was no better place to train to become a hero than the military academy at West Point, which he entered at the age of seventeen.

There he quickly built a reputation for bravery to the edge of foolhardiness. He displayed a fiery temper and a sensitivity to what he perceived as the slightest insult, particularly if uttered by a Southerner. He challenged any southern cadet he considered too arrogant, regardless of size, and almost always won his battles. Kilpatrick was becoming a warrior, and he had already chosen as his enemy anyone born below the Mason-Dixon Line.

He was a senior at the military academy when war broke out in April of 1861. So anxious was he to get to the field immediately instead of waiting two months for graduation, that he and a classmate petitioned President Lincoln asking that his class be graduated immediately. The request was granted.

Kilpatrick graduated fifteenth in a class of fifty and was selected class valedictorian. His fiancée, Miss Alice Shailer of New York City, attended the ceremony, watching in admiration as he received his degree and commission. Their wedding was scheduled for August, but at the postgraduation reception, a friend of Kilpatrick's had a better idea.

"Kill is going to the field and may not return," he told Alice. "Better get married now."

Alice and Kilpatrick thought that was a splendid idea. They summoned the school chaplain to perform the wedding ceremony. That done, Kill was ready for war.

Kilpatrick foresaw that the war would be fought mainly by volunteers and not the regular army. Therefore, promotion would be more rapid in a volunteer regiment. Within a week, the newly graduated, newly married second lieutenant was elected a captain in the Fifth New York Infantry, known as Duryee's Zouaves.

By June 11, 1861, he was in combat, leading the first charge at Big Bethel. And there, on his first day in the war, Kilpatrick was wounded by a rebel shell fragment that ripped the epaulet from Colonel Duryee's shoulder, tore through Kilpatrick's thigh, and killed the soldier behind him. Ignoring his pain, Kilpatrick rallied his men: "Are we going to stay here and be shot down, and do nothing?" He led the troops in a charge across an open field until overcome by the loss of blood.

It was a sensational beginning for a military career. As fortune would have it, he was the first West Point officer to be wounded. That distinction, plus an exaggerated report of his exploits (dictated to his wife, who happened to forward a copy to the *New York Times*), won him considerable favorable publicity. He had achieved a measure of fame, and the war was only two months old.

Alice embroidered a battle flag for him. Two eagles fought in the center, one seizing the other with its talons. Two streamers across the top bore the names Alice and Kilpatrick and the motto *Tuebor*—"I will defend."

After a three-month period of convalescence, Kilpatrick reported to duty with his new flag and the rank of lieutenant colonel in command of the Harris Light Cavalry Regiment of the Second New York Cavalry. In addition, he received an appointment as inspector general of General McDowell's division.

He was also arrested and jailed for three months, charged with stealing livestock and selling horses and tobacco he had confiscated. The charges were dropped—because the army needed daring cavalry officers—and Kilpatrick was promoted to colonel while serving his sentence.

Thus, by the time the war was a bare six months old, the young West Pointer had advanced four ranks and his name was already well known. For an ambitious man bent on promotion and greater glory, there appeared to be no limit to how far he would rise, except, as it turned out, that imposed by the same characteristic that impelled him to prominence in the first place: his brash and reckless temperament.

The next two years provided unceasing activity for Kilpatrick, leading raids and battles from Virginia to Pennsylvania. In June 1863, he was promoted to brigadier general, the first of the younger West Pointers to win a star.

Always determined to be the best, whether engaged in a favorite sport—horse racing with the daring and colorful Custer—or leading his men against the enemy, Kilpatrick was not modest about his achievements. He was a shameless self-promoter, offering sometimes enhanced accounts to his superiors and to reporters. From Big Bethel to Gettysburg to Atlanta, to the end of the war, Kilpatrick compiled an enviable record on the battlefield, but it was increasingly tarnished by his own personality.

Tragedy entered Kilpatrick's life in November 1863, when Alice succumbed to influenza. In January, their infant son died. Kilpatrick threw himself into his work but, unfortunately, there were no raids or battles, nor was there likely to be any action until spring. He planned and schemed, hunting for ways to wage war. Every winter he fretted, impatient with the long periods of waiting, training, recruiting. The inactivity was worse than usual that winter of 1864 as he tried to cope with his personal loss. "He has just lost his wife and only child," Colonel Wainwright noted, "and they say he is gloomy and desperate; just in the state to try something wild."

The "something wild" he conceived was a raid on Richmond to free the Yankee prisoners. If successful, Kilpatrick would be awarded another star, probably two. And with that rank and visibility, the White House would surely be his. He realized he could not go through normal military channels to get approval for his idea. That would take too long and might not work. Further, he considered his superior, Major General Alfred Pleasonton, to be too cautious to grasp the consequences of such a bold plan. And even if Pleasonton were to agree, he might give command of the raid to someone else.

As for General Meade, the commander of the Army of the Potomac, it was unlikely *he* would approve anything that might benefit Kilpatrick. Meade had hated Kilpatrick ever since Kill had called Meade's son incompetent and demanded he be removed as quartermaster of the Third Cavalry. Nobody understood why Kilpatrick had so publicly criticized the younger Meade. Everyone agreed Kill was rash, but he was not stupid. "Angered by the slur against his son [Meade] threatened to get rid of Kilpatrick by shipping him to a lesser post in the west."

But Kilpatrick did not need Pleasonton or Meade to advance his plan, not when the powerful Senator Jacob Howard of Michigan was in the camp as his guest. He told Howard about his scheme to raid Richmond and free the prisoners, certain the senator would inform Lincoln. And so Kilpatrick had every reason to feel smug when he got the president's telegram requesting his presence in Washington immediately. He was on his way to bigger things.

The city of Washington to which Kilpatrick traveled on the morning of February 12 had remained, as Henry Adams had described it, virtually unchanged for more than sixty years. It was "the same rude colony . . . camped in the same forest, with the same unfinished Greek temples for workrooms, and sloughs for roads." Hardly the center of the nation's cultural or commercial life as European capitals were, it was merely a place where government sat, a pretentious and unfulfilled idea placed in a wilderness. To visitors from abroad, Washington was outlandish, a "vast practical joke," one called it. Another described it as a "great, scrambling, slack-baked embryo of a city basking in the sun like an alligator on the mud-bank of a bayou in July."

Still another observer characterized the city as

one of the worst pestholes. Well water was often contaminated by nearby latrines; Constitution Avenue was an open sewer filled with dead animals; and the Potomac River was already so polluted that President Abraham Lincoln had become ill from eating its fish. Garbage was eaten by pigs rooting openly in the streets. Hospitals had over-flowing bedpans in the wards, and there were piles of trash on the grounds outside—no wonder that typhoid, dysentery, and malaria spread everywhere.

Despite these unpleasant conditions, Washington was prospering as never before. War can do that, particularly in a capital city where clever men are seeking lucrative government contracts. The population was growing, the price of real estate up, construction booming. A local citizen noted: "If the people of the Union could not win this war, at least they were making money out of it."

Ugly and muddy, noisy and dirty, the city could be toured in an afternoon. Pennsylvania Avenue was a wide but neglected street with dingy buildings and houses of prostitution on the south side, shops, restaurants, and hotels on the north. So upscale was the north side that it boasted a brick sidewalk.

Only the bravest undertook to walk the streets at night, for bands of bullies and toughs roamed at will. Vice and gambling were rampant; whorehouses, both elegant and seedy, stood in sight of the White House. There were four hundred fifty registered brothels in the city and more than seven thousand prostitutes, if one counted those working in nearby Georgetown and Alexandria.

A lot of people had a great deal of money to spend, and the cost of living rose accordingly. As a result, federal government workers, like their counterparts in Richmond, barely earned subsistence wages. These conditions led to labor strikes that winter—bookbinders at the Government Printing Office, streetcar drivers, even the police petitioned for higher wages.

A government clerk earned about fifteen hundred dollars a year, scarcely enough for food and shelter for his family. A few blocks from the White House, freed Negroes lived in shanties and lean-tos, their situation worse than in their old quarters on the plantations of the South. A former slave could be hired for as little as eleven dollars a month.

The agents and detectives who worked for General LaFayette Baker, the high-handed and heavy-handed chief of the Secret Service, were busily ferreting out traitors, deserters, speculators, fraudulent contractors, and common thieves. Washington's counterpart to Richmond's feared General Winder, Baker was called many things— cheat, liar, tyrant—but no one ever accused him of lacking diligence in his search for wrongdoers.

His men charged into gambling halls and bawdy houses, confiscated stolen supplies of morphine and quinine, nabbed hospital orderlies who preyed on the wounded, and had the temerity to arrest government officials and army officers they found in the houses of pleasure.

> In the new year of 1864, the trains of Government wagons rumbled through the streets, pigs and cows meandered on the slushy sidewalks, and dead horses lay stinking in the winter sun. On hospital cots, men languished and died. Abandoned infants wailed in alleys. Recruiting agents ran off contrabands, and deserters stealthily paddled across the Potomac. Peculating contractors and quartermasters went to jail. There were robberies and murders. . . . The grand jury brought fresh indictments against the bawdy houses. The destitute starved and shivered, and the underpaid workers scrimped.

General Kilpatrick moved freely and zestfully around the capital city, sampling its pleasures, opportunities, and intrigues. As he left the ornate wooden railway station and headed for the White House, he was on his way to becoming a central figure in a new intrigue.

The White House was a strange mix of newfound prosperity and aged dilapidation, of high taste and the banal. Ramshackle sheds and outbuildings huddled against its walls, and the curious circulated inside and on the lawns. The rugs were threadbare from the heavy traffic and mud lay all about. "The whole place had the air of a rundown, unsuccessful third rate hotel."

Congress repeatedly refused funds to repair the building from the continuing depredations of sightseers. Visitors had stripped the decorative paper from the walls, slashed swatches of brocade and damask from the curtains and sofas, and stolen tassels from the East Room's draperies and ornamental shields. Without guards, the craze for souvenirs had turned into outright vandalism.

Lincoln greeted Kilpatrick warmly. Although the president had heard the more sordid stories about Kilpatrick, he also knew of the general's courage in battle. If there was anything Lincoln appreciated—and longed for—among his generals, it was audacity and bravery, and Kilpatrick had more than his share of both.

The two men spoke only a short time; no record remains of their conversation. The president apparently articulated his hope for freeing the Union prisoners, and Kilpatrick expressed his confidence that he could carry it off. Lincoln also wanted his amnesty proclamation widely distributed in the Richmond area, hoping it would induce large numbers of Confederate soldiers to lay down their arms and return to the Union. Generously, it offered complete amnesty to all but the highest officials, if they would swear an oath to the United States.

Lincoln knew that Southerners were weary of the war, and he believed that if a significant number of people could be persuaded to swear allegiance to the Union, others would realize that a continuation of the fighting was futile. At that stage of the war, when nothing else seemed to be working, the idea was worth a try.

But the more important aim, indeed, the overriding goal of Kilpatrick's expedition, was to be the release of all Union prisoners in Richmond. That must be accomplished, Lincoln insisted. He did not ask for details of the planned raid; Kilpatrick's superiors could assess those. What Lincoln wanted to know was how certain Kilpatrick was that he could free the prisoners.

Kilpatrick had never lacked self-confidence, and in this instance he obviously impressed Lincoln. He left the president's office with full backing for the raid and instructions to coordinate the operation with the War Department, thus authorized to bypass his superiors. Neither Pleasonton nor Meade would be permitted to interfere with the mission. Kilpatrick briefed Secretary of War Stanton and was ordered to return to camp and draft a detailed plan.

Kilpatrick had the bulk of the operation outlined in his mind, so it took him little time to transfer it to paper. He proposed to set out with a force of not less than four thousand cavalry and six guns, cross the Rapidan River at Ely's Ford, and make his way south through Lee's army.

South of the Rapidan, at Spottsylvania Court House, two detachments would split off from the main force. One would move rapidly to destroy the Virginia Central Railroad in the vicinity of Frederick's Hall to prevent Lee from sending infantry reinforcements to Richmond. The telegraph wire from the Rapidan to Richmond would be cut to keep information about troop movements from rebel authorities in Richmond. Secrecy was vital.

The second detachment would tear up the tracks of the Fredericksburg Railroad at or near Gurney's Station, south and east of Spottsylvania Court House. That telegraph line connecting northern Virginia and Richmond would also be destroyed.

The main force would proceed south, crossing the North Anna River near Mt. Carmel Church and burning the railroad bridge. There, the Gurney's Station detachment would rejoin them. The other detachment would proceed independently south from Frederick's Hall to Goochland Court House on the James River, about seventeen miles west of Richmond, crossing the river to head for Richmond on the south bank. This group's task was to destroy the Confederate arsenal at Bellona, as well as the Danville & Richmond and Petersburg & Richmond railway lines.

Kilpatrick's main force would approach Richmond from due north to attempt the release of the prisoners. Regardless of the resistance they might encounter in the capital, they should have no difficulty returning to the Union lines. Kilpatrick outlined two escape routes: the way they had come, or east toward Norfolk and the safety of General Butler's lines.

Kilpatrick envisioned a speedily executed raid. He suggested five days' rations for the men and one for the horses. Only ambulances would be taken. Additional wagons would slow the march.

The proposal was ambitious and reasonably clever. With Union troops approaching Richmond from two directions, the Confederates would be compelled to split their meager defensive forces. Communications would have been disabled, so the city's defenders would receive no warning of the impending attack. Railroads and bridges would be destroyed to prevent reinforcements from Lee's army from reaching Richmond. A few other worthwhile targets, such as the arsenal, could be wrecked, and thousands of copies of Lincoln's amnesty proclamation distributed. If surprise and speed could be maintained, if the intelligence reports on the city's vulnerability were accurate, if this, if that . . . Kilpatrick's plan might succeed.

Kilpatrick, of course, was enthusiastic and optimistic. "From the information I have but lately received and from my thorough knowledge of the country, I am satisfied that this plan can be safely and successfully carried out."

One man at Union cavalry headquarters was not at all satisfied either with Kilpatrick's plan or with the cocky general himself. This was Major General Alfred Pleasonton, the commander of Meade's cavalry corps. A stubborn and proud man, Pleasonton was disturbed about the operation and irate that Kilpatrick had bypassed him to go directly to the president. Pleasonton should have been the one to forward any such plan to Washington through formal channels. He or Meade should have presented it to Lincoln and the secretary of war—not some mere brigadier leading a division.

When General Meade asked Pleasonton for his opinion of the merit and feasibility of Kilpatrick's raid, Pleasonton made his response in writing, so there would be no mistaking his position.

The raid, he declared, was "not feasible at this time." He reminded Meade of a cavalry raid on Richmond the year before, during the Chancellorsville campaign, that had cost the Union seven thousand horses and produced no lasting damage to the Confederacy. He also noted that even if Kilpatrick cut the designated telegraph lines, there were other lines from Gordonsville and Lynchburg by which Richmond authorities could be notified.

Pleasonton also felt that such a massive and dangerous operation was unnecessary to distribute Lincoln's amnesty proclamation.

I will most willingly undertake to have it freely circulated in any section of Virginia that may be desired. I do not think I am promising too much in naming even Richmond. . . . For the success of [Kilpatrick's] expedition I would be willing to sacrifice the number of horses required, but in the present state of the roads and the facilities the rebels have, with their army disengaged and distributed for frustrating such an effort, I cannot recommend it.

Meade ignored Pleasonton's recommendation; he had no choice. Lincoln and Stanton favored the expedition, and once that was known, Meade could do nothing to stop it.

But if he could not stop it, Meade at least had the option of trying to ensure its success, however slim the chances might be. On February 27, Meade wrote to his wife:

I have been a good deal occupied with an attempt I am about making, to send a force of cavalry into Richmond to liberate our prisoners. The undertaking is a desperate one, but the anxiety and distress of the public and of the authorities at Washington [about the prisoners] is so great that it seems to demand great risks for the chances of success.

Meade ordered Kilpatrick to dispatch an officer to Washington to select the best horses available, those capable of enduring the strain of five days and nights of hard riding. To enable Kilpatrick's forces to pass undetected through Lee's lines and across the Rapidan, Meade planned some diversionary moves that would be easily visible to Lee.

On the day before Kilpatrick's troops would move out, General John Sedgwick would send two regiments of Sixth Corps to Madison Court House, twenty miles southwest of Stevensburg, to serve as cover for a second force, commanded by George Custer, that would cross the Rapidan and ride south by southwest toward Charlottesville. The following morning, General David Birney would lead units of Third Corps from Brandy Station southwest toward Culpeper.

While Lee would be tracking these decoy forces, particularly Custer's, which was heading deepest into Confederate territory, Kilpatrick's men would slip across the river under cover of darkness, heading in the opposite direction, almost due east.

General A. A. Humphreys, Meade's chief of staff, informed Kilpatrick that his command would number four thousand men plus a battery of light artillery.

> With this force you will move with the utmost expedition possible on the shortest route past the enemy's right flank to Richmond and by this rapid march endeavor to effect an entrance into that city and liberate our prisoners now held there.
>
> I am directed by the major-general commanding to say that no detailed instructions are given you, since the plan of your operation has been proposed by yourself, with the sanction of the President and the Secretary of War, and has been so far adopted by him that he considers success possible with secrecy, good management, and the utmost expedition.

The raid would begin on the night of February 28.

Everything depended on secrecy—for a force of four thousand cavalry moving silently and unseen through an opposing army, more than sixty miles into hostile territory to the enemy's capital in the middle of winter. There must be no advance word that might lead rebel authorities to reinforce Richmond's defenses.

But Kilpatrick's pending raid had to be one of the worst-kept secrets of the war. On March 1, Colonel Lyman of Meade's staff wrote:

> For some days, General Humphreys has been a mass of mystery with his mouth pursed up and doing much writing by himself all to the great amusement of the bystanders who had heard, even in Washington, that some expedition or raid was on the tapis. . . . A secret expedition with us is got up like a picnic, with everybody blabbing and yelling. . . . Kilpatrick is sent for by the President; Oh, Ah! Everybody knows it at once: he is a cavalry officer—it must be a raid. All Willard's [Hotel] chatters of it. Everybody devoted his entire energies to pumping the President and Kill-Cavalry! . . . The idea is to liberate the prisoners, catch all the rebel [military commanders] that are lying around loose and

make tracks to our nearest lines. I conceive the chances are pretty hazardous.

Indeed, the raid was all the talk at Washington's fashionable Willard's Hotel after Kilpatrick had called on the president. And that was when a young one-legged colonel heard about it and decided he wanted to be part of the action.

But before the raid could take place, before the war's death and dying could resume, the Army of the Potomac had something better to anticipate—the George Washington's Birthday Ball.

Chapter 7

THE PALACE OF
PLEASURE

February was a busy and exciting time for the Army of the Potomac, busy for the enlisted men, exciting for the officers. While some plotted the details of the coming raid on Richmond, others were organizing an affair of quite a different order: a party to commemorate George Washington's birthday. All the Union's notables had been invited, civilian and military. It was to be a grand event in the army's history.

The camp along the Rapidan River seemed an unlikely spot for pageantry, dancing, and flirtation. The site looked like what it was, a desolate swath of ground fought over by marauding armies. Barely a house had been left standing; the few that remained lacked windows or doors. All the wood that could be pried loose from the frames had long since contributed to bonfires, to keep the men warm or cook their dinner. Everywhere there was mud, acres of tree stumps, tents, horses, wagons, and cursing and discontented troops.

The refuse of an army lay underfoot: canteens, pots, shell fragments, bones of horses and mules, and bones of men, too, though it was hard to tell the difference. Buzzards and crows circled, waiting their turn, the evening air heavy with their watchful cries.

The troops were housed in shanties with mud floors. The generals claimed the few habitable homes. Junior officers lived in wall tents, raised about two feet off the ground on split logs. The tents were fitted with doors, chimneys, and fireplaces; some even had glass windows.

The war was still in evidence that February, right across the muddy Rapidan. From time to time, ambulances careened through the camp, bearing wounded from a patrol or a barrage loosed by a nervous, or ambitious, artillery officer. On the riverbank itself, where pickets were within shouting distance of the other side, there was rarely any firing. The men had worked out on their own a tacit agreement that permitted long stretches without firing. When the weather changed, the killing would resume soon enough.

Sentries from both sides would cross the river to barter—tobacco for food, newspapers for coffee—returning safely to their lines. There was no need for guns, not even angry words, just one tired soldier to another talking about their disgust with the war, their comrades lost, their desire to go home. Their only fear was of their own officers, who disapproved of the fraternization. If northern and southern soldiers became too friendly, they might be reluctant to go back to war.

On the camp's periphery, a few civilian families remained in the ruins of their plantations, and many a Union officer was cheered by their hospitality. The visitors always brought food when invited to dinner, not enough to offer the offense of charity but sufficient to repay the kindness. Enemies thus passed pleasurable evenings in the ruined countryside, jarred occasionally, painfully, when a host displayed a photograph of a son killed in battle, sometimes in fighting against the very men now being entertained so graciously.

There was much work for lumberjacks and carpenters in preparation for the ball. Officers combed the ranks to find troops possessing those skills. An abandoned sawmill had been spotted nearby, and it was decided to build a grand ballroom—a palace of pleasure, it came to be called—rising out of the mud of the battlefield. Scores of soldiers were sent through miles of countryside to fell trees, which teams of horses dragged back to the mill. Orders were dispatched to Washington for kegs of nails and building supplies.

From dawn to dark, the carpenters sawed and hammered, and all in camp found an excuse to pass by to watch the progress. It was heavy work, but what a joy for the men of the Army of the Potomac to see something constructed for fun and dancing. The thought was almost unreal to some, but to others the palace of pleasure was the only reality. The rest—the mud, the misery, the killing—surely that had to be the unreal part of their lives.

Ultimately, the ballroom was ninety feet long and sixty feet wide. It smelled of fresh-cut pine. The walls and ceiling were draped with every regimental and headquarters flag owned by the celebration's hosts, General George Meade's Second Army Corps. They may have suffered nineteen thousand casualties, but they had never lost a flag. There was much honor in that. Evergreens, guidons, sabers, drums, revolvers, rifles, and bayonets completed the decoration, a fitting backdrop for the ball, just as these were fixtures in the daily lives of those who would dance there, many for the last time.

A platform at one end of the room featured, as an entertainment for the ladies, a romanticized display of army camp life. It showed spotlessly white tents tightly pulled, drums and bugles ornamentally arranged, stacked rifles, a campfire with gleaming kettles, and two small cannon, their brass as bright as a mirror. Everything was as clean as the day it came from the factory.

As the time for the event drew near, arrangements were made for a special train to bring guests from Washington, D.C. Exceptional care was devoted to the entertainment and housing of the ladies. "The army is overrun with women," wrote General Meade. "I believe half of Washington is coming down to attend."

The officers yielded their quarters, remaking the beds with the softest of cedars. Two ladies were lodged in each tent, and a sergeant placed at their disposal. Enlisted men assigned to their service built fires, brought hot water, cleaned their boots, and performed other household chores. One officer observed: "The girls thought the little canvas tents 'just too lovely for anything,' and were delighted with all they saw."

It promised to be a wondrous time, and many a northern belle's heart had been broken when she failed to receive one of the three hundred coveted invitations. The women were wooed, flirted with, and treated with all the delicacy one might lavish on the finest Dresden china.

Each morning, bands serenaded them as they dressed. While the cooks prepared breakfast, eager young officers vied for the privilege of playing escort. "Such glorious breakfasts were these," an officer wrote. "Such flirtations and conversations, where compliments flew like musket balls. . . . The sweet strains of music ever rising and falling in rhythmic waves idealized the moments, and we lived in ecstasy."

During the morning meal, with a general officer presiding, plans were made for the day's activities. There would be rides to the front line to wave at the enemy, horse races through the camp, and lavish picnics. Dinners followed, full-dress affairs in such splendor as to rival the manner of the finest homes of the North.

As part of the festivities, General Kilpatrick had invited a number of senators and their wives as his guests. They were quartered throughout the area and entertained royally at the general's mansion, for these were men who had final approval over promotions of general officers. Senator Howard's son recalled: "Kilpatrick was happy, and as active as a flea and almost as ubiquitous. Wines, liquors, and eatables were in profusion." Everyone, except Kilpatrick, made ample use of spirits.

With so many politicians present, it was inevitable that there would be an opportunity for oratory. A meeting was convened in a building in Culpeper, shortly before the ball. But it was not the politicians' speeches that held everyone's attention. It was the one delivered by the fiery General Kilpatrick. (He had been mesmerizing audiences since he was seventeen, when he had stumped New Jersey for a congressman's re-election, for which he received his West Point appointment.)

Kilpatrick had the power to capture and hold his listeners and was considered one of the best orators of his day. On that night he stirred tremendous enthusiasm by hinting that something grand would soon occur and that he would have a major role to play in it.

On the afternoon of Washington's birthday, February 22, the specially commissioned, heavily guarded train from the capital pulled into Brandy Station, with its additional complement of guests for the ball. A considerable portion of the Union's social and political leadership was now in camp, including the vice president and his daughter, the governor of Rhode Island and his wife (generally considered the handsomest woman in the country), a large delegation from the British embassy, senators, socialites, a Supreme Court justice, and every general officer with his entourage.

Even a Confederate soldier attended, dressed as a woman. Benjamin Franklin Stringfellow was a twenty-one-year-old scout for Wade Hampton's cavalry. When the war began, Frank Stringfellow had been teaching Latin and Greek at a school for young ladies in Mississippi. He returned to his native Virginia to join the army but was turned down four times because he weighed only ninety-four pounds and with his long, blond curly hair looked like a "beardless youth with a waist like a girl's."

When he finally talked his way into service he became a scout for Jeb Stuart, and then for Hampton. He spent much time behind Union lines in Alexandria, Virginia, spying and gathering intelligence while courting his future wife, Miss Emma Green.

Shortly before the George Washington's Birthday Ball, Stringfellow and others of Hampton's scouts captured a Union captain who was carrying a pass through federal lines for a woman who lived near Culpeper Court House, permitting her to attend the dance as his guest. Frank knew the girl and her family, and he asked them to loan him a ball gown and "other feminine fripperies" to disguise himself as Miss Sally Marsten.

Sally and her mother drilled Stringfellow in etiquette and feminine behavior and outfitted him for the dance. Under the hoop skirts he wore trousers, rolled up, so he could carry a pair of derringer pistols. When the ladies were finished, Sally burst out laughing. "Why, Frank!" she said. "You're positively beautiful."

At the Union checkpoint, a lieutenant examined Stringfellow and his pass with skepticism but decided to let him through. The new Miss Sally Marsten did not have to wait long for dancing partners. And how those Union officers loved to talk! Sally seemed so interested in their activities and asked so many charming and naive questions. Before long, Stringfellow had learned that Fourth Corps was being moved from the West to Virginia and that the Army of the Potomac would soon have a new commander, one U. S. Grant. A talkative major let *that* slip two weeks before the official announcement was made.

Suddenly Miss Sally was confronted by the lieutenant from the outpost. Still suspicious, he had inquired about her escort and discovered that no one had seen him for days. Quietly, the guard took Stringfellow's arm and compelled the imposter to accompany him to the provost marshal's office.

They had not gone far when Stringfellow pulled out his derringers and took the lieutenant prisoner. He forced the Yankee to drive Miss Sally's horse and buggy back through federal lines. "My God," the man muttered, "how did this ever happen to me?"

The ball was a glittering, glamorous success. The crudeness of the hall dissolved in the mellow, romantic light of hundreds of candles and Chinese lanterns. The swish of taffeta and the clinking of swords blended with the music to erase the war from memory and anticipation. Only harmony and dancing and beautiful women filled those blissful hours. When a cavalry general asked a young lady to dance, she first offered condolences, knowing that his only son had recently been killed in battle. The general took her arm and said, "Yes, madam, very sad. He was the last of his race. Do you waltz?"

The dancing continued until the early hours of the morning. General Meade, in a rare affable mood, did not return to his quarters until 4:00 A.M. "We have had quite a gay time," he noted. Horses, ambulances, and carriages transported tired young ladies back to their quarters. "Gayly sped the feet and sweetly smiled the lips of the brave and beautiful and honored of the Republic," wrote a guest. "Swiftly passed the hours of the festal night, and with the matin song of lark and blue bird and the courtesies of parting, the morning looked in upon a Banquet Hall deserted."

The celebration continued the next day with a grand parade and review of the troops. The weather was clear with a touch of warmth in the air as General Meade, with nearly two hundred ladies in his retinue, rode to the review grounds. In front of the grandstand stretched the men of Second Corps: great masses of artillery with guns gleaming on their carriages, blue-coated men erect on the caissons, officers in dark blue, red, and gold on splendid horses. Next came cavalry squadrons, several thousand strong, the men in light blue with yellow trim. Then the infantry, a multitude of men in dark blue uniforms and slouch hats.

Bugles blared and the grand maneuvers and review began. The cannon were unlimbered, batteries galloped to follow the officers' barked commands, the men executed the motions of aiming, loading, and firing.

Then the entire corps—infantry, artillery, cavalry—passed in review with bands playing, flags and guidons blowing in the breeze, the line stretching out of sight. This was the army that would end the war. When the last unit had gone by, the crowd turned, watching for the final event: Kilpatrick's cavalry charge.

Senator Howard's son recalled:

With sabers all drawn, and carbines dangling by the side, and beginning with a slow, forward movement, the skirmishers out in advance on the front and sides, the buglers at intervals sounding the orders in silvery, clear, high notes, the pace quickening as the squadrons approach the hill, the skirmishers gradually drawing in closer and closer to the main body. At last the buglers sound the charge, and with one mighty shout, the glittering sabers held high up in the flashing sunlight, every man rising in his stirrups, the vast column rushes on like a mighty river that has overflown its banks and sweeps everything before it. That sight stirs our blood the most of all.

With one accord, we all, ladies and gentlemen, hurrah. Up the hillside they sweep, yelling and flashing sabers, over the brow, and then down. It seems as if nothing could stop those reckless, brave, death-dealing troopers and their horses.

It was over. The guests were driven back to the Brandy Station platform to board the train for Washington. There had been magic and romance for those few days, but as the train passed out of sight, left behind were wrinkled dance programs, wilted flowers crushed underfoot, and a perfumed handkerchief or two kept close to the heart of a lonely soldier. In the glaring light of day, the grand ballroom, the pleasure palace, became a shoddy, makeshift building soon to be torn down. Its planks, which had framed such joy and laughter, would become firewood, coffins, and grave markers.

Chapter 8

HOW LITTLE WE KNOW
WHO WILL GO NEXT

One of the early arrivals at Brandy Station stayed behind when the ball was over. He was a twenty-one-year-old colonel, tall and slender, with reddish-blond hair, a thin goatee, and a great deal of charm. Many of the distinguished guests from Washington recognized Ulric Dahlgren as he rode about the camp on his magnificent coal-black stallion. It was well known that he knew everyone of importance in government, including the president.

People were surprised to see him looking so robust, remembering, as all Washington did, that he was near death in the weeks after Gettysburg, seven months before. He did appear thinner, however, and there was another reminder of his wound—the crutch tied to his saddle.

He was perhaps the youngest colonel in the army, the son of Rear Admiral John A. Dahlgren, the noted authority on ordnance, currently in command of the Union fleet off Charleston. Ulric Dahlgren was notable in his own right as well, not just as the son of a famous man but as a cavalry officer, frequently praised in the newspapers for his exploits.

But why had he come to the George Washington's Birthday Ball? Surely not to dance, not with his artificial leg. And another colonel was not needed in camp that winter to run the army. No, Dahlgren had come for another purpose: to join Kilpatrick's raid on Richmond. He had heard talk of it a few weeks ago in Washington and was determined to take part. He had proved to himself he could still ride, and he yearned for a chance to get back into the war.

His zeal for the Union cause was even stronger than before his mishap. Although he did not share the bitterness and personal hatred many Yankees held for the rebels, Dahlgren agreed passionately with Lincoln that the country could not be allowed to remain divided. He brooded over this issue during his months of convalescence, and over the plight of his fellow soldiers and friends held in Confederate prisons. He had long ago vowed he would never be taken prisoner, yet he felt great sympathy for those who had been. When he heard about Kilpatrick's daring plan to release the prisoners in Richmond, Dahlgren knew it was the kind of expedition that could shorten the war. He intended to do his part.

Kilpatrick needed little persuasion to include Dahlgren in his plans. He was aware of the colonel's distinguished record. More important, he knew that having Dahlgren along would bring even more publicity and prestige to his raid. The admiral's son would ensure greater attention for Kilpatrick, and so he eagerly altered his plans for the mission to give Dahlgren a key assignment.

Dahlgren would lead a unit of five hundred men across the James River west of Richmond and enter the city from the south. While the southern defenders concentrated on repelling Kilpatrick's larger force north of the city, Dahlgren's men would slip into Richmond to free the prisoners, then rejoin Kilpatrick's command before returning to Union lines. The expedition's success would depend on Dahlgren. If he could not enter Richmond, it would fail.

Young Dahlgren had grown up in Washington, D.C., living at the Navy Yard, his father's command. Naval cannon were his toys, and obliging sailors his early tutors and friends. As an adolescent, he was familiar with the modern tools and weapons of war, having had free run of the navy's ordnance department. He became an expert boatman and swimmer and excelled at other sports, taught by the rough, unschooled seamen.

Dahlgren's formal education was conducted privately, and he became articulate and well read. He spent many hours in the Capitol building, impressed by the oratory of Webster and other powerful speakers, absorbing the political heritage of the country.

One of the most striking characteristics of Dahlgren as a boy, noted by his father, was the intensity and earnestness with which he pursued his interests, whether in the schoolroom or the playing field. "It seemed as if he obeyed by instinct the scriptural injunction, *'Whatever thy hand findeth to do, do it with all thy might.'*"

Although his tutors reported that he did well in his studies, it was clear he had little interest in a scholarly career, preferring outdoor activities such as riding, hunting, and sailing. In 1858, at the age of sixteen, he decided to become an engineer—and to learn the profession on his own.

He studied the basic principles of field surveying and traveled to Louisiana where an uncle owned land. (Passing through Richmond on his journey, he spent several days exploring the city.) On his uncle's plantation, this city boy reveled in the chance to ride for hours through wild, unspoiled territory. The nearest house was twenty-five miles away. He worked at surveying tracts of land, repairing levees, and administering the plantation.

He also studied French and fencing, in which well-bred gentlemen were expected to be proficient. Not given to introspection or contemplation, Dahlgren craved action, excitement, and challenging work. He wrote to his father that he preferred work over everything else. "When I have nothing to occupy my mind, I always feel dissatisfied until I find myself busy again."

When nearly eighteen, he wrote to his father that he felt prepared to earn his own livelihood as an engineer, but he wanted to establish himself farther west, independent of his family. "The whole of it is, I want to earn my own living, which I am doing now, but in a very indefinite way." Before he left the plantation, however, a return letter arrived from his father summoning Ulric home to talk about his decision. Regardless of his own feelings, Ulric dutifully obeyed his father's call. "As you know what is best for me, dear father, I will cheerfully and willingly follow your advice."

Back in Washington, Ulric was successful in persuading the admiral of the soundness of his judgment, and after a month's stay returned to Louisiana. But four months later, his father called him home again, this time because of the political situation. The division between North and South had widened, the rhetoric on both sides increasingly provocative. Admiral Dahlgren, certain war was coming soon, did not want Ulric caught in the Deep South when fighting broke out. He advised him to move to Philadelphia, to study law at the office of another uncle.

This was a drastic change from the free, open life of the Louisiana plantation, but Ulric approached the task with characteristic diligence. He pursued his law studies during the day and at night took courses in geology at the Franklin Institute. He read the newspapers and kept in touch with his father to follow the deteriorating political situation.

By the end of January 1861, five states had withdrawn from the Union, and the Southerners in the Cabinet had resigned. In the following month, the states of the rebellion elected their own president, southern-born military officers had resigned their commissions, and Fort Sumter was under siege. Ulric was incensed. "The American flag should never have been insulted; there was no necessity for it."

Washington, D.C., with fewer than two thousand troops on hand, bordered by the states of Virginia and Maryland, was in a precarious, exposed position. A strike force from disloyal states could quickly seize the capital and the valuable Navy Yard, with its huge quantities of weapons and ammunition.

War fever swept the capital. Returning home, Ulric accompanied several detachments of sailors his father sent into Virginia in the hope that their cannon and trained men would compensate for the lack of army troops. Overall, this was an exciting time for a young man from a military family. There were bands, parades, colorful uniforms, patriotic speeches. He felt he was part of a crusade, a grand and glorious campaign to save the Union. At least so it seemed until the Battle of Bull Run and the shameful retreat to the streets of Washington.

"I am in the midst of very exciting and interesting events," Dahlgren wrote from his navy artillery outpost in nearby Alexandria, Virginia. Over the next months he had the opportunity, through his father's auspices, to observe the president, the Cabinet, indeed, all the Union's high military and civilian officials.

President Lincoln had found a friend in Admiral Dahlgren, and he visited the Navy Yard as often as he could.

> Sometimes Lincoln drove down to watch a new invention being tested, but more often he came just for coffee, cigars, and a chat with his favorite naval officer. He visited the yard almost every week . . . and usually brought along cabinet members and other top officials. Dahlgren entertained them with food, drink, and shipboard jaunts down the Potomac.

Lincoln so enjoyed the admiral's company that he frequently invited him and Ulric to the White House. Often, the elder Dahlgren would drop in of an evening, without an appointment. The president came to rely on his opinions about military developments.

Ulric spent much of the next year with naval artillery units setting up defensive positions around Washington. On May 29, 1862, more than a year after the war began, his status changed. Returning to Washington to obtain ammunition for the unit he was accompanying, he found his father and the president in the office of Secretary of War Stanton. Lincoln asked the young man for an account of his experiences. When he finished speaking, Stanton granted him a direct commission as an aide-de-camp with the rank of captain. Ulric Dahlgren was in the army.

There is no doubt he was commissioned out of favoritism, but soon there would be no question that he deserved it. A good soldier and a natural leader, he served on the staff of General Franz Sigel that summer and fall and saw action in the Shenandoah, at Second Bull Run, and along the Rappahannock.

Brave but not foolhardy, displaying initiative, strength, and fortitude, Dahlgren distinguished himself in action. He also enjoyed himself immensely. When he was occasionally sent to Washington on military business, President Lincoln often asked him to describe the recent battles in which he had fought.

In November, 1862, General Sigel asked Dahlgren to take a patrol into Fredericksburg to assess the rebel strength. With a force of sixty men, he rode nearly fifty miles in twenty-four hours through heavy snow. He led his men in a charge down the main street of the town and engaged in close street fighting, dispersing a Confederate cavalry unit four times the size of his force. He retired with a good estimate of rebel capabilities and brought back thirty-one prisoners, having lost only one man killed from his command. The exploit captured the attention of the northern press, and Dahlgren became a hero. Several months later, when opposing forces met in the heights overlooking Fredericksburg, Dahlgren was with the first troops to cross the river.

A few months later he joined the staff of General Hooker, then in command of the Army of the Potomac. In the bloody Chancellorsville campaign, Dahlgren carried out his duties in a cool and diligent way, never flustered, careless, or less than brave under the stress of continued combat. He was observed on more than one occasion to expose himself to danger by volunteering for hazardous missions.

A reporter for the *New York Times*, describing the battle of Beverly Ford, wrote: "Captain Dahlgren, of General Hooker's staff, a model of cool and dauntless bravery, charged with the regiment, and his horse was shot in two places." General Hooker noted: "I cannot too highly commend the zeal, efficiency, and gallantry which have characterized the performance of his duties."

At Gettysburg, Dahlgren asked for a small body of men to harass the enemy's rear columns. The fighting was heavy and hard. When Lee began his retreat to Virginia, Dahlgren continued to operate with his outfit and on July 6, he rode into Hagerstown, Maryland, just as a large rebel column came into town from a different direction.

Dahlgren led his men in a charge through the center of the city. The street fighting rapidly escalated, a deadly battle with bullets from all directions and sabers hacking at close quarters. Shot in the foot, Dahlgren called out to E. A. Paul, the *New York Times* correspondent, "Paul, I have got it at last." But he remained upright in his saddle until forced off by the loss of blood.

"Wounded," he wrote in his diary that night. "Did not consider it more than a ball glancing—had no idea that it went through. Soon gave way from loss of blood. Laid in an ambulance all night. Foot not very painful. Slept well."

The following day, surgeons operated on the foot. Dahlgren recorded in his diary: "4 or 5 pieces bone taken out. Foot easy and comfortable. Slept well." But the next day he wrote that some surgeons thought his foot "had better come off."

His condition worsened, leaving him too weak to make further entries in the diary. Three days later, his strength rapidly failing, Dahlgren was brought home to Washington and carried on a stretcher into his father's house. Many friends came to visit, including Abraham Lincoln, but before the week was out, he was too sick to receive anyone. General Hooker and the secretary of war were turned away. Ulric lapsed into a coma, unaware the secretary had promoted him to colonel. No one thought he would live to wear the eagles of his new rank.

Admiral Dahlgren, on duty aboard his flagship off the South Carolina coast, was devastated when he received the news of Ulric's condition. Helpless to do anything for him, he wrote to his son on July 20.

> I have been concerned beyond expression to hear of your misfortune. It was almost a foreboding with me. . . . Still I hope for the best. There is nothing good that could happen to me which by any possibility could compensate for a serious evil to any of my children.
>
> You will have the whole house at your disposal and all that I have to make you comfortable.
>
> Meanwhile I shall await for the news with the utmost solicitude.
>
> Goodbye my son—my earnest wishes will be for your happy escape from this wound.
>
> Most affectionately,
> Your Father

Ulric remained in a coma, unaware of the letter. The doorbell was taken down, wagons barred from the street, and cavalrymen placed on duty in front of the house to ensure quiet. The surgeons agreed that the only hope for saving his life lay in immediate amputation of the leg below the knee. But following the operation, he lingered near death for two more days.

On the third day he showed signs of recovery, and on the next day even more. The decision was made to inform him of his promotion. A magistrate was called and Colonel Dahlgren summoned the strength to raise his right hand to take the oath.

Within the week there was a second invalid in the house. Ulric's older brother, wasted by malaria contracted during the Vicksburg campaign, was brought home.

The long days of recuperation and the adjustment to the loss of his leg altered Dahlgren's temperament, giving him reason for introspection and contemplation. He spent much time reading the Bible. In a letter to his aunt Patty, he wrote:

> Often while lying down in my room, I think over what I have seen and what has taken place since I first came home wounded. It seems like a dream and puzzles me to think of "Death" and wonder what it is. . . . How little we know who will go next.

His father wrote letters of encouragement:

> It is not so much what we have in the world as the use we put our means to. You can do a great deal more minus a foot than most young men who have two. It's no small matter to have fought your way to a colonelcy at 21, and that must lead to more.

Ulric was pronounced out of danger in August and traveled to Newport, Rhode Island, to escape Washington's oppressive summer heat. He visited friends in Philadelphia, and by mid-November was on his way to see his father with the fleet off Charleston.

Three months after the amputation, he got back on a horse. Once in the saddle, he found he could ride just as well as before his wound. He lived aboard his father's flagship and frequently went ashore, accompanying the sailors in small-boat maneuvers and training exercises.

He quickly recovered his strength and vitality and walked a great deal, practicing on crutches on land as well as on the rolling decks of the ship. He rode as often as he could and began to nurture the hope that his service to the Union was not finished. To his father's dismay, he expressed his eagerness to return to the fighting.

In late December, he asked to command a landing force being put ashore at Murrill's Inlet on the South Carolina coast. Admiral Dahlgren refused to let him lead the expedition but permitted him to go along as a volunteer. He also joined scouting parties, going ashore under cover of darkness to reconnoiter behind rebel lines.

Ulric returned to Washington in late January 1864, and occupied himself for several days with social calls. He wanted to return the kindness of friends who had been so attentive during his convalescence, including the president. He wrote to his father on January 31:

> I called at the White House matinée yesterday. Abe told me to come up soon, he would like to have a talk with me and I intend to call every day until I find him in.

On February 1, at four o'clock that afternoon, Ulric was ushered into the president's private quarters. The two men talked while Lincoln was being shaved. It was the last time they saw each other.

Not long after that, Dahlgren heard the rumor about Kilpatrick's planned raid on Richmond to free the Union soldiers, and on February 18, he arrived at Brandy Station to join the expedition. On February 26, he wrote to his aunt Patty, enclosing a letter for his father. She was to send it to the admiral in the event Ulric did not return from the raid.

> We will start soon and I think will succeed and if so it will be the grandest thing on record. I have not the slightest fear about not returning, but we can't always tell, so don't be uneasy *nor say a word to anyone.*

In the letter enclosed for his father, Ulric wrote:

I have not returned to the fleet, because there is a grand raid to be made, and I am to have a very important command. If successful, it will be the grandest thing on record; and if it fails, many of us will "*go up*." I may be captured, or I may be "*tumbled over*"; but it is an undertaking that if I were not in, I should be ashamed to show my face again. With such an important command, I am afraid to mention it, for fear that this letter might fall into the wrong hands before reaching you. I find that I can stand the service perfectly well without my leg. I think we will be successful, although a desperate undertaking. . . .

If we do not return, there is no better place to "*give up the ghost.*"

Your affectionate son,
Ulric Dahlgren

Chapter 9

DON'T KNOW YET
WHERE WE ARE TO GO

Headquarters Cavalry Corps
Army of the Potomac
February 26, 1864
Brigadier-General Kilpatrick,
Commanding Third Cavalry Division:
General: Your command, increased to 4,000 men with one battery, will be placed in readiness to move on a raid to Richmond for the purpose of liberating our prisoners at that place.

You will start on Sunday evening, the 28th instant, and will proceed by such routes and make such dispositions as from time to time you may find necessary to accomplish the object of the expedition. You will not be confined to any specific instructions in reference to such matters. Col. Ulric Dahlgren is authorized to accompany you, and will render valuable assistance from his knowledge of the country and his well-known gallantry, intelligence, and energy. Important diversions will be made in your favor, the particulars of which you have already been advised.

With my best wishes for a perfect success, and the assurance that every effort will be exerted by the service here to insure it,
    I remain, very respectfully, your obedient servant,
    A. Pleasonton
    Major-General, Commanding

With his best wishes for success but doubtful of achieving it, General Pleasonton had carried out General Meade's orders to facilitate the raid in every way possible. General Meade, still unconvinced, though believing there was some slim chance of success, had carried out his orders from the War Department and the president. Kilpatrick, Dahlgren, and their officers had carefully crafted their plan. Everyone had done his part. In two days' time, the operation would begin.

On the northern side of the Rapidan there was a bustle of activity. All items of equipment were cleaned, repaired, or replaced, and every horse checked for its shoeing. "This looks extremely raidish," one officer remarked.

There was also noticeable chaos and a surprising amount of disorganization in the northern camp as various cavalry units were ordered to Kilpatrick's headquarters on February 27 and 28. The men came from several commands—Third Indiana, Fourth New York, Seventeenth Pennsylvania, First Maine, Second New York—and most were elated by the prospect of a raid. For a cavalryman, daily life in winter camp was dreary. It was far easier to recruit volunteers for a raid than to get them excited about grooming yet another horse.

Major W. H. Spera of the Seventeenth Pennsylvania Cavalry received his orders on February 27 to select two hundred of the best men and horses available and report to General Thomas Devin. When the men were outfitted and ready, Spera led them to Devin's headquarters. The general, greatly perplexed, had no idea why the unit was there, so he passed them along to a major, who didn't know what to do with them either. He ordered Spera to report to First Division Headquarters, a considerable distance away. There they encountered a similar confusion; no one had orders for the disposition of such a unit.

After hours of wasted time and miles of riding from one encampment to another, they stopped at Kilpatrick's headquarters. Major Spera expected Kilpatrick to be furious about his delay in reporting for duty. Instead, one of the general's aides told Spera to set up camp and make the men and horses comfortable. Armies, it seems, do not change.

That same lack of order was evident almost everywhere. Lieutenant Sam Harris of the Fifth Michigan Cavalry was told to take twenty-five men of Company K and report to Colonel Ulric Dahlgren at Stevensburg. But Company K was not Harris's outfit; it was led by another officer who knew the men well. Why couldn't Harris take his own men? His superior had no answer. Harris ended up in charge of a group unfamiliar to him amid a growing body of veteran cavalrymen from four other regiments.

In one regiment, ten men were selected from each company, hastily formed into a unit, and rushed to Kilpatrick's camp, only to sit idle for a day before being issued supplies. Men returning from leaves or furloughs found themselves stepping off the train and immediately being assigned to units of complete strangers.

Kilpatrick's was a hodgepodge little army, seemingly thrown together with little rhyme or reason, the men uninformed but intensely curious. They suspected they were there for something big.

On the morning of February 28, orders were dispatched to the assembled units to replace any man or horse not in condition to make a long ride. That afternoon, rations for three days were issued to each man: hard bread, sugar, coffee, salt, but no meat. Whatever they were going to do, the men told one another, it apparently wasn't going to take long.

Elsewhere along the Rapidan, the commanders set in motion the various diversionary movements. On the 27th, two regiments of Sixth Corps, under the command of General Sedgwick, moved out, heading west toward Madison Court House. The long column—complete with ambulances, hospital wagons, and headquarters wagons—had only one purpose: to be seen by Confederate observers. The regiments were to remain at Madison, providing cover for another, more daring, diversion.

On the afternoon of February 28, the Second Michigan Cavalry Brigade, Brigadier General George Armstrong Custer commanding, left camp. Although the weather was raw, wet, and windy, the conditions did not prevent Custer's bride of three weeks from coming out to see her husband off. The raid would be their first separation since the wedding, and twenty-two-year-old Libby Custer was frantic with worry about whether she would see him again. Eliza Brown, Custer's black servant, tried to reassure her. "He'll come back," Eliza said. "He always does, you know."

Custer ordered his troops to make as much noise as possible, to be sure they were noticed by the Confederates. Heartily singing "The Girl I Left Behind Me," Custer's renowned Wolverines—Old Curly's Blue-Devils—some fifteen hundred strong, formed up and rode out behind their flashy, long-haired general.

The plan called for Custer's brigade to ride southwest toward Charlottesville, forty miles into enemy territory, to destroy a railroad bridge and supply depot, and to return to camp. The real purpose of the mission was to persuade Robert E. Lee to focus on his left flank, so Kilpatrick and Dahlgren could penetrate on the right. To hold Lee's attention on his left flank, General Birney led units of his Sixth Corps to Culpeper. There, band playing, men marching in maneuvers, they set up camp with as much commotion as they could create.

Back in Stevensburg, the newly organized and thoroughly confused units assembled for the raid waited and wondered. "Don't know yet where we are to go," wrote a captain of the Eighteenth Pennsylvania. Finally, at 6:15 that evening, General Humphreys, Meade's chief of staff, sent a confidential dispatch to Kilpatrick:

"The Major-General commanding, directs that you move tonight."

The flag was up.

While confidential messages sped to and from Kilpatrick's headquarters, delivered by escorted, armed couriers to keep the raid's details secret even from those who were participating in it, the full plan—including maps—was spread out in the offices of the New York newspapers. Even before specific units had been chosen, someone—apparently seeking publicity—had given the information to reporters. As a result, many journalists, editors, and typesetters knew more about the upcoming raid on Richmond to free the Union prisoners than most of the officers and troopers themselves.

At Ely's Ford, the point on the Rapidan where the Union force was to cross, two men lounged in the brush on the rebel side of the river. They laughed and joked but kept watch on the opposite bank, never letting their vigilance lapse. They were Hugh Scott and Dan Tanner, two of Wade Hampton's best Iron Scouts, so called by the Yankees because of their reputation for being so hard to kill. The Iron Scouts were the very effective eyes and ears of Hampton's cavalry. Not much happened on the Yankee side of the river that they did not hear about, sooner or later.

At the headquarters of the Army of Northern Virginia, the Confederates had been expecting an attack on Richmond since the previous November. At that time, Lee had written to Jefferson Davis that scouts had reported plans for a raid to release the Union prisoners. Lee noted that northern newspapers carried many articles on the plight of the captives at Libby and Belle Isle. He gathered his staff for a meeting and tapped his finger on the map at Ely's Ford; he was certain that was where Meade would cross the Rapidan.

The Confederate spy network had kept the Union's Army of the Potomac under close observation throughout the winter. With help from southern sympathizers inside Union lines, the Iron Scouts were able to learn precisely what troops and supplies were moving over the Orange & Alexandria Railroad, the vital link between Washington, D.C., and Brandy Station.

The Iron Scouts were known as unusually brave and resourceful soldiers. In February, one Channing Smith had been able to ride casually through Meade's artillery park, counting the numbers and kinds of weapons stored there. He went on to Fifth Corps headquarters and sat for quite a while with his hand on the headquarters flagstaff, hoping for the chance to take it as a souvenir. He wasn't able to do so, but it made a great story to tell back in camp.

The Iron Scouts operated largely from two secret base camps within the Yankee picket lines. As one historian described the situation:

> The largest camp was a permanent base for Confederate scouts and spies, at times perhaps as many as a hundred. Here the Confederates were so secure that they seem to have given up grey uniforms almost entirely, living permanently in the uniforms of the enemy. The false uniforms were a great advantage. In the fastnesses of the swamp, there was little chance of being caught and hanged for wearing them, and any genuine Yankee scout, wandering into a rebel lair, would imagine himself among friends—until it was too late. The rebel spies were so completely and comfortably established that they kept with them a Confederate Army medical officer.

In addition to the Iron Scouts, the rebels had other efficient sources of information. The Confederacy had entered the war with a highly organized spy system already in place in Washington that included the large number of government employees still loyal to the South. Southerners had worked in all areas of government long before the war began, and the fortuitous result was just as beneficial as if it had been planned.

Union intelligence services were never able fully to protect government secrets from rebel spies. Until the end of the war, Confederate agents remained on the job in the highest government offices, even on the staff of General LaFayette Baker. Southern agents visited Washington so often that a well-known hotel kept a room permanently reserved for them.

One piece of information the Iron Scout Frank Stringfellow, disguised as Sally Marsten, overheard at the George Washington's Birthday Ball was that something big would be happening soon—some sort of cavalry raid that was expected to give the rebels quite a shock.

From a variety of sources, then, the Confederates had ample warning that the Union was about to attempt a raid on Richmond. On February 27 and 28, they received reports that three large commands—Sedgwick's, Custer's, and Birney's—were on the move south-west.

This could be the start of the raid they had been anticipating, an attempt to bypass Lee's troops by going far out on his left flank. Or it could be a diversion or an independent operation designed to create havoc in the Shenandoah Valley, nowhere near Richmond.

Lee faced a difficult decision. Where should he commit his troops? He could not cover the entire Rapidan front and also protect Richmond; he didn't have enough men. But he couldn't ignore the troop movements led by Custer and the other Yankee units in case their forays were *not* deceptions. Lee decided to send Jeb Stuart and his cavalry toward Charlottesville and hold the remainder of the army in place behind the Rapidan. Richmond would have to remain virtually defenseless until he had more information.

Chapter 10

A DARKNESS THAT
COULD BE FELT

The sky was clear on the night of February 28, the stars bright. The moon cast a pale glow over the northern Virginia countryside. The five hundred men of Colonel Dahlgren's command, each armed with a carbine and two Colt revolvers, had ridden out of Stevensburg late that afternoon and were within two miles of Ely's Ford, waiting for darkness.

By ten o'clock the column moved up to within a few hundred yards of the ford and halted again. Those nearest the front heard Dahlgren issue a few hasty orders. They watched a lieutenant, fifty troopers, and two scouts dismount and make their way down to the water, where they waded across.

Led by Martin Hogan, a nineteen-year-old scout who had emigrated from Ireland three years before, the soldiers crossed the river above the ford, surprising the rebel pickets on the southern side. A quick rush, a brief struggle, two wild shots fired—and the entire Confederate picket force of two officers and sixteen men were captured.

With the pickets safely out of the way, a courier was dispatched to

Kilpatrick with the news. Dahlgren's main force proceeded across the Rapidan. The colonel rode to the head of his column, a ghostly figure outlined in the moonlight, the crutch strapped to his saddle. Orders were passed to prepare for the next stage of the raid, a high-speed ride to Spottsylvania Court House.

Dahlgren was pleased to have brought his men across the ford so smoothly, without alerting the Confederates. He was unaware that two of Hampton's Iron Scouts, Hugh Scott and Dan Tanner, had joined the rear of his column. They had watched the capture of the Confederate pickets, then slid two logs into the icy river and paddled across. They easily made an estimate of the size of the raiding party, stole two horses from the unit's herd, and took their place in line, riding calmly along with the Yankees. Once across the river again, the rebel scouts broke away to ride like hell, so they could tell Wade Hampton the Yankees were coming.

General Kilpatrick's main Union force of thirty-five hundred men departed Stevensburg around eleven o'clock that night and crossed the Rapidan two hours later. Captain Joseph Gloskoski was so impressed by the beauty of the evening that he recorded his feelings in the florid prose of the day:

> Myriads of stars twinkled in heaven, looking at us as if in wonder why should we break the laws of God and wander at night instead of seeking repose and sleep. The moon threw its silvery light upon Rapidan waters when we forded it, and it seemed as if the Almighty Judge was looking silently on our doings.

Kilpatrick sent a more prosaic message to headquarters, informing Meade of the capture of the rebel picket force: "It was a complete surprise. No alarm has been given. The enemy does not anticipate our movement." According to a *New York Tribune* correspondent, Kilpatrick also sent a message to Pleasonton, offering to double his bet of five thousand dollars that he would enter Richmond successfully.

Both Kilpatrick's and Dahlgren's forces rode throughout the night, sometimes at a trot, sometimes at a gallop. The pace was so fast that men at the rear had difficulty keeping up. By dawn, the columns had passed through the grisly Chancellorsville battlefield. To the northeast, toward Fredericksburg, they could see the rebel campfires.

The commanders allowed only a few brief breaks, and by eight o'clock on the morning of February 29, Kilpatrick's main column entered Spottsylvania Court House. Dahlgren had passed through earlier and was now leading his troops southwest, toward the James River.

Kilpatrick halted briefly at Spottsylvania, where the men, a little crazed with exhaustion and hunger, had their first skirmish of the expedition—with a flock of geese. An elderly woman armed with a broom made up the entire defensive force. She screamed at one trooper after another, striking wildly about with her weapon, while the riders thundered through her farmyard, sabers flashing, feathers flying. Captain L. B. Kurtz tried to calm her. "Madam," he said gallantly, "these Yankees are hell on poultry."

At his Stevensburg headquarters, General Meade wrote to his wife:

> My cavalry expedition for Richmond got off last night, and at 2 A.M., the last I heard from them, they were getting on famously, not having met any one or being, as far as they could tell, discovered by the enemy. I trust they will be successful; it will be the greatest feat of the war, if they do succeed, and will immortalize them all. Young Dahlgren, with his one leg, went along with them. The weather from having been most favorable, now that the expedition has gone begins to look suspicious.

Kilpatrick, too, was concerned about the weather. Observing the masses of dark clouds that were forming, he told his staff he hoped the storm would hold off for twenty-four hours. Then they would be fine.

The columns pushed on, never stopping long enough for sleep or a cooked meal. Even though their rations had not included meat, they were well supplied. Since Kilpatrick had issued orders to live off the land, foraging in the countryside had proceeded diligently. Almost every saddle had a chicken, goose, or ham dangling from it, but the men couldn't take the time to eat.

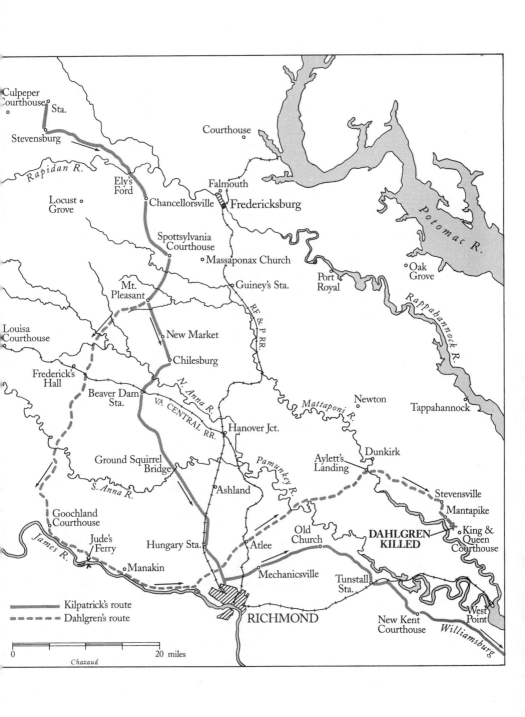

Culpeper
Courthouse ○
○ Sta.
Stevensburg
Rapidan R.
Ely's
Ford
Locust
Grove ○
Chancellorsville ○
Courthouse ○
Falmouth
Fredericksburg
Spottsylvania
Courthouse
○ Massaponax Church
Mt.
Pleasant
New Market ○
Louisa
Courthouse ○
Guiney's Sta.
RF & P RR
Port
Royal ○
○ Oak
Grove
Potomac R.
Rappahannock R.
Chilesburg ○
Frederick's
Hall ○
Beaver Dam
Sta.
N. Anna R.
VA. CENTRAL RR.
Hanover Jct. ○
Ground Squirrel
Bridge ○
S. Anna R.
Mattaponi R.
Newton ○
Tappahannock ○
Dunkirk ○
Aylett's
Landing
Stevensville ○
Mantapike
Goochland
Courthouse ○
Jude's
Ferry
Hungary Sta. ○
Pamunkey R.
Ashland
Atlee ○
Old
Church ○
**DAHLGREN
KILLED**
King &
Queen
Courthouse
James R.
○ Manakin
Mechanicsville ○
Tunstall
Sta. ○
West
Point
RICHMOND
New Kent
Courthouse
Williamsburg

——— Kilpatrick's route
- - - - Dahlgren's route

0   20 miles
Chazaud

At ten o'clock in the morning, General Meade telegraphed General Halleck, the army chief of staff:

A cavalry expedition left last evening with the intention of carrying Richmond by a *coup de main*, General Kilpatrick in command. If successful, expects to be there by tomorrow P.M., March 1, and may the next day be in the vicinity of General Butler's outposts and picket. Will you please notify that officer, that his advanced posts may be warned?

The forces rode into the afternoon without detecting any sign of the enemy, except for a few isolated pickets who were promptly captured. But the signs of the war were everywhere, the destroyed homes, deserted farms, abandoned churches. The very landscape itself looked neglected. The few inhabitants were poorly fed and clothed, defeat and weariness etched in their gaunt faces.

Many of Dahlgren's troops were serving with him for the first time. Ordering a brief rest, he rode slowly along the length of his formation as if measuring each man. One officer wrote that Dahlgren's appearance "gave general satisfaction, and expressions of confidence were heard all around." There was no mention of his missing leg.

Early on the morning of February 29, the Iron Scouts Scott and Tanner reined in at Wade Hampton's house to report their encounter with the Yankee forces. Without waiting for orders, General Hampton assembled all the men he could muster from his scattered and understrength command—only three hundred six troopers and two cannon. Undaunted, he led them out to pursue a raiding party ten times the size. Wade Hampton was used to being outnumbered.

In Richmond, General Lee's concern was mounting over the continuing reports of troop movements from the other Yankee outfits— led by Sedgwick, Custer, and Birney—but he remained ignorant of the main force, deep into Confederate territory and moving on the capital. He boarded a train for his headquarters at Orange Court House, unaware he would be passing through territory the Yankees were invading.

Dahlgren's men pushed on toward Frederick's Hall Station. About a mile out of town, they cut the telegraph wire and tore up the track of the Virginia Central Railroad. In the distance, to the north, they detected the sounds of a train receding. By minutes they had missed capturing Robert E. Lee, the only person capable of holding the Confederacy together.

Dahlgren's men also missed another prize. The entire artillery of the Confederate Second Corps—more than eighty pieces of every caliber—was massed outside of Frederick's Hall Station. Dahlgren learned of the stash from rebel captives, including eight officers and men taken prisoner while holding a court martial in an empty house. Questioning a private who did not seem too intelligent, Dahlgren found out that the guns were guarded by five cavalry regiments. Because he did not believe the soldier, Dahlgren questioned some slaves from the nearest plantation. They told the same story: The guns were defended by many troops. The officers from the court martial were interrogated individually; all insisted the guns were heavily guarded.

Dahlgren decided not to attack a force that was clearly so much larger than his own five-hundred-man outfit, even though the capture of the artillery would have been a significant setback for the South. As it turned out, all those he questioned had lied. The guns were protected by only a handful of soldiers.

Wade Hampton's troops were racing to catch up with the Federal raiders. Hampton sent a courier to Colonel Bradley Johnson of the Maryland Line Cavalry stationed around the New Kent Court House, ordering him to locate and track the invaders. Equipped with a mere sixty men and two cannon, Johnson rode out to do battle.

By late in the day, Kilpatrick's men were closing in on Beaver Dam, another stop on the Virginia Central Railroad line. Sweeping down on the station, the troopers surprised the telegraph operator before he could tap out a warning message to Richmond. The men set fire to the small settlement. Twenty buildings and hundreds of cords of wood were set ablaze, sending flames rising above the treetops. Captain Gloskoski wrote: "The dark forms of our soldiers jumping and dancing around it seemed from a distance like demons on some hellish sport." An oncoming train blew its whistle and men were sent to intercept it, but the engineer saw the blaze in time and reversed course, back in the direction of Richmond.

After dark, the column marched away from the ruins of Beaver Dam. Heavy rain mixed with snow had begun to fall. The men were hungry and had been in the saddle nearly twenty-four hours. The horses, too, were suffering. The woods were dense, making passage difficult. Bitter winds drove stinging rain and sleet into tired eyes. Captain Gloskoski recalled:

> Now it stormed in earnest. Sharp wind and sleet forced men to close their eyes. The night was so dark that even the river in front could not be seen and trees on the roadside could not be distinguished. So complete darkness I never saw.

And Colonel James Kidd remembered "a darkness that could be felt":

> On and on, for hours and hours, facing the biting storm, feeling the pelting rain, staring with straining eyes into the black night, striving to see when nothing was visible to the keenest vision.

Some of the men began to gripe, but Dahlgren set an example. One soldier wrote: "Who could complain of weariness when he looked at the colonel, still weak from his wound, riding along quietly, uncomplainingly, ever vigilantly watching every incident of the march."

At midnight, Dahlgren halted the exhausted five hundred at a crossroads beside a small store. As he was helped from his horse, a trooper asked if he wasn't tired. "We'll have some supper and two hours' sleep," Dahlgren said, "then you'll see how bright I am."

Kilpatrick led his force south from Beaver Dam. As the snow, sleet, and wind intensified, men were forced to depend on the instincts of their horses to follow the ones ahead, because it was impossible to see the next man in line. Their misery was compounded by sniper fire.

Rebel soldiers on leave, home guards, farmers with old muskets—indeed, anyone who could shoulder a gun—harassed the Yankees, fired into their ranks from the cover of darkness. They often had to stop to clear away barricades hastily erected from fence posts and felled trees. The rebels would hide, fire a volley, and disappear, only to snipe again a half-mile farther on. One Union soldier noted that the scattered shots in the darkness reminded him of fireflies.

Horses foundered, forcing some troopers to proceed on foot, carrying their saddles and clutching a comrade's stirrup for balance. Some men became separated from the main column. A wrong turn, a momentary daze, and a soldier would be alone in the night, afraid to cry out lest the rebels hear. Ice formed on beards and overcoats, scabbards and rifles. The men swayed in their saddles, drugged with fatigue.

At ten o'clock that night, Kilpatrick paused so the men could build fires to make coffee, eat a little cold food, and try to get some rest. By then his column was strung out so far that it took two hours for the rear units to reach camp.

Confederate home guards watched the Yankees huddling around their fires. Some rebels were prepared to shoot, but their commander, Dr. L. B. Anderson, argued against it. His group was too badly outnumbered to stage a proper fight. But he sensed that the column might be heading into a trap as it approached Richmond, and he wanted to help ensure that the trap closed. Anderson wrote out a dispatch noting the size and location of the enemy force and its direction of march, and sent it off with a fast rider to Richmond.

At one o'clock in the morning, Kilpatrick ordered his men to mount up. Their hard ride continued.

That same day, in New York City, the *Herald* published a story outlining in remarkably accurate detail "a grand expedition" under way in Virginia. All that was omitted was the raid's objective: no mention was made of Richmond.

By the evening of February 29, Confederate authorities in Richmond had been alerted to the danger, although no one was certain of the size or precise location of the enemy force. Lee, however, knew even less. Back at his headquarters at Orange Court House, the general remained preoccupied by the presence on his left flank of Custer's cavalry, relentlessly moving toward Charlottesville.

Suddenly Lee received word of another Federal cavalry unit on the right, in the vicinity of Frederick's Hall. Where had they come from? Several reports came in that his major artillery reserve at Frederick's Hall had been captured. He was greatly relieved when these turned out to be false.

Neither Lee at Orange Court House nor Jefferson Davis in Richmond could sleep that night. Both had reason to be worried; they still didn't know what the Yankees were up to.

WE ARE GOING ON

Dahlgren was on the move by dawn on the morning of March 1, after a few hours of fitful sleep in the icy rain. He halted his column about twenty-one miles from Richmond and ordered Captain John Mitchell to take a detachment of a hundred men, with the ambulances and prisoners, down the Kanawha Canal on the north side of the James River.

Mitchell's task was to destroy canal locks, boats, mills, and grain. When his force reached Westham Creek, about six miles outside Richmond, he was to send the ambulances and the prisoners north to Kilpatrick and rejoin Dahlgren in the city. Meanwhile, Dahlgren would cross the James and enter Richmond from the south.

Mitchell's party moved slowly, finding that thorough destruction takes time. His men methodically set buildings afire. Cattle and horses that could not be taken along were shot. The area being systematically pillaged contained some of the finest homes and plantations in all Virginia, among them Sabot Hill, the home of the Confederate secretary of war, James A. Seddon.

Earlier that morning, Dahlgren's column had stopped to rest on the grounds of the Seddon plantation. Dahlgren rode up to the great white house to inquire whether the honorable gentleman was at home. Even if not, Dahlgren thought it only polite to leave his card.

Mrs. Seddon came to the door; the house servants were too fearful to answer the knock, what with four hundred Yankees lounging on the grounds. She raised an eyebrow at the caller, supported by his crutch, and demanded his name. When he identified himself, her expression softened and she inquired of his relationship to Admiral John Dahlgren. That settled, Mrs. Seddon smiled. "Then I knew you as a boy," she said, "and I knew your father when I was one of your mother's schoolmates in Philadelphia. He was a beau of mine."

Mrs. Seddon invited Colonel Dahlgren inside and sent a servant to the cellar for a bottle of 1844 blackberry wine. For a time they sat together, making pleasant conversation about Philadelphia, the admiral, and mutual friends. Toasting one another's families with silver goblets of wine, they might have been neighbors visiting of a Sunday after church. The talk was light, charming, and witty. The war was not discussed.

When it was time to go, Mrs. Seddon watched from the veranda as Dahlgren slowly mounted his horse. He removed his hat and bowed deeply, assuring her that his men would not harm the property.

Although thoroughly charmed by her young visitor and the memories of her girlhood his appearance occasioned, Mrs. Seddon did not forget that "little Ully" was the enemy. While one servant had fetched the wine, another had been sent riding to Richmond. The government had to be warned that a band of Yankees was nearby. A southern writer later suggested, in the absence of any firm evidence, that "Mrs. Seddon saved Richmond." And, indeed, she had tried to.

Mrs. Seddon was not alone in finding Colonel Dahlgren agreeable. Some Confederate officers captured by his outfit later reported that he had treated them decently, sharing his food and drink. "He was most agreeable and charming," one recalled, "very fair-haired and young looking, with manners as soft as a cat's."

Dahlgren reached the James River at eleven o'clock that morning and led his men to the point where their guide said they would be able to cross. The guide, Martin Robinson, was an ex-slave who had

become a bricklayer. He had been recommended by the provost mar-
shal-general's office:

> At the last moment I have found the man . . . well acquainted
> with the James River from Richmond up. . . . Question him five
> minutes and you will know him the very man you want. . . . He
> crossed at Rapidan last night, and has late information.

In talking with Robinson, Dahlgren learned that the guide had
lived nearby. Robinson confirmed that he had crossed the Rapidan
only the night before and therefore had the latest information on
troop concentrations. He had also lived in Richmond and had escorted
some of the Libby Prison escapees on their journey north.

Dahlgren told Robinson before they left that he would pay the
guide generously for getting them safely across the James River. But
Dahlgren warned Robinson that if he were found to be deceiving or
lying, he would be hanged.

When the column reached the riverbank at the crossing point,
they found the water swift and deep, with no sign of the promised
ford. Robinson appeared confused, staring open-mouthed into the
depths that should have been shallow enough for horses to cross.
Dahlgren asked if there was another spot nearby where they could take
the horses across. The guide slowly shook his head. One of Dahlgren's
officers recalled:

> The colonel then told him he would have to carry out his part of
> the contract, to which the guide assented and admitted that was
> the agreement and made no objection to his execution. He went
> along to the tree without any force and submitted to his fate
> without a murmur.

Dahlgren ordered a sergeant to commence the hanging. A stout
rope was fashioned into a noose, an oak tree with a thick branch over-
hanging the bank was chosen, and the deed was done.

The Yankees were left with no way to cross the James, losing their
opportunity to slip into Richmond from the south while the rebels
were occupied, defending the city in the north. Dahlgren rallied his

troopers and headed southwest at a trot, following the James River's northern bank in the direction of Richmond.

The body of Martin Robinson was left to dangle in the wind, silhouetted against the overcast sky. The local residents let the body remain there for a week as a lesson for their slaves, to show them what Yankees really thought about Negroes.

Captain Mitchell and his men continued their mission of destruction. At each plantation, the scene was the same. Frightened slaves or friends rushed to each house, bearing the news that Yankees were on the loose. The family silver was buried in the yard as the residents saw smoke rise in the distance from the fires on the neighboring plantation. The men of the house ran for the barn to saddle up and ride away. There followed the thundering approach of many horses, shouted commands, pounding at the door. Finally, the torch was applied.

Not knowing of Dahlgren's promise to Mrs. Seddon, Mitchell's men entered Sabot Hill, burning the Seddons' barn, stables, and corn houses. They left the mansion untouched. At Dover plantation, the soldiers set fire to the great house three times; each time house servants extinguished the fire with buckets and brooms. Disgusted, the Yankees gave up, but not before looting the cellar of vintage wines and cordials.

As Mitchell made his way to the river road, he was surprised to see tracks from a large body of cavalry heading southwest. He was sure they could not be Dahlgren's because he was supposed to be across the James by then. Mitchell was alarmed, wondering whether a rebel force was close. A little farther on, he found an explanation.

At a place on the river called Jude's Ferry, he discovered Martin Robinson's body. Consulting his map, Mitchell wondered why Robinson had led Dahlgren's force there to cross the river instead of the ford at Dover Mill two miles away. Apparently, Robinson simply had gotten lost.

At 3:30 that afternoon, Mitchell caught sight of Dahlgren's forces. Together, the two men reformulated their plan for approaching Richmond. As they hovered over a campfire, they heard the sounds of fighting north of the capital. Assuming it was Kilpatrick attacking the Confederates, Dahlgren dispatched a detachment, with prisoners and ambulances, in the direction of the firing. At five o'clock, Dahlgren's men mounted up and resumed their march to Richmond, following the road to the village of Westham. Dahlgren was determined to attack, to come to Kilpatrick's support.

General Kilpatrick and his troopers had ridden through the night, harassed by snipers and bushwhackers. By dawn they had reached the Brook Pike, within five miles of Richmond. But where was Dahlgren? The hour for the joint attack was at hand, and Kilpatrick did not know if Dahlgren's men were in position to charge into Richmond from the south. The two forces were supposed to have communicated with flare signals, but the rain and low clouds had made them worthless. Maybe Dahlgren was on schedule and just waiting to hear evidence of Kilpatrick's attack before commencing his own.

Although Kilpatrick was uncertain of Dahlgren's whereabouts, the rebels of Colonel Johnson's Maryland Line Cavalry were not. The Southerners had captured five troopers of Dahlgren's command who were carrying a dispatch for Kilpatrick, a message telling of Dahlgren's lack of success in crossing the James River. Dahlgren suggested that both forces attack Richmond at sunset; Kilpatrick never received the message.

Kilpatrick was hesitant, unsure how to proceed. His characteristic brashness had deserted him and he was reluctant to move out. He surveyed the perimeter fortifications of Richmond's defenses along the Brook Pike. He considered the information he had obtained from a prisoner that two thousand infantry and six cannon were nearby. Obviously, one objective must be to neutralize that force—assuming it existed. He decided to divide his command, assigning Major Hall and four hundred fifty men the task of attacking the rumored force, to keep it away from Kilpatrick's main body. Before long, Kilpatrick could hear rebel artillery firing at Hall's men.

The general continued to question civilians and prisoners; all assured him that Richmond was calm. No one was expecting a Yankee attack. The capital was his for the taking. And with it, he thought, a sure promotion, glory, even the presidency—in time. Who would not vote for the man who had captured Richmond?

Still, Kilpatrick had misgivings. His exhausted men had been in the saddle thirty-six hours, but they were eager to attack, perhaps more so than their commander. They were only five miles from the enemy capital. The city was at their feet, nearly defenseless. Why hadn't Kilpatrick sounded the charge?

Kilpatrick's optimism, which had flamed so high in Washington and at Stevensburg, was fast dimming in the pale dawn light on the Brook Pike. Ahead of him, for more than a thousand yards, stretched clear fields crisscrossed with earthworks and trenches. The defensive force appeared under strength; there did not seem to be many soldiers in the trenches. The Union's three thousand troopers could easily ride through them to storm down the streets of the rebel capital.

The soldiers watched expectantly. Finally, after a long silence, Kilpatrick turned to an aide and issued an order. The men tensed with excitement. But instead of ordering the anticipated massive charge, all Kilpatrick did was send skirmishers forward on foot, to feel out the defenses. In advance of them, six field guns were brought up and opened fire.

All the speed, thrust, and pulse-pounding urgency of the last thirty-six hours ground down to the cautious footsteps of a line of skirmishers. The cannon fired, a few rebel cannon answered. Sporadic rifle shots rang out. The skirmishers overran some forward rifle pits and found a second line of breastworks empty. There were hardly any defensive forces at all.

Behind the skirmishers, Kilpatrick sent columns of mounted troopers moving slowly forward, watching and listening. Farther back on the Pike, a reserve brigade, mounted in columns of fours, waited, uneasy at the delay. Suddenly, a hard-riding staff officer from Kilpatrick overtook them. Surely this was the order for the charge by the entire command. The lift in morale was visible.

It was not a signal to attack. Kilpatrick had sent word that the wounded would have to make their own way back to the Rapidan because no ambulances were available. If ever a message was received at the wrong time, it was that one! Colonel Kidd recalled, with sarcasm:

> Cheerful intelligence, surely, and well timed to put men and officers upon their fighting mettle! From that moment, the mental attitude of the bravest was one of apathetic indifference. Such an announcement was enough to dampen the ardor of men as brave as those.

By one o'clock in the afternoon, having advanced only two miles nearer Richmond in the hours since dawn, Kilpatrick's men met with heavy resistance. His delay had given the rebels sufficient time to bring up reinforcements. At dawn, there had been few troops to contest the Union advance; now their number had grown. Kilpatrick's men were facing heavier and more accurate fire from trained soldiers, not what could be expected from amateur home militia units. Brigadier General Henry Davis, commanding Kilpatrick's advance force, judged the situation to be increasingly dangerous. They had much open terrain to cross where the Confederates could sweep the attackers with cannon fire. Worse, the muddy, slippery ground was making it difficult for the cavalry to operate.

General Davis continued his advance, pushing the skirmishers onward. Kilpatrick, watching from behind, worried about the mounting resistance. He told an aide the rebels had too many damned guns and were bringing up too many new ones. The rain was beginning to fall again, and soon it turned to snow.

Davis organized his men for a charge when a messenger galloped up with new orders from Kilpatrick. Davis was to fall back and cover the rear of the main force. The attack was over. Just at the moment when victory, glory, and fame were so near, Kilpatrick had lost his nerve. Thus, his dreams of advancement were shattered by the threat from a small force of local guardsmen that he could have defeated easily.

That was as close as Kilpatrick and his men came to capturing

Richmond. The highly touted raid had failed. The only goal left was to survive, to escape the marauding Confederates and retreat.

Unaware of Kilpatrick's hesitation and the collapse of the attack, Dahlgren was racing toward the battle sounds he heard from the west. Five miles outside the city, as dusk began to settle, his advance party met with heavy fire. At the same time, the firing north of the city, from the direction of Kilpatrick's force, suddenly ceased. Dahlgren sent scouts to find out what had happened to Kilpatrick's attack but none of them returned.

Now Dahlgren heard train whistles from the far side of the James River, indicating to him that reinforcements were coming from Petersburg. He faced a dilemma: Should he continue with the mission, which was seeming increasingly hopeless, or try to save his men and ride for the Union lines? Scouts brought word of several sizable Confederate cavalry units in the area. He interrogated newly captured prisoners, who told him the assault from the north—by Kilpatrick—had been repulsed.

It looked hopeless to continue, but after conferring with his officers, Dahlgren elected to press on with his advance toward the city. He knew the opportunity to release the Union captives in Richmond's prisons had been lost. Without Kilpatrick's force to keep the rebel army occupied, Dahlgren had no chance to undertake that raid. Nor could he hope to invade the city with a mere five hundred men. But Dahlgren would not allow himself to retreat in the face of the enemy without a fight.

The only honorable way to proceed, Dahlgren decided, was to charge. First he ordered the lone remaining ambulance—which contained the signal rockets, oakum, and turpentine for burning bridges—to be destroyed. There was no point in leaving it to the enemy. And several hundred slaves would have to be abandoned. They had joined Dahlgren's column to escape to freedom, but he could not afford to be encumbered by them now.

As Dahlgren mounted his horse, he remarked on how awkward it was for him with one leg. He added, "We are going on; and if we succeed, I'd gladly lose the other."

They prepared to move out. An officer later commented on "the colonel's coolness. He rode along the line, speaking to the men, so calm, so quiet, so brave that it seemed to me the veriest coward must needs fight, if never before."

The force of fewer than five hundred men made a bold charge into a fortification of unknown strength, and at first they were successful. For two and a half miles, they charged in waves, with Dahlgren always in the lead. Each time, the rebels broke under the impact of the Yankee force, abandoning their trenches, and racing away across the fields toward the city.

> It was a scrub race—across fields, fences and stone walls, we pressed after them, rallying and scattering them repeatedly as they attempted to dispute our advance whenever a wall or house afforded shelter. Between formidable works, over rifle pits, ditches and every obstruction, with a cheer, a run and a volley from our Spencers, we crowded them back to the edge of the city. It was now dark and the gas lights burning. We were inside the city limits, though the houses were scattered.

There, the advance stopped. It was as far as they could go. Dahlgren had lost too many men to continue the attack. He passed the word to withdraw, ordering Captain Mitchell to serve as a rear guard. Speed was imperative. There was no choice but to leave the wounded behind. A young assistant surgeon volunteered to remain with them, knowing he faced capture. Snow and sleet were falling and the wind blowing hard as Dahlgren's weary troopers rode northwest toward Hungary Station. Their retreat had begun.

In Stevensburg, General Meade paced, awaiting word from Kilpatrick. Custer's force had returned from its diversionary foray without losing a man. They had covered almost a hundred miles in forty-eight hours, through ice, snow, and freezing rain. They had burned a railroad bridge and depot, taken fifty prisoners, and evaded Jeb Stuart's cavalry. More important, they had kept Stuart occupied so Kilpatrick and Dahlgren could push through to Richmond unimpeded.

The last message Meade received from Kilpatrick was when the raiders were thirty miles from Richmond. Meade wrote to his wife:

> Of course you can imagine our anxiety to know his fate. If he finds Richmond no better guarded than our information says it is, he will have a great chance of getting in and liberating all the prisoners. . . . God grant he may, for their sakes and his.

Chapter 12

THE CHASE WAS A
NIGHTMARE

Throughout the morning of March 1, the citizens of Richmond listened with growing fear as the sounds of war drew closer. Couriers dashed through the streets, bearing urgent messages for Jefferson Davis or for army headquarters. Wagons filled with ammunition rumbled by, heading north to the front. The tension was fed by rumors whispered softly from one person to another, as though the Yankees might overhear if they talked in normal voices. "Mr. Seddon's family has been captured." "Did you hear? The government is preparing to evacuate the city." "There are five thousand Yankees out there." Or was it fifty thousand? No one knew.

Davis sat in his office, listening to the cannon fire, his West Point–trained mind calculating how far the enemy was from the gates of his capital. It put him in a bad temper for the rest of the day.

The firing got closer. Elizabeth Van Lew remembered that "every reliable man was called out. There was an awful quiet in the streets; the heavy silence was impressive." A congressman told friends that the raiders were shelling his house, only a mile and a half distant. Silent crowds milled about outside the capitol building, waiting for word of Richmond's fate.

In homes throughout the city, men barricaded their families in upstairs rooms and showed them once again how to use the rifles and pistols, in the event those people—the cursed Yankees—bent on murder and rapine, broke into their homes. Churches opened their doors and hundreds filed in to kneel and pray for deliverance from the evil that was out there all around them, as signaled by the cannon and rifle fire.

People became agitated about the Union captives caged up in their midst. Suppose they became emboldened by the Yankee raids so close by and broke out of their prisons? The defensive forces included only old men, boys, and crippled veterans to protect the citizenry. They would never be able to stop thousands of enraged Yankees from pouring out of their cells and rampaging through the streets, lusting for revenge.

The person responsible for Richmond's defense, Colonel Walter Stevens, had moved some artillery and additional men into the northern fortifications the night before. Before Kilpatrick attempted to attack that morning, Stevens had ridden out to inspect the defenses. No sooner had he returned to his office when the firing started.

Stevens concentrated his entire force, all six hundred men, against Kilpatrick. They were the ones who would stop Kilpatrick's three thousand trained troopers and force them to retreat. Elizabeth Van Lew had been right; Richmond was highly vulnerable to attack, but it needed someone with more nerve than Kilpatrick to take advantage of the city's weakness.

Early in the afternoon, however, the people of Richmond faced a new terror when word came of another Union force bearing down from the west. That was Dahlgren and his five hundred men. The only rebel troops to throw against them were those of the home defense brigade.

The old bell on Capital Square rang out the alarm, calling the home defense brigade into action. Instantly, throughout the city, men stopped their work. Clerks put down their pens, factory workers their tools, boys laid down their schoolbooks. There was only a moment's hesitation—just enough for the mind to register the bell's significance—then the men and boys rushed home to don their uniforms and report for duty.

As they dashed through the crowded streets, they heard the

rumors and snatches of conversation. "The enemy's in sight, coming from the north and the west." "Yankee cavalry's already loose inside our lines. . . ."

The defense brigade was organized into five battalions. Some of the men had received cursory military training. The group included old men and boys, intellectuals, businessmen, government officials, and illiterate factory hands. But they were dedicated. They knew that whenever the bell rang, calling them to service, it was to defend their city, their homes, their loved ones from imminent disaster. They also understood that they were the last line of defense. There was no one else to hold the Yankee hordes at bay.

Many of the workers had been up since five o'clock in the morning and had walked miles to their jobs, but now they ran those miles again to take up their positions. One battalion of two hundred twenty factory workers formed up and moved off to the western section of the city, led by Major Ford, an Englishman, astride a magnificent stallion. Rain and sleet were falling, the clouds low and dark.

The force grew larger as it made its way through the streets. Regular army soldiers and officers on leave, or just passing through, joined the column. Although some high-ranking officers were among them, all served as privates in this expedition.

As they neared Westham, Dahlgren's men attacked. For a band of local militia, the defenders held their ground better than expected, but eventually had to fall back under the impact of Dahlgren's larger and better-trained force. Even then, the Richmond guard carried out the retreat in an orderly fashion.

John Jones, the Confederate War Department clerk, wrote in his diary that night:

> The enemy's cavalry charged upon them, firing as they came; they were ordered to lie flat on the ground. This they did, until the enemy came within fifteen yards of them, when they rose and fired, sending the assailants to the right and left, helter-skelter. How many fell is not known.

As the fight continued and the defensive line was pushed back toward the capital, a battalion of government clerks joined the defense.

Their commander, Captain John McAnerny, a regular army soldier recovering from a severe wound, deployed his men well. Despite the darkness, cold, and rain, he sent a group of fifty men forward to fire one round simultaneously. They fell back so a second group of fifty, loaded and ready, could fire as one. Each action poured forth a deadly volume of fire until Dahlgren was forced to call off his attack. McAnerny's battalion was causing the Union troops to lose too many men. On into the evening, the battle raged. But even when it stopped, the fear and uncertainty gripping Richmond did not.

The prison guards at Libby and Belle Isle were scared. They were only a handful, equipped with antiquated rifles, left to deal with thousands of desperate, angry men. General Winder was also worried. He believed the purpose of the Union raids was to free the prisoners. And even if not, Winder thought the prisoners might stage an escape on their own, knowing their comrades were close by. Through his network of informants and spies, Winder knew the imprisoned Union soldiers had accumulated crude weapons—clubs, homemade knives, and slingshots. If those men were let loose on Richmond, the result would be mayhem.

It was too late for Winder to find additional troops to help guard the prisoners. He had to devise an alternative plan. That night, he proposed to Secretary of War Seddon that a large quantity of powder be placed in the basement of Libby's main building. If the prisoners made any attempt to escape, they would all be blown sky high.

The secretary of war, mindful of his place in history if he were judged responsible for the deaths of hundreds of prisoners, refused to order such a drastic measure. However, he impressed on Winder that the prisoners must not be allowed to escape. And Seddon issued his directive with such emphasis that Winder considered it sanction enough, and so he ordered it done.

Guards dug a large hole in the prison basement and crammed it with several hundred pounds of gunpowder. The work could hardly remain a secret. Libby's highest-ranking prisoner, the Union general Neal Dow, wrote in his diary on March 2:

Last night, a hole was dug in the centre of the *middle cellar* of this prison, about 3 feet square and 3 feet deep! *This morning, we heard a rumor that the prison officials had put a large quantity of powder in a hole in the middle cellar, dug last night!*

A southern clergyman visiting one of Libby's prisoners "assured him that we were sleeping over a volcano: that the prison is undermined and powder placed beneath it—*'to blow you (us) to atoms'*—that there is no mistake about it."

If anyone harbored doubts about the explosives, they were dispelled by the commandant, Major Thomas Turner:

I do not expect to live, if your cavalry get into the city. I shall stick to my post of duty until Kilpatrick reaches here, then every damned Yankee in this place will be blown to hell.

The prison guards now had even more reason to be terrified. If the powder were touched off, they would disappear with the prisoners, and several square blocks of Richmond as well.

Kilpatrick's men rode northeast from Richmond along the Mechanicsville Pike, toward the safety of General Ben Butler's lines. After dark, they made camp between Mechanicsville and Atlee Station. A wet, cold, dispirited lot, they had been sixty hours without sleep. They had no tents and only a few fires could be started. One trooper recalled:

A more dreary, dismal night it would be difficult to imagine, with rain, snow, sleet, mud, cold and wet to the skin, rain and snow falling rapidly, the roads a puddle of mud, and the night as dark as pitch.

Another soldier, with a more literary bent, recorded his thoughts:

It was a wild Walpurgis night, such a night as Goethe paints in his Faust while demons hold revel in the forests of the Bracken.

Kilpatrick told the men to make themselves as comfortable as possible and to try to brew some coffee over the fires. Characteristically, he did not put out a strong picket line, leaving the camp only lightly guarded. Saddles were left on horses with the girths loosened. The men lay in the mud in front of their horses with the bridle reins looped over one arm, ready to come awake, "stand to horse," and mount at a moment's notice.

Colonel James Kidd was so exhausted that he told his orderly to unsaddle his horse and put up his shelter tent. Kidd crawled inside the tent, out of the rain, and fell asleep, confident he would have time to saddle the horse in the morning while his regiment was preparing to move.

General Kilpatrick was wide awake, restless, and anxious about the impact on his reputation of the aborted raid to free the prisoners. Once he reached Butler's lines, his failure to take Richmond would be broadcast throughout the North in record time. No promotion would be forthcoming from this mission, not when he had promised so much to Lincoln himself. And how that old fool, Pleasonton, would gloat! He would tell everyone who mattered how he had always known Kilpatrick could not succeed. He had to salvage something out of this fiasco.

By one o'clock in the morning, Kilpatrick had devised a new plan to capture Richmond. Scouts had told him that most of the Confederate troops were now concentrated north of the city, leaving the capital nearly defenseless on the eastern side. Kilpatrick ordered two detachments of five hundred men each to prepare to move toward Richmond as quickly as possible. He would hold the main force in reserve to protect the rear of those columns from a surprise attack.

The troopers were shaken out of dazed sleep. Because of the weather and their terrible fatigue, it took quite some time for them to get ready. They shuffled about in the darkness, hardly aware of what they were doing. As they coaxed new campfires into existence to fix their coffee, the blazes were spotted by Wade Hampton's scouts, who quickly carried the news back to the general. Hampton approached the Union camp with three hundred six men. There was no need for stealth. The storm and darkness—and Kilpatrick's poor preparation—concealed everything.

Hampton spotted a lone Union picket and ordered Hugh Scott and Dan Tanner to take him without firing any shots. The scouts circled the guard and approached him from the direction of the camp. The man was captured easily, giving Hampton an opening in the camp's perimeter.

He moved all his men and two cannon within sight of Kilpatrick's camp. One hundred troopers dismounted and the cannon were trained on the exhausted Yankees. The rebels were reminded to yell as loud as they could when the order was given to attack. Hampton wanted the Yankees to believe they were being overrun by a superior force.

Both cannon fired at once, producing an eruption of screams as deadly shrapnel found targets among the Union soldiers in the closely packed camp. Fourteen times the cannon roared before Hampton's troopers charged.

The surprise was total, the sight and sound of the Confederate cavalry terrifying. Many Union troopers fled in panic, scattering in the woods, some on foot, others leading their horses, though many horses had bolted from fright.

Colonel Kidd slept through the commotion.

> I was for the time dead to all the surroundings. There was firing among the pickets. I did not hear it. A cannon boomed. I did not hear it. A second piece of artillery added to the tumult. I did not hear it. Shells hurtled through the trees, over the camp and the waves of sound did not disturb my ear. At last partial consciousness returned. There was a vague sense of something out of the usual order going on.

He awoke to find his orderly trying to drag him out of the tent by his heels. The man hastily saddled Kidd's horse, but when Kidd put his foot in the stirrup and started to mount, the saddle slipped off. The orderly had forgotten to fasten the girths. Kidd saddled the horse himself, "making all tight, mounted and gave the horse the spur, when to my dismay he proved to be still tied to the tree. . . . By this time it is needless to say I was getting 'rattled.'"

Some Union soldiers had regrouped and were returning the rebel fire. Bullets whistled in all directions, and in the darkness, not a few of

Kilpatrick's men were shot down by their own forces. Finally, some order was reestablished, and the Yankees proceeded down the road east toward Old Church. Mud slopped over their shoe tops, rain and sleet stung their faces, and every step was dogged by Confederate bullets and those chilling rebel yells.

A group of Hampton's men stopped to snatch food from the Union's cooking kettles, but their officers urged them down the road to pursue the Federals. The chase lasted throughout the night. Many men became separated from the main body. A few of these soldiers eventually found their way back to safety, but most were caught by southern cavalry patrols. A few unfortunate Northerners were taken by local posses. They were shot on the spot and left for the buzzards.

With the first light of dawn, Kilpatrick chose to make a stand near Old Church, ten miles from his last camp. There, his men were able to stop the rebels. Wade Hampton realized that his soldiers could not continue to harass a force ten times larger, once it was organized. In Kilpatrick's mind, so he later reported, he had been attacked by a "large force of mounted infantry and cavalry and four pieces of artillery."

Dahlgren was leading a hundred men of his advance party away from Richmond, north toward Hungary Station. He deployed pickets on white horses at intervals to mark the route along the backwoods trails. Captain Mitchell followed with the main force of approximately three hundred troops.

A furious storm lashed at them, driving freezing rain, sleet, and snow into eyes and mouths. Pine trees formed a canopy over the narrow road, and low-hanging branches whipped the men with icy skeletal arms. The soldiers stopped frequently to clear fallen trees from the path. The night was so dark that they sometimes had to feel their way through the woods with their hands. Some men fell asleep in the saddle, until their horses stumbled or fell in the mud. And if a horse had failed to follow the one in front, the rider would awaken along an unfamiliar trail, alone, lost, and frightened.

When Dahlgren's advance unit reached Hungary Station, he

ordered a rest. He wanted to confer with Captain Mitchell, whose troops were supposed to be only a few hundred yards behind. He waited impatiently for them to appear. Five minutes passed, then ten, and there was no sign of Mitchell or his men. Thinking they might have stopped elsewhere, Dahlgren sent two scouts back over their route to tell the captain to press forward.

In an hour, the scouts returned. They had not found any trace of Mitchell's outfit, and it was useless to continue to search for tracks in the mud and darkness. Although sources do not agree on precisely how the men lost contact, reports suggest that one of the units took a wrong turn sometime during the night and headed down a different trail toward Hungary Station.

Dahlgren's command had become dangerously divided. With growing numbers of Confederate patrols combing the area, Dahlgren had no option but to take his small advance party and try to rejoin Kilpatrick on his own. However, while circumstances drove Dahlgren and his men northeast to meet Kilpatrick, the general himself was heading southeast.

Chapter 13

RETURN THEIR FIRE!

On the morning of March 2, in bold headlines, the *Richmond Daily Dispatch* proclaimed the end of the raid:

DARING RAID OF THE ENEMY
THEY APPROACH WITHIN 3 MILES OF THE CITY
THEIR REPULSE ON THE BROOK ROAD
REPORTED FIGHTING ON THE WESTHAM PLANK ROAD

The raid of the enemy, so sudden and unexpected, has so completely interrupted telegraphic communications that little is known of the damage inflicted by them on the Virginia Central Railroad. But what little we have been able to ascertain leads to the belief that the injury to that road has been comparatively trifling.

The sounds of battle, so close the previous evening, had gone mercifully silent, but the results of the fighting were all too visible. Confederate wounded streamed into the city. The dead were borne in wagons or tied across saddles. Families of the clerks and factory workers who had marched off to defend the city awaited word of their fate. They peered at the bodies, curious yet afraid of what they would discover. When a loved one was recognized, the cries and screams of agony were horrifying.

Captain Albert Ellery, a sixty-three-year-old chief clerk, popular in many Richmond circles, was mourned by all. And there was Lieutenant John Sweeney of the Armory Battalion, whose corpse had been looted by the Yankees for his watch and the four hundred dollars in salary he had received moments before going off to war.

There were also some happy reunions. Men returned to Richmond who had been captured by the Federals but were later released as the Yankees made a desperate bid to escape. People gathered around to hear stories of how the enemy had been beaten back.

Late in the morning, seventy-seven prisoners, including a colonel, were paraded through the city. These were some of Kilpatrick's men, captured by Wade Hampton's troops and now destined for confinement in the very prisons they had come to liberate.

In trenches and breastworks outside the city limits, the men of the home-defense brigade kept watch, shivering in the cold, staring down their long rifle barrels, prepared in case the Union troops should come again. They had beaten back a force far larger than their own. Today, ever more confident of success, they felt they could fight off twice that number.

Near Atlee Station, Hampton's regulars were gathering up the spoils of their rout of Kilpatrick's column. Many supplies had been left behind that the Confederates could sorely use: a caisson full of ammunition, rations, clothing, rifles, pistols, and a number of horses.

While the rebels were congratulating themselves on their victory and consolidating their defenses, General Meade and other Union leaders were wondering what had happened to Kilpatrick. At the same time, three separate Union forces—Kilpatrick's, Dahlgren's, and Mitchell's—were trying desperately to reach the safety of their own lines.

In the early hours of March 2, Captain Mitchell was convinced he had lost contact with Dahlgren and had no choice but to proceed on his own. Continuing in the direction of Hungary Station, Mitchell's advance unit soon came under rebel attack from small arms and cannon fire.

Mitchell stopped the column to confer with his officers. They could not retrace their steps; the Confederates were behind them. There was no other way to reach Union lines except the path straight ahead. Their only course of action was to charge down the road at the enemy.

Shouting to give themselves courage, Mitchell and his three hundred troopers, closely packed on the narrow road, thundered ahead. Heavy fire from Confederate soldiers forced them to fall back, leaving their dead and wounded behind.

Mitchell sent patrols to probe other trails, seeking a way out. One group found a little-used road that was clear. This time, Mitchell's men got away, but throughout the day they encountered one defended roadblock after another and frequently were forced to change direction. Isolated bands of bushwhackers harassed them from the protection of trees and fences. Sometimes the Yankees were fired on by a single, angry farmer. But Mitchell was determined to goad his column on at a furious pace. He later recalled:

> Every few minutes the advance guard would have a skirmish with some of the enemy, till finally, about 8 miles from Tunstall's Station, the enemy seemed to have collected their forces, about 200 in number, and opposed our farther passage by well directed volleys from the pine woods in front. We determined to charge through them. . . . In this charge we lost about 20 men.

At 5:30 that afternoon, they came upon Kilpatrick's force. The general had remained near Old Church most of the morning and then moved cautiously southeast to Tunstall Station. There, Kilpatrick had spotted Mitchell's exhausted command, now down to two hundred sixty men. He was discouraged by their poor condition, and even more so at the news they brought about their failed mission. The two forces joined up and rode out in the direction of Williamsburg, hoping to reach Ben Butler's army before Wade Hampton caught up with them again.

Dahlgren's command, now reduced to eighty troopers, reached Hanovertown Ferry on the Pamunkey River at eight o'clock that morning. The men had ridden nearly twenty miles since the previous night's fight. The river was running unusually high and swift because of the heavy rain and snow. The troopers moved warily down to the river bank, hoping to find the ferry boat, but it was gone. They could not attempt to cross without a boat, which was why the rebels had moved the ferry upriver.

Dahlgren called for volunteers to brave the current and swim across and look for a boat on the other side. Two men made it. They found a small skiff under some bushes and rowed back, bringing enough rope to stretch between the banks so the boat could be towed back and forth. It took well over an hour to ferry the eighty men to the opposite shore. The horses were able to swim alongside.

Once safely across, Dahlgren's unit pushed on to the northeast, toward the Mattaponi River some twelve miles away. The successful crossing of the Pamunkey had brightened their spirits. Better yet, they had seen no signs of rebels all morning.

The rebels had seen them, however, and scouts and couriers were riding over the countryside to alert patrols and farmers to the Yankees' presence. Several Confederate units were in the area. A regular army detachment was on picket duty in King and Queen County—seasoned troops enjoying well-deserved furloughs.

One band already searching for Dahlgren was Company H of the Ninth Virginia Cavalry, sent out from Richmond. Known as Lee's Rangers, they were led by Lieutenant James Pollard. His command consisted of only twenty-five men; the rest of the company had been sent out individually to reconnoiter.

Lieutenant Pollard learned from his scouts the direction Dahlgren was heading, so he knew the Yankees would have to cross the Mattaponi. He ordered his men to hide the ferry boat at Aylett's Landing, the likely crossing point, and wait in ambush at Dunkirk, the only other possibility for fording the river. Dahlgren had to appear at one or the other.

At two o'clock that afternoon, Dahlgren's column arrived at Aylett's Landing to confront the same problem as at the Pamunkey River: high water, a fast current, and no boat in sight. Dahlgren sent men along the river bank in both directions until someone found an old flatboat that had been pulled up on land and covered with branches.

When half the outfit had crossed in the flatboat, some local home-guard militia spied the Yankees and opened fire. Dahlgren had remained on the west bank of the river, dismounted, and resting on his crutch. His men had urged him to cross in the first boat load but, as was his way, he insisted on being the last to leave. At the sound of firing, the troops scattered. Tired, hungry, and demoralized once again, they were in no mood for a fight.

Dahlgren mounted his horse and rode forward until he was in clear view of the enemy. Ignoring the bullets whizzing past him, he shouted to his men, taunting them, daring them to stand with him and fight. The men rallied and fired enough rounds to hold off the rebels so their comrades could cross. Defiant and stubborn, Dahlgren fired with them until the little boat returned for the last group of men. Only then did he permit himself to cross the river.

There was no respite for the Union troops when they reached the far side of the Mattaponi River. As they continued their way eastward that afternoon, they met with constant skirmishing. There was only one road, and as soon as Dahlgren sent out scouts to hunt for new trails, they were shot at or captured.

The countryside swarmed with rebels alerted to Dahlgren's location. Shortly after Dahlgren's men had crossed the Mattaponi, scouts brought the news to Lieutenant Pollard at Dunkirk. His force, larger now with the addition of local militiamen and small regular units, set off in pursuit.

Later that afternoon, they caught up with the rear of Dahlgren's column. For more than an hour they pursued the Yankees, forcing Dahlgren's rear guard to stop several times to pepper the rebels with gunfire and hurry away, only to stop again a few hundred yards farther. Despite this harassment, Pollard knew he could not stop the Yankees unless he could get in front of Dahlgren's column and set up an ambush.

At a fork in the road Dahlgren stopped for a moment and chose the turn to the right. Pollard consulted the local farmers and learned that hard riding on the road to the left would take him to a spot the raiders would have to pass, if he could get there first. He sent a small unit to follow Dahlgren and continue the sniping, and led his main body to the left, in the direction of Stevensville. If he arrived first, he would have Dahlgren trapped.

By six o'clock that evening, Dahlgren called a halt. The men and horses were exhausted. The soldiers took some corn from a nearby barn and cooked their first hot meal in more than thirty-six hours. The rain had stopped and the sky showed signs of clearing.

Dahlgren's Negro servant gathered some fence rails and covered them with blankets to make a bed for the colonel. After seeing to his men, Dahlgren stretched out and immediately fell asleep.

Lieutenant Pollard's men reached a crossroads about a mile forward of Dahlgren's camp. Near King and Queen Court House, the area was known as Mantapike Hill. Unless Dahlgren's men turned around, they would have to pass Pollard's position. All Pollard had to do was wait for the Yankees to appear.

The rebel force had grown considerably in size. Many local civilians had grabbed their rifles and left their homes, eager to join Pollard's men. Among them was the local schoolmaster, Edward W. Halbach, accompanied by his thirteen-year-old pupil William Littlepage. Some of the men were anxious and afraid; they had never fired a gun in anger.

Pollard had relinquished command to a superior officer, Captain Edward C. Fox of the Fifth Virginia Cavalry. A dispute arose among the officers about how to proceed. Some wanted to attack the raiders while they were encamped, but others persuaded them to wait for the Federals to come to them.

The officers also disagreed about when to expect the Yankees. Some said they would probably stay in camp only a short time. Others believed they would want to rest through the night and not head out until the morning. Lieutenant Pollard and the other officers who believed it would be a nightlong vigil decided to seek quarters in the homes nearby, leaving enough men at the ambush site to stop the raiders, should they arrive earlier than expected.

At eleven o'clock that night, Dahlgren roused his men and ordered them to saddle up and prepare to move out. As the troopers mounted to ride off into the darkness, it started to rain. The road took them through thick pine woods, which at night seemed gloomy, menacing, and impenetrable.

Dahlgren's force had been reduced to seventy troopers. Their ammunition was almost gone; most men had none at all. A number had suffered wounds. Even those who had not been hit were so tired they were virtually useless as fighters.

Dahlgren rode in the second set of fours with Major Edwin Cooke, his second in command. He had ordered one of their few remaining prisoners, Captain William Dement, to ride in the first set. Dahlgren hoped the sight of the captain's gray uniform would forestall an ambush. Perhaps the rebels would be reluctant to open fire on one of their own.

The men rode cautiously through the rain, anxious for word from the advance pickets who had been sent out three hours earlier. The fact that they had not returned was worrisome.

Up ahead, the Confederate soldiers waiting in ambush were also tense and uncertain. They whispered nervous assurances to one another, fingered their rifles, and peered down the long, dark road. Then they heard noise, a rattle, metal on metal, the whinny of a horse, the sound of men approaching. The rebels wiped their damp palms on their trousers, swallowed with dry throats, and tightened their fingers on the triggers.

Dahlgren's men drew closer, and then they, too, heard noise. Everyone stopped, and for a moment all was silent and still. Dahlgren spurred his horse forward, dashing up to join the advance guard. Major Cooke was right behind him. Private Louis Beaudrye in the advance cried out the challenge: "Who are you?" There was no answer.

"Surrender or we will shoot you," Dahlgren shouted. He pointed his pistol and fired, but only the cap exploded.

Beaudrye recalled:

The next instant a heavy volley was poured in upon us. The flash of the pieces afforded us a momentary glimpse of their position stretching parallel with the road about fifteen paces from us. Every tree was occupied, and the bushes poured forth a sheet of fire. A bullet grazing my leg and probably striking my horse somewhere in the neck, caused him to make a violent swing sideways. I was aware of some one dropping beside me, and attracted by a movement upon the ground, demanded who it was. Major Cooke replied, that his horse had been shot.

The Union raiders, strung out along the road, stampeded, frantic to evade the bursts of fire that surrounded them, but they were trapped between the fences on both sides of the road. In their panic, riding in all directions, they quickly created such a jam that no one could move. Finally, a Confederate prisoner in their ranks tore down some fence rails. Dahlgren's men poured through the opening like water from a broken dam.

Several men lay behind in the road. Face down in the rain and mud was Colonel Ulric Dahlgren.

LIKE A PARCEL OF
OLD WOMEN

At the first sound of firing, Captain Fox and Lieutenant Pollard rushed from the house where they had been sleeping. By the time they reached the ambush site, the fight was over. Darkness and quiet had descended. Although it seemed as though the Yankees had been beaten off, the officers were apprehensive. They could not know how many might be wandering about in the night, or whether they were regrouping, planning to attack before morning.

The Confederate troops were ordered to remain alert and to be prepared to round up the Union raiders in the morning. While the men held fast to their posts, thirteen-year-old William Littlepage crept out onto the road. He had long coveted a gold watch, and now he thought he had his chance. Surely one of the dead Yankees would have one.

On the first body he touched, Littlepage found a cigar case and a notebook containing several sheets of folded paper. Since the boy was barely literate, the papers were of no interest to him, but he took them anyway. Finding nothing more in the corpse's pockets, he went back to his schoolmaster, Mr. Halbach. At first, Littlepage said nothing about the papers. Halbach recalled:

We were just getting our places for the night, and wrapping up with blankets, garments, etc., such as we had, for the ground was freezing, and we dared not make a fire, when Littlepage pulled out a segar-case, and said: "Mr. Halbach, will you have a segar?"

"No," said I; "but where did you get segars these hard times?"

He replied that he had got them out of the pocket of the Yankee who had been killed, and that he had also taken from the same man a memorandum-book and some papers.

"Well," said I, "William, you must give me the papers, and you may keep the segar-case."

Littlepage then remarked that the dead Yankee had a wooden leg.

At that point, a rebel lieutenant, who had been a prisoner of the Federals, and who had escaped in the darkness, asked the boy how he knew the dead man had a wooden leg.

"I know he has," replied Littlepage, "because I caught hold of it, and tried to pull it off."

"There!" replied the lieutenant, "you have killed Col. Dahlgren, who was in command of the enemy. His men were devoted to him, and I would advise you all to take care of yourselves now, for if the Yankees catch you with anything belonging to him, they will certainly hang us all to the nearest tree."

The lieutenant was not the only person who tried to persuade Halbach to destroy the papers, for fear of what the Federals would do if they caught him with them. But Halbach was determined to hold on to the documents, at least until morning, when he could read them by the light of day. His curiosity would change history.

Other men went to look at the Yankee colonel's body, taking much more from the corpse than Littlepage had. They removed Dahlgren's wooden leg and stripped off most of his clothing. Cornelius Martin of Company H, Ninth Virginia Cavalry, severed the little finger of Dahlgren's right hand to take his ring.

The body was dumped into a shallow grave, really just a muddy hole at the fork of two roads. This was only the first of several burials before Colonel Dahlgren's body found its final rest.

During the long, cold night hours, soldiers on both sides, blue and gray, remained within several hundred yards of one another. Neither adversary knew the location of the other or what he might do come dawn.

After the ambush, Dahlgren's men found themselves trapped once they poured through the gap in the fence to get off the road. The field they were caught in was bordered by the road, the Mattaponi River, and a canal—and on the far side was thought to be the rebel force that had ambushed them. The surrounding terrain was either swamps or rough, wooded hillsides, difficult for the debilitated troops to negotiate.

Major Cooke, now senior officer commanding, conferred with Lieutenant Reuben Bartley and Private Louis Beaudrye. A quick check revealed only thirty rounds of ammunition left. The men were at least twenty-five miles from Union lines and believed that their position was surrounded by a large rebel force.

The idea of trying to fight their way out with so little ammunition seemed suicidal. Cooke decided to break up the command into small groups—three or four each—and try to sneak out on foot before morning. They thought it best not to kill the horses—which was standard procedure in that situation, to deny them to the enemy—because the noise might draw the Confederates' attention. They could see rebel campfires at several points around them and occasionally could hear their conversation. The only recourse the Union troops had was to drive their sabers into the ground and tie the horses to them. They destroyed their carbines by removing the chambers and burying them.

Cooke advised the men to travel light, taking only revolvers and haversacks, nothing else that might be discarded and leave a trail. But to Cooke's surprise, some of the men had no interest in trying to escape. They felt too despairing and helpless to believe they stood any chance of reaching Union lines alive. It was better to be taken prisoner. They had heard the southern voices all around them and concluded it was pointless to try to flee. They told Major Cooke they would wait for daylight and give themselves up.

Before dawn, about forty men slipped away, creeping out of the field on hands and knees, to begin their trek across twenty-five miles of hostile Virginia countryside. They were on their own, without horses or food, with nothing but a grim determination to stay out of Libby and Belle Isle prisons.

Cooke, Bartley, and Beaudrye left together and by daybreak had managed to crawl a half mile from the ambush site. They found a grove of young pine trees and bedded down for the rest of the day. At night they continued to walk toward the east until hunger forced them to risk a stop at a cabin to ask for food.

The old man who answered their knock invited them in for supper. The Northerners accepted eagerly and warmed themselves at the fire, amazed at this stroke of good fortune. They could not know that their host was the overseer of a plantation owned by Captain Richard Hugh Bagby, one of the men involved in the Dahlgren ambush and the pastor of the Baptist church. While preparations were being made for dinner, he sent a Negro servant out a back window to run to the big house and tell the captain the Yankees were there.

Captain Bagby and his party had spent the day searching for the raiders. They had just sat down to their own dinner when the servant brought the news. Gathering up their weapons, they raced the few hundred yards to the cabin, burst in, and took Cooke, Bartley, and Beaudrye by surprise.

For the three Union men, this was a bizarre beginning for their long period of captivity. Marched under heavy guard to Bagby's elegant plantation house, they were served supper in the formal dining room. All ate at the same table, but Bagby and his men kept cocked revolvers by their plates. Their host said grace, gun in hand.

Except for the weapons, it might have been a peacetime gathering of amiable dinner companions. The conversation was gracious, and the neighbors dropped by to meet the Yankee guests.

The captives enjoyed a good night's sleep, guarded by five men with revolvers at the ready. In the morning they joined Bagby for a lavish breakfast, the last good meal they would have for a long time.

When they were ready to leave, to be taken to Richmond under guard, Captain Bagby "politely but firmly" demanded their watches, money, and all other personal property of value.

As the three captives handed over their possessions, Bagby explained that his own loss in the war had been great, and that now he was recouping some of what had been taken from him. Also, he added, if *he* didn't take their valuables, they would end up being stolen by those thieves and rascals in Richmond.

At the Mantapike Hill camp, Edward Halbach read the papers young Littlepage had found on Dahlgren's body. Halbach noted the official stationery—Cavalry of the Third Division—and assumed these were the orders for Dahlgren's party. He said later that he thought they were important enough to send to Richmond, to Jefferson Davis himself. Halbach entrusted the papers—and the wooden leg—to Lieutenant Pollard, who showed the papers to Colonel R. L. T. Beale, commanding the Ninth Virginia Cavalry. Beale told Pollard to convey the orders either to Wade Hampton or Fitzhugh Lee, whichever officer he could contact first. Beale knew that high-ranking officers were always interested in captured orders. (The papers also included a notebook that Beale kept for some time, for reasons he never explained.)

During the morning hours, Pollard's men rounded up the rest of Dahlgren's unit, those who had not attempted to escape. They were captured quietly, without resistance, at first light. The ambush site itself was chaos as officers, men, and horses milled about. And soon there were mounting piles of valuables as the rebels recovered goods the Yankees had looted from homes along their route of march—mostly silverware, candlesticks, and china.

At eight o'clock on the morning of March 3, while Dahlgren's men were being marched into Richmond, Kilpatrick's ragged force was twenty-five miles away to the east. At the crest of a hill, they spotted a large body of cavalry heading in their direction. Kilpatrick sent out skirmishers and the men prepared themselves for what they sensed would be a major battle, but as the cavalry approached, Kilpatrick saw they were dressed in blue. General Butler had sent a force of thirty-eight hundred men to rescue him.

That night, word reached Butler that Kilpatrick's men had been found. Butler wrote out a telegram for Secretary of War Stanton, his first word of the expedition in three days.

> Arrived all safe. General Kilpatrick is here, having lost less than 150 men, among whom were Colonel Dahlgren and [Major] Cooke [who] are supposed to be prisoners.

An hour later, Kilpatrick dispatched a message to General Pleasonton, exaggerating his accomplishments and the condition of his men.

> I have reached General Butler's lines with my command in good order. I have failed to accomplish the great object of the expedition, but have destroyed the enemy's communications at various points on the Virginia Central Railroad; also the canal and mills along the James River, and much other valuable property. Drove the enemy into and through his fortification to the suburbs of Richmond; made several unsuccessful efforts to return to the Army of the Potomac. I have lost less than 150 men. The entire command is in good order, and needs but a few day's rest. I respectfully ask for instructions.

At Mantapike Hill, Martin Hogan, one of Dahlgren's scouts, was distressed over the condition of Dahlgren's body and its lack of proper burial. He pleaded with his Confederate captors for a coffin or some boards so he could fashion one himself. Most of the rebels ignored him, but Edward Halbach, the schoolteacher, agreed to help. He obtained a wooden coffin and carved Dahlgren's name on a small headboard.

The northern newspapers, lacking substantive information, fabricated glowing descriptions of Kilpatrick's raid on Richmond. The March 4 edition of the *New York Times* headlined:

GREAT CAVALRY RAIDS IN VIRGINIA; KILPATRICK IN
SPOTTSYLVANIA COURTHOUSE ON SUNDAY MORNING;
PROSPECTS ENCOURAGING AT LATEST ADVICES.

The accompanying story reported that Kilpatrick's troops had "formed a junction" with a force sent by General Butler. "General Kilpatrick is thus within a few miles of Richmond, and, as General Butler is cooperating with him, we may expect to hear of startling news from that quarter in a day or two."

What a prophetic statement that was, but the startling news would be unexpected—and certainly unwelcome.

The Richmond newspapers were more accurate, though no less zealous in their attempt to gain favorable propaganda from the raid. The *Richmond Daily Dispatch* of March 4 told its readers:

> Thus ends the great raid which was designed for the destruction of General Lee's communications and the liberation of the Yankee prisoners in Richmond. The injury to the communications of the Army of Northern Virginia can be repaired in three days and instead of releasing the prisoners already in our hands they have added not less than 250 to their number.

An editorial writer lambasted Kilpatrick personally:

> His highest exploit has thus far consisted in robbing hen-roosts and stealing negroes. He has never fought a fair fight with any of our forces. He runs as soon as he is brought face to face with real danger. Nothing could have been more disgraceful than his flight, when he was attacked by General Hampton at Atlee's. The Yankee General Meade knew what he was fit for and chose him accordingly. He is a mere hen-roost general and nothing more.

No one in the North had received word of Dahlgren's death. Indeed, there was reason to believe he had been captured. A Confederate deserter told Butler's men that a one-legged colonel and one hundred men had been taken prisoner. This information was sent directly to

President Lincoln, who was awaiting news about the expedition—*his* expedition—with mounting concern.

Later, Kilpatrick noted in his official report: "It is impossible to estimate the amount of property destroyed and damage done to the enemy during this raid." Then he went on to estimate the amount of property destroyed and damage done, implying all of northern Virginia lay in ruins. The main railroad line between Richmond and the Rapidan, which Kilpatrick claimed to have rendered impassable for at least three weeks, was back in operation in one day.

In a craven but typical effort to shift the blame for the operation's failure, he wrote that "if Colonel Dahlgren had not failed in crossing the river," or if there had been an attack from the east by Butler's forces to coincide with his own (conveniently forgetting that such an attack was never envisioned), "I should have entered the rebel capital and released our prisoners."

At Brandy Station, Colonel Lyman, General Meade's aide, summed up the situation more bluntly, and a good deal more accurately.

Behold my prophecy in regard to Kilcavalry's raid fulfilled. I have heard many persons very indignant with him. They said he went to the President and pressed his plan; told Pleasonton he would not come back alive if he didn't succeed. . . . I fancy Kill has rather dished himself. It is painful to think of those poor prisoners hearing the sound of his guns and hoping a rescue was at hand! Now all that cavalry must be carried back in steamers, like a parcel of old women going to market!

Chapter 15

ULRIC THE HUN

At ten o'clock on the morning of March 4, Lieutenant Pollard arrived in Richmond. He called on General Fitzhugh Lee, nephew of Robert E. Lee, and handed over the Dahlgren papers and Dahlgren's wooden leg. One of the more crucial items was an undated document on official stationery: "Headquarters Third Division Cavalry Corps." It contained a two-page address to Dahlgren's officers and men, written in ink.

A second important document was a list of instructions to Dahlgren's men, written in ink on both sides of a single sheet of official stationery. There was no date or signature with these instructions. Other papers appeared to be military orders of a more routine—and decidedly less volatile—nature.

Fitzhugh Lee read the two key documents and declared himself outraged, incensed by the exhortation in the Dahlgren papers for Union soldiers to destroy Richmond and "kill Jeff Davis and cabinet . . . on the spot." The president and the entire Confederate Cabinet were to have been murdered!

Lee took the papers to Davis at once. The president read them but was far less annoyed than Fitzhugh Lee. Indeed, Davis did not seem to take this threat to his life very seriously. He read the papers aloud to Judah P. Benjamin, the secretary of state, and burst out laughing when he reached the part about killing the Cabinet members.

"This means you, Mr. Benjamin," he joked.

And that was the extent of the president's initial reaction to Dahlgren's papers. Indignation would come later, urged on him by others. But at the moment, he simply told Fitzhugh Lee to forward the papers to Sam Cooper, the adjutant general, to be filed away.

As ordered, Lee sent the papers to the adjutant general, accompanied by the following note:

> General: I have the honor to transmit the inclosed papers found upon the body of Col. U. Dahlgren, of the U. S. Army, who was killed by a portion of my command. . . . These papers were sent by Lieutenant Pollard, commanding a detachment of the Ninth Virginia Cavalry, to Colonel Beale, and by him transmitted direct to me. They need no comment. Colonel Dahlgren commanded a force picked to co-operate with Brigadier-General Kilpatrick in his ridiculous and unsoldierly raid.

General Cooper did not file the papers away quietly. He passed them around the War Department for everyone to read. "Some extraordinary memoranda were captured from the raiders," the War Department clerk John Jones recorded in his diary, "showing a diabolical purpose, and creating a profound sensation here."

Later that same afternoon, the papers reached the desk of General Braxton Bragg, newly appointed as Jefferson Davis's chief military adviser. Bragg was not "noted for calm judgment and an equable disposition." Unlike Davis, he did not find the Dahlgren papers amusing, nor was he prepared to file and forget them. He was irate, and he wanted the papers made public, so all the world would see the perfidious nature of the Union enemy. Bragg swore vengeance against the Dahlgren raiders who had been captured.

Bragg quickly penned a note to Secretary of War Seddon:

> Dear Sir: It has occurred to me that the papers just captured from the enemy are of such an extraordinary and diabolical character

that some more formal method should be adopted of giving them to the public than simply sending them to the press. My own conviction is for an execution of the prisoners and a publication as justification; but in any event the publication should go forth with official sanction from the highest authority, calling the attention of our people and the civilized world to the fiendish and atrocious conduct of our enemies.

On the following day, March 5, the story of this Yankee treachery was published in every Richmond newspaper, unleashing a storm of public horror and indignation. The *Richmond Daily Dispatch* devoted an unusually long editorial to what it headlined as:

THE LAST RAID OF THE INFERNALS: THEIR PLANS UNVEILED.

People read each issue with shock and disbelief. For many days, the signal topic of conversation was the Dahlgren papers and the fate of the city of Richmond, its people, and the leaders of the Confederacy had the Yankee plan succeeded. Would the enemy stop at nothing? Would they stoop to the cold-blooded murder of civilians? The Dahlgren papers answered those questions all too clearly.

The *Richmond Daily Dispatch* editorial read:

The reader will be startled this morning by the diabolical plans of the Yankee raiders who have just been driven in disappointment and disgrace from the very edge of Richmond. A lucky shot has sent to his long account one of the three leaders of the three bands into which Kilpatrick's band was divided and upon his person were found the papers making the important development of their whole plan. It was quite complete in itself involving the MASSACRE OF THE PRESIDENT AND HIS ENTIRE CABINET and the destruction of Richmond, the hated city, as one of the orders style it.

All this was to have followed the releasing of all the Federal prisoners. . . . The men were required to keep together and well in hand and once in the city it must be destroyed and Jeff. Davis and cabinet killed. The address setting forth these objects and signed by Col. Dahlgren, on whose body it was found, appeals to the men under his command to engage heartily in the enterprise and taunts contemptuously any man who would decline.

To any such man Col. D. says, "let him step out and he may go home to the arms of his sweetheart and read of the braves who have swept through the city of Richmond." A memorandum discovered imparts the information that none declined. . . . Not the blandishments of a sweetheart could tempt any of the band of robbers and thieves to forgo the booty and butchery, the robbing and marauding that would inevitably fall to the lot of the braves who swept through the city of Richmond.

And the pious as well as brave Dahlgren concludes his address to his cutthroat followers: "Ask the blessing of the Almighty and do not fear the enemy." And they came and the Almighty blessed them not, and Dahlgren is dead and gone to answer for his crimes and several hundred of his partners in the plot concocted so deliberately are now our prisoners. They every one richly merit death. . . .

And thus concluded the grand plot which was to have achieved results which Dahlgren assured his men would "write their names on the hearts of their countrymen in letters that can never be erased." Their failure deprives them of any such inscription on the pages of history which will hand them down to the execration of mankind through all future ages. . . . Let us redouble our energies and our vigilance to guard against the schemes and plots of a foe who has proved himself to be the most unscrupulous as he is the most brutal and fiendlike that ever made war on a people.

With such inflammatory statements from the daily papers, is it any wonder the people of Richmond were shocked? Still embedded in the culture was a gentlemanly code of honor, and that unwritten law restricted war and its consequences to those who actively bore arms. Armies fought against armies, soldiers against soldiers. They did not wage war on civilians and most certainly did not attempt to assassinate political leaders.

Another Richmond newspaper, *The Whig*, posed rhetorical questions about Dahlgren's men:

Are these men warriors? Are they soldiers, taken in the performance of duties recognized as legitimate by the loosest construction in the code of civilized warfare? Or are they assassins, bar-barians, thugs who have forfeited (and expect to lose) their lives? Are they not barbarians redolent with more hellish purposes than were the Goth, the Hun or the Saracen?

Ulric the Hun quickly became a common appellation in the lan-guage of a generation, symbolizing to Southerners the barbarity, cruel-ty, and uncivilized nature of their northern enemy. Thousands of Confederate supporters clipped from the newspapers the published copies of Dahlgren's orders to his men. Pasted into scrapbooks, they would be read by their children and grandchildren, keeping regional hatred alive for a century.

The *Richmond Examiner* printed the full text of Dahlgren's written address.

HEADQUARTERS
Third Division Cavalry Corps
_____, 186_____

Officers and Men:
You have been selected from brigades and regiments as a picked command to attempt a desperate undertaking—an undertaking which, if successful, will write your names on the hearts of your countrymen in letters that can never be erased, and which will cause the prayers of our fellow-soldiers now confined in loath-some prisons to follow you and yours wherever you may go. We hope to release the prisoners from Belle Island first, and having seen them fairly started, we will cross the James River into Richmond, destroying the bridges after us and exhorting the released prisoners to destroy and burn the hateful city; and do not allow the rebel leader Davis and his traitorous crew to escape.

The prisoners must render great assistance, as you cannot leave your ranks too far or become too much scattered, or you will be lost. Do not allow any personal gain to lead you off, which would only bring you to an ignominious death at the hands of citizens. Keep well together and obey orders strictly and all will be well; but on no account scatter too far, for in union there is strength. With strict obedience to orders and fearlessness in the execution you will be sure to succeed.

You will join the main force on the other side of the city, or perhaps meet them inside. Many of you may fall; but if there is any man here not willing to sacrifice his life in such a great and glorious undertaking, or who does not feel capable of meeting the enemy in such a desperate fight as will follow, let him step out, and he may go hence to the arms of his sweetheart and read of the braves who swept through the city of Richmond.

We want no man who cannot feel sure of success in such a holy cause. We will have a desperate fight, but stand up to it when it comes and all will be well. Ask the blessing of the Almighty and do not fear the enemy.

U. Dahlgren
Colonel, Commanding

Others among the papers found on Dahlgren's body were also reprinted. These included separate orders given to Captain Mitchell, a page of general instructions, the early itinerary, and some notes in a memorandum book. All of these items stated explicitly that "Jeff. Davis and cabinet must be killed on the spot."

A March 5 editorial in the *Richmond Inquirer* challenged Southerners to consider the significance of the Dahlgren papers for the Confederacy's future conduct of the war:

> Soldiers, read these papers and weigh well their purpose and design. Will not these documents take off the rosewater sentimental mode of making . . . campaigns? Should our army again go into the enemy's country, will not these papers relieve them from their restraints of a chivalry that would be proper with a civilized enemy, but which only brings upon them the contempt of our savage foe? Decidedly, we think that these Dahlgren papers will destroy, during the rest of the war, all rosewater chivalry, and that Confederate armies will make war afar and upon the rules selected by the enemy.

For the South, the nature of warfare changed forever. Gone was the gentility and idealism of the past. "The papers taken from the slain young colonel convinced Davis that Lincoln and Stanton had approved a new level of warfare—including arson, pillage, and assassination." The result would be total war, carried directly to the people of the Union, as Dahlgren had tried to carry that terrible fate to the people of Richmond. If Federal leaders were prepared to loose murder and rapine on the citizens of the South, then the South was free to respond in kind.

For Davis and the other Confederate leaders, how better to respond than with the program of terror, arson, and murder proposed by Captain Thomas Hines—his Northwest conspiracy—to carry the fight to the faraway cities of the Union? Any scruples they had professed earlier about initiating such a plan were overruled when Dahlgren's plot was exposed. The Confederate government could not have had a better justification for sanctioning this type of warfare than if it had written the Dahlgren papers itself.

Behind the Union lines in Brown's Lock, Kentucky, some five hundred miles away, a party was in progress. Many of the guests, including the guest of honor, had risked their lives to ride through enemy-occupied territory to attend. But it was worth it to them because of the purpose of the party—to celebrate the engagement of Miss Nancy Sproule and Captain Thomas Henry Hines.

The evening at the Sproule house brought much singing and dancing, and for a time the war was forgotten, even though Union troops were quartered in town. Miss Sproule's father rapped on the table, calling for quiet so he could make his announcement.

He had just started to speak when someone knocked loudly on the kitchen door. It was a member of the Confederate underground with an urgent message for Hines from Secretary of State Judah Benjamin: the captain was to report to Richmond at once. The engagement announcement was made and the guests informed that Hines had to leave.

On the back porch, the couple said hasty goodbyes. Hines rushed to a friend's house where a horse was saddled and ready. He knew he was on his way, as he put it, "to play a dangerous game." The Northwest conspiracy had begun.

In Richmond, the growing public furor about the Dahlgren papers was focusing on the men of Dahlgren's command who had been captured. There were insistent calls that action be taken against them; they should be hanged like common criminals.

Once again, the newspapers both inflamed and reflected the popular sentiment. The *Daily Examiner* exclaimed:

> Our soldiers should in every instance where they capture officers engaged in raids characterized by such acts of incendiarism and wanton devastation and plunder, as this last raid has been, hang them immediately. If they are handed over as prisoners of war, they at once come under the laws of regular warfare and are subject to exchange. . . . therefore we hope that our soldiers will take the law in their own hands . . . by hanging those they capture.

Sentiments were taking a dark turn. It was not only editorial writers arguing for such drastic measures, but Confederate leaders as well. General Braxton Bragg had already urged the execution of the prisoners in his letter to Jefferson Davis. General Josiah Gorgas, the army chief of ordnance, declared that "Hereafter those that are taken will not be heard of."

Jefferson Davis discussed the matter with his cabinet for many hours. Most of his advisers were in favor of hanging the Union prisoners. Secretary of War Seddon was particularly vocal in urging such retribution on the captives. But Davis did not agree. He decided to ask Robert E. Lee for his opinion; the fate of the prisoners would be left to him.

Seddon wrote to General Lee:

> I inclose to you herewith a slip from one of the morning papers containing an account of the disposal of a portion of the enemy's force which recently attacked this city and a copy of the papers found on the body of Colonel Dahlgren who was killed. The dia-

bolical character of those papers and of the enterprise they indicate seems to require at our hands something more than a mere informal publication in our newspapers.

My own inclinations are toward the execution of at least a portion of those captured at the time Colonel Dahlgren was killed, and a publication of these papers as its justification. . . . General Bragg's views coincide with my own on this subject. The question of what is best to be done is a grave and important one, and I desire to have the benefit of your views and any suggestions you may make. . . . as well as your judgment of what would be the sentiment of the Army on a course of severe but just retribution.

While the disposition of the Union prisoners was thus under consideration, President Davis personally intervened to take an unusual action with regard to Dahlgren's corpse. He sent a courier to the home-guard headquarters at King and Queen Court House ordering them to remove the body from its grave and convey it to Richmond. His implied purpose was to arrange a proper identification for the body. In truth, Dahlgren's corpse was to be put on public display.

1. Ulric Dahlgren (STANDING), then on General Meade's staff, with (left to right) Major Ludlow; Lieutenant Colonel Dickinson, of General Hooker's staff; Count von Zeppelin, the Prussian army observer later known for his dirigibles; and Lieutenant Rosencranz, of General McClellan's staff, at Headquarters, Army of the Potomac, near Fairfax, Virginia, June 1863. *Signal Corps photo, National Archives.*

2. Guard mount, Headquarters Army of the Potomac, Brandy Station, Virginia.
Signal Corps photo, National Archives.

3. George Washington's Birthday Ball, February 22, 1864, at Second Corps camp near Brandy Station, Virginia.
Library of Congress.

4. Richmond, Virginia, showing 20th Street in foreground; Grace Street right of center.

Brady photo, National Archives.

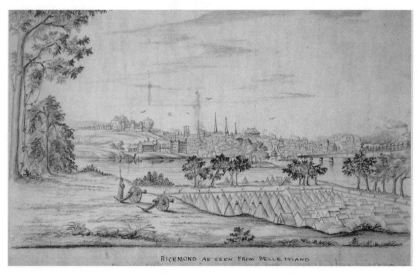

RICHMOND AS SEEN FROM BELLE ISLAND

5. Richmond as seen from Belle Isle: pencil drawing by a Union prisoner.

Library of Congress.

6. The warehouse that became Libby Prison; the U.S. flag can be seen in this photo, taken soon after Richmond's occupation by Union forces.
Brady collection, National Archives.

7. Brevet Brigadier General Thomas E. Rose, Colonel, Seventy-seventh Pennsylvania Infantry, who led the Libby Prison escape.
Library of Congress.

8. Brigadier General John Hunt Morgan, the Confederate raider. *National Archives.*

9. Ulric Dahlgren.
Brady photo, National Archives.

10. Brigadier General Hugh Judson Kilpatrick, Headquarters Third Division, near the Rapidan River, 1864, just prior to the raid on Richmond. *Library of Congress.*

11. Elizabeth Van Lew.
The Valentine: The Museum of the Life and History of Richmond.

12. Captain Thomas
Henry Hines.
*The Filson Club Historical
Society, Louisville, Kentucky.*

13. Ohio Congressman
Clement L. Vallandigham,
Grand Commander of
the Sons of Liberty, a
Copperhead organization.
Brady photo, National Archives.

14. The Honorable Jacob
Thompson of Mississippi,
confidential agent of
the Confederate States
of America mission
to Canada.
Library of Congress.

15. The Confederate
White House (Jefferson
Davis's residence in
Richmond, Virginia).
Brady photo, National Archives.

16. Confederate Secretary of
War James A. Seddon.
National Archives.

17. Confederate Secretary
of the Treasury Judah P.
Benjamin.
Brady photo, National Archives.

1 8. Kilpatrick's raid to Richmond: pencil drawing by Edwin Forbes. *Library of Congress.*

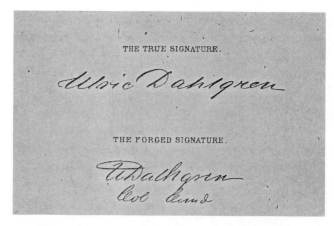

THE TRUE SIGNATURE.

THE FORGED SIGNATURE.

1 9. Reproductions of the allegedly forged signature (bottom) and the true signature (top) of Ulric Dahlgren.

Chapter 16

AN EXPRESSION
OF AGONY

On March 6, General Meade received a copy of the *Richmond Sentinel*, bringing him his first information about Dahlgren's death. General Kilpatrick didn't believe it; he maintained that Dahlgren was alive. Kilpatrick dispatched a message to General Pleasonton that same day, reporting that Dahlgren, with about one hundred men, had been heard from, close to King and Queen Court House. Meade, more inclined to accept the account of the Richmond newspaper than the word of Kilpatrick, wrote to his wife: "You have doubtless seen that Kilpatrick's raid was an utter failure. I did not expect much from it. Poor Dahlgren I am sorry for."

Others lamented Dahlgren's death. Colonel Charles Wainwright wrote in his diary:

> Poor Dahlgren is killed. He had let his men disperse into small bodies; nearly all of them got in safely, but he is said to have been betrayed by his negro guide, and murdered in cold blood. All who knew him regret his loss exceedingly.

The *New York Times* boasted in bold front-page headlines about the raid's success. It said nothing about Dahlgren's death:

THE CAVALRY RAID; GREAT DESTRUCTION OF RAILROADS,
CANALS AND BRIDGES; SUBLIME AUDACITY OF KILPATRICK;
HE FIGHTS ALL DAY INSIDE THE REBEL WORKS;
REBEL CAPITAL AGAIN THROWN INTO PANIC.

The story described the raid as follows:

a complete success, resulting in the destruction of millions of dollars of public property . . . some of which cannot be replaced at all, and the whole of it valuable to the rebel Government as a means of carrying on their infernal schemes against the United States.

Also on the morning of March 6, a train pulled into Richmond's York River Railroad Station. In the baggage car was a pine coffin, accompanied by a guard detail. Shortly after the train halted, one of the Confederate officers Dahlgren had captured during the early stages of his raid arrived to identify the body.

The baggage car was opened to the public. A newspaper article described the condition of the corpse:

It would seem something of the curse he came to bestow on others lighted upon his own carcass, when it fell riddled by Southern bullets. Stripped, robbed of every valuable, the fingers cut off for the sake of the diamond rings that encircled them [only one finger had been cut off; the stolen ring was a plain gold band] . . . when the body was found by those sent to take charge of it, it was lying in a field stark naked, with the exception of the stockings. Some humane persons had lifted the corpse from the pike, and thrown it over into the field to save it from the hogs. The artificial limb worn by Dahlgren was removed. . . . It is of most beautiful design and finish.

Another journalist described the body as that of "a small man, thin, pale, and with red hair and a goatee of the same color. His face wore an expression of agony."

A great many curiosity-seekers visited the depot to gaze on the remains of Ulric the Hun and his artificial leg, the latter object put on display in a nearby shop window. One of those who came was Elizabeth Van Lew, who left quickly, repulsed by the vulgar spectacle.

Another woman viewing the dead Yankee raider was shocked to see a face from her past. She rushed from the station to find her companions—the father and uncle of a young Confederate private, Thaddeus Walker, and other neighbors from Old Church. Agitated, she led them to the depot and waited while they stepped into the baggage car. When they emerged, Mr. Walker took her arm and led her away. All agreed: The corpse was that of Lieutenant Murray, the Union deserter who had stayed in their home a month earlier.

The woman suggested they tell the authorities, but Mr. Walker was emphatic; they must keep that knowledge to themselves. Winder's agents were everywhere, he reminded her, and people had been arrested for considerably lesser offenses than harboring an enemy soldier, particularly one as notorious as Colonel Dahlgren.

At two o'clock that afternoon, Lieutenant Colonel John Wilder Atkinson and a detail of six men brought a wagon to the railroad depot to carry out a direct order from President Davis. Their charge was to bury Dahlgren's body in a secret grave. More than forty years later, Atkinson wrote:

> With a detail of some half-dozen men and a wagon, I went to the York River depot, and was shown the body of a man in a rough undressed pine coffin, and found it marked in stencil on the lid of the coffin with his name—"Ulric Dahlgren." . . . The lid of Dahlgren's coffin when I saw it had been removed, and was lying by the side of the rough box in which the body had been placed. He was apparently a young man . . . dressed in an unbleached cotton shirt, and in green pants, apparently uniform parts. . . . I at once had the lid of the coffin screwed on, and it

was placed in the wagon, which proceeded immediately to Oakwood [Cemetery] for burial. He was buried near the entrance, a young sapling only marking his grave, and there we left him, as we supposed, until the great resurrection.

Atkinson failed to mention a crucial instruction in his orders from Jefferson Davis. No one was ever to learn the location of the burial site. To ensure this secrecy, Atkinson took precautions so that no one followed the wagon or was present at the cemetery to observe the burial. He placed no marker on the grave.

How peculiar it all was. The bodies of enemy officers were routinely transported back to their families for burial, certainly not dishonored by a public display or interred in an unmarked grave. For the president of the Confederate States personally to concern himself with such a matter was even stranger. And for him to so mistreat the body of Ulric Dahlgren, a brave Union soldier whose family he and his wife had known before the war, was almost beyond explanation.

The Richmond newspapers were continuing to keep alive the hatred and heat of revenge. The *Richmond Inquirer* of March 7 asked its readers to imagine

What would have been the condition of Richmond this day one week ago had Dahlgren succeeded? Imagine ten to twelve thousand brutal soldiers released from captivity, inflamed with liquor and burning with lust, turned loose with arms in their hands, without officers to restrain their violence. . . . picture the smoking ruins, the dishonored women and the murdered men of Richmond.

The Whig wrote, simply, that "Henceforth the name of Dahlgren is linked with eternal infamy."

General Robert E. Lee had considered Secretary of War Seddon's question about the fate of the Union prisoners, and on March 6, he offered his response. Lee agreed with Seddon that the papers found with Dahlgren's body be made public, so that "our people and the world may know the character of the war our enemies wage against us, and the unchristian and atrocious acts they plot and perpetrate."

But Lee opposed Seddon's wish to execute the soldiers captured in the raid.

I cannot recommend the execution of the prisoners that have fallen into our hands. Assuming that the address and special orders of Colonel Dahlgren correctly state his designs and intentions, they were not executed, and I believe, even in a legal point of view, acts in addition to intentions are necessary to constitute crime.

These papers can only be considered as evidence of his intentions. It does not appear how far his men were cognizant of them, or that his course was sanctioned by his Government. It is only known that his plans were frustrated by a merciful Providence, his forces scattered, and he killed. I do not think it right, therefore, to visit upon the captives the guilt of his intentions. . . .

I presume that the blood boils with indignation in the veins of every officer and man as they read the account of the barbarous and inhuman plot, and under the impulse of the moment many would counsel extreme measures. But I do not think that reason and reflection would justify such a course. I think it better to do right, even if we suffer in so doing, than to incur the reproach of our consciences and posterity.

Nor do I think that under present circumstances policy dictates the executions of these men. It would produce retaliation. How many and better men have we in the enemy's hands than they have in ours?

Lee's eloquent letter put an end to the emotional clamor for hanging the Union captives. Such an action could, indeed, have led to death for Confederate prisoners in retaliation. Lee himself was well aware of the horror of that possibility; his son Rooney was a prisoner of the Yankees.

Because of Robert E. Lee's counsel, the lives of Dahlgren's men were spared, but they would not be well treated. The officers, who had been marched through the gates of Libby Prison after Dahlgren's death, were locked in basement dungeons. Their cellmates, deliberately selected by the Confederates, were black soldiers.

Colonel Thomas Rose felt sympathy for the new prisoners. Rose had led the digging of the escape tunnel and been recaptured and confined, for a time, to one of the basement dungeons. With his characteristic tenacity, he carved a hole between floors into the basement "and dropped down playing cards, telling the raiders to turn a king face-up on their table when the guard was not looking. Then he fed cornbread and substitute coffee down to them through a funnel made from a broken bottle."

On the morning of March 7, the USS *Morse*, a Union navy gunboat, cruised up the Mattaponi River toward King and Queen Court House. Periodically it fired a signal gun, hoping to attract any stragglers from Kilpatrick's or Dahlgren's commands. Four troopers from Dahlgren's unit, plus his personal servant, heard the *Morse* and rowed out to board her. After the men were interrogated, word was dispatched to navy headquarters in Washington that Dahlgren was dead, last seen by his servant lying naked in the mud with one finger cut off.

Abraham Lincoln grieved when informed of the death of his young friend, and he immediately sent a condolence message to Admiral Dahlgren at the Navy Yard. The elder Dahlgren asked the president for permission to depart for Fortress Monroe, the formal contact point between representatives of North and South for prisoner exchanges and the return of remains. Dahlgren told Lincoln he was praying for a miracle, that Ulric was still alive and his reported fate a case of mistaken identity.

"Go," Lincoln told him. "I authorize it. Ask no one. I will stand by you."

Admiral Dahlgren arrived at Fortress Monroe the following night. There would be no miracle; the fate of his son had been confirmed. Ulric was dead, and his body had been exhibited in Richmond, then consigned to a secret location. He also learned that the body was missing a finger with the plain gold ring Ulric wore in memory of his dead sister.

He read the Richmond papers. Ulric was called a barbarian, a fiend, deservedly given a dog's burial. And the wild story about a plot to murder Jefferson Davis and his Cabinet! Admiral Dahlgren didn't know what to make of that.

He asked Kilpatrick if there were any truth to the so-called Dahlgren papers. Kilpatrick assured him there was not. They were fabrications of the southern newspapers. There had been no plan for burning Richmond or attempting political assassinations. In his diary, Admiral Dahlgren recorded his judgment about the Richmond papers: "May an avenging God pursue them."

General Kilpatrick set out to avenge Dahlgren's death. At least, that was what he said he was going to do. In his report he wrote that

> the outrageous treatment of the remains of Colonel Dahlgren and the cruel and barbarous manner in which his men were hunted down and captured by citizens and soldiers with dogs determined me to visit the neighborhood of King and Queen Court-House with a sufficient force to punish those who had been engaged in the murder of Colonel Dahlgren and the capture of his men.

Kilpatrick's visit was to be a complex foray led by General Isaac Wistar. The operation involved twenty-seven hundred infantrymen, conveyed up the York River on a small fleet of ships, plus eleven hundred cavalry. Kilpatrick proceeded by ship and played little active role in the expedition. General Wistar became so frustrated with Kilpatrick's unwillingness to fight that he ordered him back to Monroe and continued without him. Kilpatrick's thirst for vengeance apparently did not extend beyond his official report.

The elaborate plan went awry. The timing for the coordination of the various units was off, the rain was heavy, and the mission accomplished nothing more than the burning of the settlement at King and Queen Court House. Even so, Kilpatrick managed to claim credit for what little damage had been inflicted on the enemy. "My cavalry has returned," he telegraphed General Butler. "The people of King and

Queen Court-House have been well punished for the murder of Colonel Dahlgren."

Kilpatrick's cavalry was brought back to Alexandria by ship—"like a parcel of old women," as Colonel Lyman had predicted—where they were to rest for several days before returning to camp at Stevensburg. When a trooper went into town and slashed a Negro soldier with his saber on the street, the whole command was sent back to the Rapidan immediately. Thus, Kilpatrick's raid on Richmond officially ended, and his weary men returned to where they had started nineteen days before. The impact of the raid was far from over, however. In both North and South, much sound and fury were to come.

On March 9, the *New York Times* became the first northern newspaper to carry the story of Dahlgren's death and the orders found on his body:

IMPORTANT FROM RICHMOND; THE MANNER OF COL. DAHLGREN'S DEATH AND THE CAPTURE OF HIS MEN; THEY ARE SHOT DOWN FROM A MIDNIGHT AMBUSH; CONFINEMENT OF THE PRISONERS IN DUNGEONS AND IN IRONS; THEIR PROMPT EXECUTION DEMANDED; BARBAROUS INDIGNITIES, CRUELTIES AND PASSIONS.

Reprinting the Richmond accounts, the *New York Times* told its readers of the pursuit of Kilpatrick's and Dahlgren's men, the setting of the trap, and the death of the popular young colonel. The Dahlgren papers were published intact.

The correspondent E. A. Paul, who had been with Dahlgren when he was wounded in Boonesboro, composed a eulogy for his friend.

Brave almost to rashness, and prompted by as high order of patriotism as ever inspired a hero, he was the man of all others to lead a daring enterprise. . . . while fully realizing the desperate character of the expedition [he] expressed a willingness to sacrifice his own life in an effort to rescue his brave countrymen from the Bastille in which they have been for months confined. . . .

He has fallen, and the grave has closed over one of the most manly forms that has succumbed during the present war. He dies just where he would have wished most to die—fighting the enemies of the Union.

In Washington, a reporter asked President Lincoln about the expedition and his part in the planning of it. Lincoln, after expressing his pleasure in Kilpatrick's safe return and sorrow for the loss of Dahlgren, replied that he had given his consent to the raid. He added that, even though some of his generals had pronounced the scheme impracticable, he had been willing to attempt it. Releasing the prisoners had seemed worth the risk.

Northern newspapers, particularly the anti-administration publications, were quick to air their criticisms and to affix blame. Some of the fury was directed against Kilpatrick, but most was reserved for Lincoln. The *New York World* wrote on March 15:

General Kill . . . who is an enthusiastic and hopeful officer, supposed the thing could be done and the President, with his usual want of discretion, told him to go ahead.

In Richmond, the *Daily Dispatch* told its readers:

the chief criminals are Lincoln, Seward, and the Black Republican crew in Washington, men who have deliberately planned and directed the commission of one of the most gigantic crimes in the annals of human warfare.

And all the while, Jefferson Davis was preparing to plan and direct another.

A PRETTY UGLY PIECE
OF BUSINESS

Captain Hines arrived in Richmond during the second week of March and went immediately to meet with Secretary of War Seddon and Secretary of State Benjamin. Both Seddon and Benjamin agreed with Jefferson Davis that the Dahlgren papers provided the perfect justification for beginning the campaign of arson, assassination, and violence against civilians that Hines had proposed to them the month before.

Hines's Northwest conspiracy could be the Confederacy's last hope for winning the war, or at least for negotiating a settlement with the North. If the mission resulted in Lincoln's defeat in the coming election, then the war would be as good as over.

Some said later that having those papers surface when they did seemed downright providential. Without them, Davis would not have had the alibi for responding to terror with terror.

Davis instructed Seddon and Benjamin to work out the details with Hines and to provide whatever assistance he needed to take the war directly to the people of the North. Hines met once more with Davis, who gave Hines certain verbal orders, the nature of which have never been made known. On March 14, Seddon wrote to Hines, formally ordering him to implement the Northwest conspiracy. Hines was to be the military commander and was to "travel to Toronto to carry out the orders which we discussed last night."

Two days later, Seddon gave Hines another letter, amending his authority in the operation. Hines would remain military commander, but the overall mission based in Canada would be supervised by three commissioners—civilian officials of the Confederacy. They would have authority to approve or disapprove all plans for military operations.

This letter, like the earlier one, described Hines's orders in broad terms. Nothing specific was written about arson, assassination, or fomenting revolution in the Northwest. Perhaps Seddon was mindful of his place in history, not wanting his name linked directly with spreading terror in the city streets.

> Confederate States of America
> War Department
> Richmond, March 16, 1864
> Captain T. Henry Hines:
> Sir—You are detailed for special service to proceed to Canada, passing through the United States under such character and in such mode as you may deem most safe, for the purpose of collecting there the men of General Morgan's command who may have escaped, and others of the citizens of the Confederate States willing to return and enter the military service of the Confederacy. . . .
>
> In passing through the United States you will confer with the leading persons friendly or attached to the cause of the Confederacy, or who may be advocates of peace, and do all in your power to induce our friends to organize and prepare themselves to render such aid as circumstances may allow; and to encourage and animate those favorable to a peaceful adjustment to the employment of all agencies calculated to effect such consummation on terms consistent always with the independence of the Confederate States.
>
> You will likewise have in view the possibility, by such means as you can command, of effecting any fair and appropriate enterprises of war against our enemies, and will be at liberty to employ such of our soldiers as you may collect, in any hostile operation. . . .
>
> Reliance is felt in your discretion and sagacity to understand

and carry out, as contingencies may dictate, the details of the
general design thus communicated. More specific instructions in
anticipation of events that may occur under your observation
cannot well be given.
    Respectfully,
    James A. Seddon
    Secretary of War

What all this circumlocution referred to was, as Hines later wrote,
a plan for creating a revolution in the United States by releasing
Confederate prisoners, attacking northern cities, and killing political
leaders. Hines said he was commissioned to carry out such a mission
and given whatever he needed to execute the plan.

Curiously, only two days after this letter was written, the Union
general Ben Butler telegraphed Secretary of War Stanton, suggesting
that John Hunt Morgan's men who were being held in Union prisons
in Ohio—one of the states in which Hines was expected to operate—
be sent to Butler's jurisdiction for confinement at Point Lookout.
There is no written record of why Butler made this suggestion, but
such a move (which was not carried out) would have ensured that
Hines would have no opportunity to release Morgan's men. The fact
that only two days elapsed between Seddon's order to Hines and
Butler's telegram is a fascinating coincidence. One possible explanation is that Elizabeth Van Lew, in Richmond, learned of Hines's mission and got word of it to Butler.

The financing of the operation was also unusual; Secretary of War
Seddon gave that responsibility to Hines himself. The actual fund-
raising would be disguised through the sale of two hundred bales of
cotton that Seddon had transferred to Memphis. Hines would handle
the sale, and the proceeds—some seventy thousand dollars—would be
placed in his name in a Canadian bank in Montréal.

Hines traveled through several southern states to recruit men,
amass supplies, and supervise the cotton sale. During this period he
sent some of his personal papers to his father to pass on to a local historian who was writing a book about Hines's exploits.

Hines also contacted the *Atlantic Magazine* in Boston, proposing
that he write an article about his escape, and General Morgan's, from

the Columbus jail. How bizarre that Hines should initiate business dealings with a northern magazine publisher at the very time he was planning a terror campaign against the North.

By the middle of April, all preparations made, Hines returned to Richmond, ready to embark on his dangerous enterprise. His son later told the story that Hines was honored at a banquet the night before he left. Allegedly, the elder Hines proposed a wager during the dinner, boasting that he could travel through Washington, D.C., and shake hands with President Lincoln, with the bonds to finance the Northwest conspiracy sticking out of his coat pocket. Given Hines's resemblance to John Wilkes Booth, it is conceivable Hines was able to pass himself off as the famous actor when he visited the White House.

Confederate leaders wasted no time capitalizing on the propaganda value of the Dahlgren papers, in their continuing efforts to win foreign support for their cause. Sometime in the middle of March, Secretary of State Benjamin ordered fifty copies to be made of the papers, each set including five photographs of the actual documents. Earlier, he had sent a Catholic priest to the European cities of Paris, Madrid, Vienna, and Rome, to solicit aid for the Confederacy of both a moral and a material nature.

Benjamin shipped the papers to the priest and described the planned sacking of Richmond and the "exposing of its women to nameless horrors." He added that the Union "spares neither age nor sex, nor do they even shrink from the most shameful desecration of the edifices in which the people meet for the worship of God."

Details of Kilpatrick's raid and additional copies of the Dahlgren papers were sent to John Slidell, the representative of the Confederate States based in Paris. Benjamin wrote to Slidell that the papers revealed the barbaric nature of the war waged by the Federals. Referring to the photographic copies of the Dahlgren papers, he commented:

> They speak for themselves and require no comment. . . . You will agree with me that they should be circulated, as the most conclu-

sive evidence of the nature of the war now waged against us by those who profess a desire that we should live with them as brethren under one Government.

The Union command was in an uproar over the Dahlgren papers. Even before Kilpatrick's men returned to their winter camp along the Rapidan, General Meade had ordered a full investigation into the legitimacy of the documents. The charges being printed in the southern newspapers were serious, and it was expected that the Confederate government would file a formal protest. Meade would have to be prepared with a response, and he was determined that it would clear him of any complicity in the matter. As commander of the Army of the Potomac, he would bear the ultimate responsibility for the orders. He had to find out who had issued them. Was it Dahlgren? Or was it Kilpatrick?

On March 14, Meade directed his chief of staff, General Humphreys, to contact General Pleasonton, ordering that

careful inquiry be made to ascertain whether Colonel Dahlgren made or issued such an address to his command as that which has been published in the journals of to-day; and also whether any orders or directions of the character of those contained in the memorandum following the address were given to his command or to any part of it.

On receipt of that order, Pleasonton's adjutant general wrote to Kilpatrick:

General: The major-general commanding directs that careful inquiries be made to ascertain whether Colonel Dahlgren made or issued such an address to his command as that which has been published in the journals of the day. Every effort will be made by you to learn the truth of this matter, and the officers and men of his command will be carefully questioned on this point, and the result of the investigation and whatever you may yourself know of the matter will be reported at the earliest practicable moment.

The general also desires to know whether any orders or directives of the character of those contained in the "memorandum" following the address, as printed in the public journals, were given to his command or to any portion of it.

Kilpatrick was on the spot. He had to ascertain whether Dahlgren had ever issued any orders to kill Jefferson Davis as every newspaper in the North was saying. At the same time, Kilpatrick had to make sure no suspicion fell on him. If the papers were genuine, then Kilpatrick's superiors had to be made aware that he knew nothing about them and was in no way implicated in their preparation.

Two days later, Kilpatrick replied to the directive, claiming to have examined the officers and men of Dahlgren's command who survived the raid. All of them, he wrote, "testify that he published no address whatever to his command, nor did he give any instructions, much less of the character alleged in the rebel journals."

If there had been any such instructions in the Dahlgren papers, as the South was claiming, no member of Dahlgren's command seemed to be aware of them. However, just because such orders had not been issued to the men did not mean the orders never existed. But Kilpatrick had no doubts: the men had never heard of such orders, and the orders never existed, at least not in the form published by the rebels. Kilpatrick wrote:

> Colonel Dahlgren, one hour before we separated at my headquarters, handed me an address that he intended to read to his command. That paper was indorsed in red ink, "Approved," over my official signature. The alleged address of Colonel Dahlgren published in the papers is the same as the one approved by me, save so far as it speaks of "*exhorting the prisoners to destroy and burn the hateful city and kill the traitor Davis and his cabinet.*" All this is false and published only as an excuse for the barbarous treatment of the remains of a brave soldier.

Meade had his answer. Neither Dahlgren nor Kilpatrick had written or issued any orders to assassinate Jefferson Davis and the Confederate Cabinet. But there was another question: Could Meade trust Kilpatrick to reveal information that might further damage his already tarnished reputation? It was possible Kilpatrick was covering up the truth to protect himself.

Meade cast his investigatory net wider. On March 22, he sent for Captain Mitchell, Dahlgren's second in command. The captain, after providing General Meade with a full report of his part in the expedition, denied any knowledge of the Dahlgren papers. Mitchell noted:

> With regard to the address and memoranda of plans alleged by rebel papers to have been found on Colonel Dahlgren's person, I would state that no address of any kind was ever published to either officers or men; that none of Colonel Dahlgren's plans, save what I have mentioned in the first part of my report, were ever made known to either officers or men in the expedition, and that I know it was not Colonel Dahlgren's intention to kill Jeff. Davis, in case he could be captured.

The *New York Times*, on March 14, printed the first public suggestion that the Dahlgren papers were not genuine. The correspondent E. A. Paul, who had accompanied the expedition and claimed to have seen Dahlgren's orders the day the raid began, denied the rebel account. Paul wrote:

> The simple fact [is] that in the so-called programme of operations found upon the body of the lamented Col. Dahlgren, they have interpolated words of their own coining to the effect that Jeff. Davis and his Cabinet were to be killed. . . . The writer was privileged to see the documents which Col. Dahlgren had the day he started on the expedition . . . and although having no copy of these papers before him now, he is satisfied that there is no expression therein written which could reasonably be construed even as to express a determination to murder any person or persons.

The following day, the *New York Times* published an editorial, "The Rebel Calumny on Col. Dahlgren," which took even a stronger stand. Paul had written that the rebels had interpolated words, a fairly polite and restrained indictment. The editorial accused the rebel government of deliberate forgery.

The editor cited Paul's statement that he had seen Dahlgren's orders, adding that

> no officer of the American army would ever dream of putting to death civil officers taken captive by such a raid, and no officer in his senses, even if he were barbarous enough to contemplate such a result, would ever put such orders in writing . . . simply to damn himself to lasting infamy.

Other people also voiced disbelief. If Dahlgren had been intent on political assassination, why put it in writing? Verbal orders would have sufficed. Yet his men insisted they received no such orders—verbally or in writing. Dahlgren's fellow officers raised an additional point: If the orders existed in the form alleged by the Confederates, so damning to Dahlgren, why did he keep them during his retreat from Richmond?

Any officer less experienced than Colonel Dahlgren would have known to destroy incriminating documents in the chaos of a running retreat, with death or capture imminent. In such circumstances, it made no sense to keep such potentially damaging papers.

Toward the end of March, Confederate President Jefferson Davis directed General Robert E. Lee to file a formal protest with General Meade over the Dahlgren papers. On March 30, the adjutant and inspector general in Richmond sent Lee the original Dahlgren papers, and photographic copies, with a cover letter:

> [T]he Government is in possession of ample and incontestible evidence that the papers were taken from the body, which was identified as that of Colonel Dahlgren. . . .
>
> The President directs that you open a correspondence with the general commanding the Federal Army of the Potomac to ascertain if the orders and instructions of Colonel Dahlgren, as contained in these papers, were in conformity to instructions

from his Government or superior officers, and whether the Government of the United States sanctions the sentiments and purposes therein set forth.

Lee made his protest to Meade on April 1:

General: I am instructed to bring to your notice two papers found upon the body of Col. U. Dahlgren, who was killed while commanding a part of the Federal cavalry during the late expedition of General Kilpatrick. To enable you to understand the subject fully I have the honor to enclose photographic copies of the papers referred to, one of which is an address to his officers and men, bearing the official signature of Colonel Dahlgren, and the other, not signed, contains more detailed explanations of the purpose of the expedition.

Lee went on to quote the most incriminating passages from the papers—referring to the destruction of the city of Richmond and the killing of Davis and the Cabinet. Lee concluded:

In obedience to my instructions, I beg leave respectfully to inquire whether the designs and instructions of Colonel Dahlgren, as set forth in these papers . . . were authorized by the United States Government or by his superior officers, and also whether they have the sanction and approval of those authorities.

Two weeks passed before Lee's letter reached General Meade. Heavy rains had swollen the rivers and streams in northern Virginia, making them impassable until April 16. Meade forwarded the letter to Washington, and he asked Kilpatrick for another copy of the report of his investigation of Dahlgren's men.

Instead of routing a second copy of his report to Meade's attention, Kilpatrick prepared a new version. Although in other respects virtually a duplicate of the first, Kilpatrick added the following sentence: "Colonel Dahlgren received no orders from me to pillage, burn or kill, nor were any such instructions given me by my superiors."

Meade's reply to General Lee—a direct and brief denial—was sent to Confederate authorities April 17, with General Kilpatrick's letter enclosed. Meade wrote:

> In reply, I have to state that neither the United States Government, myself, nor General Kilpatrick authorized, sanctioned, or approved the burning of the city of Richmond and the killing of Mr. Davis and cabinet, nor any other act not required by military necessity and in accordance with the usages of war.

This outcome left both Kilpatrick's and Meade's reputations intact. "Everybody's reputation was safe—except that of Dahlgren now [conveniently] dead."

In a letter to his wife, Meade admitted feeling differently.

> This was a pretty ugly piece of business, for in denying having authorized or approved "the burning of Richmond or killing Mr. Davis and cabinet," I necessarily threw odium on Dahlgren. I, however, enclosed a letter from Kilpatrick, in which the authenticity of the papers was impugned; but I regret to say Kilpatrick's reputation, and collateral evidence in my possession [the copy of the papers received from Lee], rather go against this theory. However, I was determined my skirts should be clear.

And so they were.

Chapter 1 8

FULL AND BITTER TEARS

An ugly piece of business, General Meade had called it, but the affair of the Dahlgren papers was not yet finished. More intrigue and uncertainty were to come, and more grief for Admiral Dahlgren, who wanted only to bring his son's body home. Throughout the month of March, the elder Dahlgren made four trips to Fortress Monroe to try to make the necessary arrangements so that Ulric could have a proper burial in his hometown of Philadelphia.

As early as March 11, General Butler contacted Judge Robert Ould, the Confederate Commissioner of Exchange, to request formally the return of Dahlgren's body.

> Sir: I have the honor to request that the body of Col. Ulric Dahlgren, late of the U. S. Army, which we learn is buried in Richmond, be permitted to be forwarded by flag-of-truce boat, to be delivered to his afflicted father, who is waiting here to receive it.
>
> As remains of officers have been forwarded to their friends in this manner I trust this request may be granted: specially so because I see by the Richmond papers that some circumstances

of indignity and outrage accompanied the death. You do not war upon the dead as these papers would imply, and would it not be desirable to prevent all supposition that your authorities countenance such acts by delivering the remains to the bereaved family?

Thus, Butler passed the challenge to the rebels. Was it true Dahlgren's body had been submitted to "indignity and outrage?" Of course, Butler already knew that was the case, because Dahlgren's servant had personally witnessed the condition of the colonel's body. If the remains were returned, then the matter could be settled. The evidence of the mutilated body could be used to advantage by northern propagandists to counteract the southern charges of barbarity levied against Dahlgren. Two weeks later, Butler received a reply from Ould; Butler immediately wrote to Admiral Dahlgren.

Dear Sir: I have received the most positive assurances from Judge Ould upon two points that may interest you. First, that the statements in the Richmond papers of any indignities to the remains of your son are false; that they were decently and properly buried under the direction of an officer of equal rank in the Confederate service. Secondly, I have the most positive assurances from him that you shall receive the remains of your son by next flag-of-truce boat.

I beg leave to add my own assurances that the moment Colonel Dahlgren's remains arrive at this point they shall be safely and most speedily forwarded to you.

The Richmond press learned about these negotiations to return Dahlgren's remains from accounts printed in Union newspapers. On April 5, the *Richmond Examiner* fumed:

Northern papers hint significantly that the body of Ulric, the Hun . . . is to be disinterred from its unknown grave, and delivered over into the embrace of an impious father. . . . What has become of the gusty pronunciamento of the Confederate Government that Ulric Dahlgren's body should be disclosed only by the trump of the last judgment? Butler's trumpet call for it has been far more potent than Gabriel's, and behold he appeareth!

Judge Ould had not foreseen any difficulty in returning the remains of Colonel Dahlgren to his family in the North. It was a straightforward procedure that had been carried out routinely many times before. When Ould had received Butler's request, he had gone to see Lieutenant Colonel Atkinson, the man charged by Jefferson Davis with overseeing the secret burial.

Atkinson recalled Ould saying to him that:

> he knew I had superintended the burial of Colonel Dahlgren, and that he wanted me to show him the grave; that he wished to disinter the body and take it down in the next leaving exchange boat and deliver it to his father. . . . Having received an order from President Davis not to divulge the burial spot of Dahlgren to any one, I felt obliged to refuse.

Ould was surprised. Never before had his government denied a request to return the body of a fallen soldier. What possible purpose could be served by such a refusal? A few days later, it was Atkinson's turn to be surprised; he received a signed directive from Jefferson Davis authorizing him to show Judge Ould, or Ould's sergeant, the location of Dahlgren's grave. This time Davis wrote that the return of the body "would be of material advantage to the Confederacy." Atkinson wondered what advantage could possibly accrue now that would not have pertained earlier, when Ould had come to see him.

Davis's latest directive in hand, Atkinson rode to the grave site with the sergeant who delivered the directive and pointed out Dahlgren's grave. Several days later, on Judge Ould's orders, the sergeant returned to the cemetery with a wagon, prepared to disinter the body. The grave was a shallow one, and it took little digging to discover that the grave was empty. Dahlgren's body was gone.

Atkinson was alarmed. Who would have taken the body, and for what purpose? Jefferson Davis had made a great effort to keep the burial site secret. Who else could have known its location? And why had Davis so quickly reversed his decision and authorized Atkinson to reveal the location of Dahlgren's grave?

More puzzling was that, when Davis was informed of the missing corpse, he blamed Atkinson. As Atkinson recalled: "I received a sharp reproach direct from Mr. Davis." Apparently, Jefferson Davis blamed Atkinson because the body was missing.

Did Davis have the corpse removed so the Federals would not have proof of the indignities perpetrated on the colonel's body? Had some other government agency acted to move the body without the president's knowledge? Acting on orders from the president, General Winder's agents attempted to find the guilty party, but whoever had done the deed left no clues. Even the tree had been replanted over the empty grave.

On April 17, General Butler informed Admiral Dahlgren that Ulric's body was missing. As Ould recounted to a Union officer:

> upon going to the grave of Colonel Dahlgren it was found empty, and that the most vigorous and persistent search fails to find it; that the authorities are making every exertion to find the body, which shall be restored if found.

Admiral Dahlgren was heartbroken at the thought that he might never be able to give his son a decent burial. However, three days later, Butler wrote to him again.

> I have reliable information from Richmond that Colonel Dahlgren's body has been taken possession of by his Union friends, and has been put beyond the reach of the rebel authorities.

The following day, Butler was able to provide additional information.

> The remains are not so far within my control as to be able to remove them from Richmond, where every effort is being made by the detectives to find them; but they are, I am informed and believe, in the hands of devoted friends of the Union, who have taken possession of them in order that proper respect may be shown to them at a time which I trust is not far distant.
> I hardly dare suggest to Ould, when he reports to me, as he will, that he cannot find them, that I can put them into his possession, because that will show such a correspondence with

Richmond as will alarm them, and will redouble their vigilance to detect my sources of information. I am, however, under the direction of the president.

Shortly after Admiral Dahlgren received the second message from General Butler, a stranger called on the admiral at home in Washington, D.C. He had recently come from Richmond and had been sent, he said, to inform the admiral that the body had been removed from its burial site by Union agents and had been reburied in a safe place, to await the end of the war.

Years later, the truth was revealed. The removal of Dahlgren's corpse had been arranged by Elizabeth Van Lew. She wrote:

> [T]he heart of every loyal person was stirred to its depths by the outrages committed upon his inanimate body, and to discover the hidden grave and remove his honored dust to friendly care was decided upon.

For her daring and dangerous plot, she had enlisted the assistance of other northern loyalists and spies living in and around Richmond. One of her operatives was F. W. E. Lohmann, a German who ran a grocery store and restaurant. Lohmann, who was also a dealer in gold, greenbacks, and the black market, had been entrusted with the task of locating the grave site and carting off the remains.

One of Lohmann's customers, Martin Meredith Lipscomb, was in charge of burying the bodies of Federal soldiers who died in Richmond. "Pickling pork and burying dead Yankees," was how Lipscomb described his business interests in a rally in support of his mayoral campaign. (He lost the election.) Lohmann tried discreetly to sound Lipscomb out on where Dahlgren might be buried. Unfortunately, Lipscomb did not know; he had been banished from Oakwood Cemetery the night of the burial. Lohmann asked directly if Lipscomb could find out. At first, Lipscomb refused, but Lohmann persuaded him that he wanted to disinter the body solely for humanitarian reasons, to assure a decent funeral in a metal casket for a brave young man.

Lipscomb made inquiries among the cemetery's Negro workmen to see if they knew anything about a secret burial that had occurred around midnight some time early in March. One man recalled a four-mule government wagon with an armed escort late one night. He noticed that an officer had ridden ahead of the wagon as if checking to see whether they were being observed.

The workman had hidden behind a tree to watch. When the soldiers left, he marked the shallow ditch and returned in the morning to mark it again. He did not know who was buried there, but the procedure was so unusual that he wanted to remember the grave's location.

The night of April 6 was cold and damp. Patches of snow lay on the ground, and another storm was threatening. A wagon stopped at the entrance of Oakwood Cemetery, and Lohmann, accompanied by his brother John and by Martin Lipscomb, checked to make sure they had not been followed. The wagon creaked ahead, stopping not far from the entrance, where the Negro workman and two companions were waiting with their shovels.

They opened the grave, heaved the coffin out, and pried off the lid. Lohmann probed inside with his hand to make sure the corpse had only one leg. They could not risk a light, and that was the only way Lohmann could think of to confirm that the body was Dahlgren. Lohmann paid the cemetery workers fifteen hundred dollars in Confederate money and reminded them to refill the grave and replant the small tree over top.

The men loaded the coffin onto the wagon and drove a short distance out of the city to the farm of William S. Rowley. At forty-eight, Rowley was the oldest of the conspirators. He had been arrested twice and had received frequent threats from his neighbors for his Union sentiments. Since January he had been an agent for General Butler and had worked with Elizabeth Van Lew. The coffin was carried into a workshop where Rowley sat up through the night keeping watch. The next morning, the Lohmann brothers arrived with a metal casket obtained by Lipscomb and placed Dahlgren's body in it.

Several Union sympathizers stopped by the farm to pay their respects. Elizabeth Van Lew recalled:

> Dahlgren's hair was very short, but all that could be spared was cut off and sent to his father before Richmond fell. . . . The body, except the head, was in a perfect state of preservation, fair, pure and firm the flesh; here and there a purple spot as of mildew. . . . The comeliness of the young face was gone, yet the features seemed regular and there was a wonderful look of firmness or energy stamped upon them. His dress was a shirt of the coarsest kind, not even fastened; pantaloons of dark blue cloth; a fine cotton sock was on his left foot, the right leg was wanting beneath the blanket. . . . Around the body was wrapped a blue military blanket.

About midday, the metal coffin was sealed with a compound of chalk and oil, because there was no putty to be had in all of Richmond. The box was placed on Rowley's wagon and covered with young peach trees. Along the route to the new burial site, Rowley passed through several picket posts.

Elizabeth Van Lew wrote:

> Wary and vigilant were our pickets, and if one had run his bayonet into this wagon only a few inches, death would *certainly* have been the award of this brave man; and not only death; but torture to make him reveal those connected with him—his accomplices. The forged papers said to have been found on Colonel Dahlgren's body had *maddened the people;* and Southern people, when maddened . . . stop not at trifles.

Rowley passed each successive guard post undetected. As he drove up to the guard's tent at the final stop, he let the reins of the horses fall casually, with "the appearance of perfect indifference." The lieutenant on duty ordered a private to search the wagon, then he disappeared into his tent.

"Whose peach trees are those?" the guard asked.

Before Rowley could answer, the guard spoke again.

"I think I have seen your face before."

"Yes," Rowley said, "and I have yours."

They chatted a moment and discovered that Rowley had once attended a party at the guard's home. The guard asked again about the peach trees.

"They belong to a German in the country to whom I am carrying them," Rowley said.

Another wagon drew up, and the guard examined it carefully, poking through the contents. Rowley tried to keep his nervousness under control. When the soldier returned, he remarked that it seemed late in the season to transplant peach trees.

For another half hour Rowley kept up a lively conversation about the trees, and mutual acquaintances, and anything else he could think of to keep the guard from probing the wagon's cargo. While he waited for clearance, nearly a dozen other wagons approached the picket post. The guard had examined each one thoroughly. Finally, the lieutenant emerged from his tent. Noticing that Rowley was still there, he ordered the private to finish searching the wagon and let Rowley go on.

"It would be a pity to tear those trees all up," the guard said, "when you have them packed in there so nicely."

"When I packed them," Rowley said, "I did not expect them to be disturbed; but as it is, being a citizen, I know a soldier's duty and expect him to do it."

When another wagon arrived, the lieutenant reminded the guard to finish the search and let Rowley get on with his business.

"I don't want to hinder you any longer," the guard whispered, so his lieutenant would not overhear. "I think it all right, at any rate your honest face is guarantee enough for me—go on."

Rowley conveyed Dahlgren's coffin to a farm near Hungary Station belonging to a Scotsman, Robert Orrock. There the coffin was buried. A peach tree was planted to mark the grave.

Admiral Dahlgren was increasingly frustrated in his attempts to recover his son's body. Now he had been told it would be necessary to wait for the end of the war. How ironic that Elizabeth Van Lew's humanitarian deed served to prolong the admiral's grief. Because the

Confederates had already decided to return the body, Admiral Dahlgren had made arrangements for the funeral. The family preacher had prepared a two-hour sermon. But it would be more than a year before he could deliver it.

Miss Van Lew's plan had been dangerous not only for the conspirators, but also could have harmed all northern agents in Richmond had any of the plotters been captured and made to talk. The Confederate government was embarrassed, even humiliated, that Dahlgren's body could not be found, but they were also outraged and, as a result, intensified their efforts to ferret out Union sympathizers. The futility of their search, however, indicated how effective and widespread the Union network was. The whole effort proved a major defeat for the Confederates on the home front.

It was also a setback for Admiral Dahlgren, depressed over his failure to retrieve the body and by southern allegations that Ulric was a common murderer who deserved to lie dead in a ditch. "Full and bitter tears do I shed for my dead boy," he wrote in his diary. He told Ulric's aunt Patty: "He has given limb and now life for his country."

Friends became concerned for the elder Dahlgren's sanity. He talked of nothing but recovering the body, of erecting a statue in his son's honor, of writing a book to memorialize him. When Secretary of War Stanton met him on the street, all he would speak about was his son. Secretary of the Navy Sumner Welles noticed his morbid obsession and advised him "to get abroad and mingle in the world, and not yield to a blow that was irremediable."

But Admiral Dahlgren seemed possessed. He collected every scrap of paper written about Ulric. He obtained reminiscences from Ulric's friends. In a macabre gesture, an aide "had Ulric's amputated leg sealed inside the cornerstone of a gun foundry being built at the Washington Navy Yard to honor the only portion of the youth's remains that the Confederates had not defiled."

"Occupied in collecting every item about dear Ully," Admiral Dahlgren confided to his diary on April 15.

> Old letters &c every day some extracts are sent me showing how deeply the brave fellow had taken hold of the feelings everywhere—

Letter from Capt. Mitchell 2d NY Cavalry, who was in his command and saw much of him—took his meals with him and assisted him off and on his horse writes in glowing terms of the noble boy so brave under fire,—so enduring of hardship,—and his presence so influential with the men—

Dear Ully you have fought your last battle—Rest my son in peace.

Determined to clear his son's name, he scoured the southern newspapers, searching out allegations to refute. In the *Richmond Examiner* of June 16, he came across a curious item:

Dahlgren a spy—The correspondent of the Charleston *Mercury* says that Dahlgren played spy in Richmond for six weeks last winter, and extended his observations to Petersburg and Wilmington. His assumed name was Lieutenant Murray. He had a pass to go where he pleased from General Winder.

Admiral Dahlgren was certain this was yet another lie. He did not know that Thaddeus Walker's father and uncle, and several family friends, had identified Dahlgren's body as that of Lieutenant Murray. The admiral was positive Ulric could not have been in Richmond for six weeks that winter; only seventeen days had elapsed between his visit to President Lincoln on February 1 and his arrival at Brandy Station February 18 to join the raid on Richmond.

In July, Admiral Dahlgren got the opportunity to prove that the Dahlgren papers were more rebel calumny. He received a photographic copy of the orders the rebels claimed had been found on the body. What he saw persuaded him beyond any doubt that Ulric could not have written them. On July 28, he wrote to the *New York Times*, hoping to use this forum to influence public opinion.

I have patiently and sorrowfully awaited the hour when I should be able to vindicate fully the memory of my gallant son, Col. Ulric Dahlgren, and lay bare to the world that atrocious imposture of those who, not content with abusing and defacing the remains of the noble boy, have knowingly and persistently endeavored to blemish his spotless name by a forged lie. . . . That hour has at last come. . . .

I can now affirm that this document is a forgery—a barefaced, atrocious forgery—so palpable that the wickedness of the act is only equaled by the recklessness with which it has been perpetrated. . . .

I felt from the first . . . that my son never wrote that paper— that it was a forgery; but I refrained from giving utterance to that faith until I had seen a sample of the infamous counterfeit. . . . I say now, that a more fiendish lie never was invented . . . they forged the lie, and gave it currency in all the minuteness of a fac-simile . . . the shameful deceit could not fail to be apparent to any-one having the least knowledge of Col. Dahlgren's handwriting.

He pointed out that the handwriting on the so-called Dahlgren papers was markedly different from Ulric Dahlgren's handwriting; clearly, someone else had written those pages. But there was an additional point the admiral did not mention until some years later, when he wrote a reminiscence of his son. Then he noted:

the document alleged to have been found upon the person of Colonel Dahlgren is utterly discredited by the fact that the signature attached to it cannot possibly be his own, because it is not his name, a letter is misplaced, and the real name *Dahlgren* is spelled *Dalhgren*; hence it is undeniable that the paper is not only spurious, but is a forgery.

Admiral Dahlgren stated that the signature on the papers provided additional support for the charge of forgery.

Evidence almost as positive, is to be found in the writing of the Christian prefix of the signature. The document is signed "U. Dahlgren," whereas Colonel Dahlgren invariably signed himself "*Ulric* Dahlgren," *never with the bare initial of the first name.* Among all the letters of his writing which can be collected, not an instance to the contrary occurs, down to the last that he ever wrote, just before starting for Richmond . . . I pronounce those papers a *base forgery.*

Relieved at being able to prove that his son was not a murderer, that the accusations reported and repeated in the southern papers were lies, he began to come to terms with his loss, but he never recovered fully from Ulric's death. In his diary the following Thanksgiving, he wrote:

> My son, my son, how much better that I had passed away in your stead—The most loved and cherished of all things to me, in all life—gone,—and how sadly—It is the Thanksgiving day of the nation,—but what shall I be thankful for!—not for life surely nor for happiness.

On the first anniversary of Ulric's death, the admiral cursed the rebel government. "May God scourge them and send them to wander unpitied over the world." His campaign to restore his son's honor and good name had no effect in the South. However, by then it made no difference who had written the Dahlgren papers. Whether genuine or forged, fact or fiction, they had served their purpose. The Confederacy's campaign of terror in the North, for which the papers provided justification, was under way.

Chapter 19

ON THE EVE OF
GREAT EVENTS

Captain Thomas Henry Hines arrived in Toronto the third week of April, some seven weeks after Ulric Dahlgren's death. He took a room in a boardinghouse and set about the task of fomenting a revolution to topple the government of the United States of America. Although this might have seemed to others an impossible task, Hines did not think so, and by his second day in Canada he was no longer alone. His army of revolutionaries had begun to assemble.

Hundreds of Yankees and Confederates were living in Toronto— deserters from the Union army, Northerners who had fled to Canada to evade the draft, rebel soldiers who had escaped from Yankee prison camps, spies from both sides, and assorted adventurers and soldiers of fortune ready to spy or fight for whichever side paid better.

Most of the Southerners congregated in the lobby and bar of the Queen's Hotel. It was easy to spot these escapees from Yankee prisons—emaciated, hollow-eyed men who faced an uncertain future in a strange, cold land. They made an effort to keep their tattered Confederate uniforms clean and to find sufficient cheap food to keep themselves alive. They lived a hand-to-mouth existence, surviving on the modest funds their relatives could provide.

They could not afford the expensive ship passage to the Bahamas and from there back home via Charleston or Wilmington by fast blockade runner, so they languished in Toronto's Queen's Hotel, hoping to meet someone who would lend them money, and waiting for the war to end. It was from among these men that Hines expected to recruit the nucleus of his army.

On his second morning in Toronto, he walked into the hotel bar and found his first ally, a rebel captain whom he had met when they rode with John Hunt Morgan. The man had escaped from prison and was nearly destitute. Hines bought him breakfast, and from the amount of food the man consumed, it was obvious he hadn't eaten so well in a long time. Hines outlined his plan to carry the war to civilians in the North, and by the time the man finished breakfast, he had agreed to join Hines's cause and to enlist other escaped prisoners.

By the end of Hines's first week in Toronto, he had found more than a hundred escaped Confederate officers and men. He knew some from his days with Morgan. Those he believed were trustworthy were asked to join for what he called special service in the northern states. Those he judged unsuitable for the mission were given money for the journey home, along with notarized identification papers certifying their Confederate citizenship. He made sure his recruits knew and accepted the dangers. If caught in enemy territory in civilian clothing, they would be hanged. The men were willing; to have the chance to fight Yankees again was worth the risk.

Jefferson Davis had chosen three civilian commissioners to head the official Confederate commission operating out of Canada. The group was apparently intended to be the "political counterpart and, in a sense, the diplomatically respectable front for Hines's assignment." The chief commissioner, Colonel Jacob Thompson, was a former U.S. congressman from Mississippi. He had served as Secretary of the Interior under President Buchanan and as a staff officer to General P. G. T. Beauregard. On April 27, Davis issued the following charge to Thompson:

Sir: Confiding special trust in your zeal, discretion and patriotism, I hereby direct you to proceed at once to Canada; there to carry out the instructions you have received from me verbally, in such a manner as shall seem most likely to conduce to the furtherance of the interests of the Confederate States of America which have been entrusted to you.

A tall, handsome, well-spoken man in his early fifties, Thompson was obstinate, inflexible in his opinions, and lacking in imagination. He was easily awed by anyone who claimed to have high connections in the Confederacy. He was also naive, "inclined to believe much that was told him, trust too many men, doubt too little, and suspect less." And Thompson was careless in spending the government's money.

He had been entrusted with one million dollars in gold for the mission, and more would be forthcoming. Hines was appalled at the sums Thompson gave freely to anyone who claimed to have a scheme to advance the Confederate cause. The gullible commissioner financed idle daydreamers and crooks as well as genuine but misguided patriots, bestowing as much as fifty thousand dollars on any man with an attractive idea, even if he had never met the person before. Often, once the money was turned over, Thompson never saw the fellow again.

One man approached Thompson with a demand for ten thousand dollars to buy weapons and ammunition. He claimed Secretary of State Benjamin had sent him to Canada but had misplaced his formal orders. He offered to return to Richmond to obtain another copy if Thompson would provide three thousand dollars to tide him over. Thompson gave the man the funds. The commissioner may have been the only one surprised when the man never returned. For all his faults, however, it was fortunate for the Confederacy that Thompson was chief commissioner, because he was considerably more competent than the others, Clement C. Clay and James P. Holcombe.

Clay, a former U.S. congressman from Alabama, loved the good life, fine food and wine, and elaborate dinner parties at which, to Hines's dismay, he tended to discuss confidential matters with new acquaintances. Clay was also in poor health, which should have been sufficient to prevent Davis from assigning him to such an important position. Sometimes Clay was little better than an invalid. Holcombe, a scholarly, erudite lawyer from the University of Virginia, invariably appeared in public wearing a black suit and tie and carrying a red book of poetry. He was clearly out of place dealing with spies, revolution, and undercover operations. Apparently he recognized his limitations and stayed very much in the background.

Hines met the commissioners for the first time on May 19. He was unimpressed with their qualifications but was relieved when he learned they did not intend to interfere with his activities. They had their own ideas about planning diversions against the Union, and agreed to leave Hines free to fight his own war in his own way. However, the temptation to meddle in Hines's operations turned out to be too great to resist.

What better day for the commencement of an uprising against the United States than the Fourth of July? This was an inspired choice on the part of Captain Hines. Not only was it Independence Day for the Union, but it was also the opening day of the presidential nominating convention of the Democratic party, meeting in Chicago. It would be the perfect opportunity to begin a terror campaign to bring down the Republican president.

Hines had the men to accomplish his task, thousands of them, armed and ready to strike at arsenals, military bases, and supply depots in the Northwest. The Copperheads alone claimed they could muster fifty thousand fighters. Hines also counted five thousand rebel officers and men confined at Camp Douglas, near Chicago, and seven thousand at Rock Island, one hundred twenty miles west. All were trained military men.

A force that size would spread so much destruction and fear throughout the North that General Grant would be compelled to shift half his army away from Lee to deal with the threat. That move would leave Lee free to strike against the remnants of Grant's army and perhaps to reinvade Pennsylvania, this time with happier results.

In June, Hines traveled through Illinois, Indiana, and Ohio to talk with local Copperhead leaders. In Chicago, he visited Charles Walsh, the political boss of Cook County and the man slated to command the Copperhead uprising there. Hines made good use of Walsh's home, within sight of Camp Douglas, as an observation post, carefully studying the prison compound and preparing maps for the attack.

Hines also made contact with Morgan's men who were among the captives at the camp. Many had relatives who had migrated from Kentucky to Chicago before the war. It was easy for these families to obtain passes to visit their kin, and Hines freely used them as couriers to pass information in and out of the compound.

Hines planned the assault with thoroughness and precision. By night the Chicago Copperheads would attack the prison from outside on three sides while the prisoners fought the guards inside. They would be equipped with the weapons and ammunition rapidly filling Walsh's house and barn, materiel purchased with money Hines supplied. As soon as the prisoners were freed, some would travel by train to release their comrades at Rock Island and capture its arsenal. Hines had already bribed railroad officials to insure that trains would be ready for them with a clear right of way to Rock Island, to arrive before dawn.

On June 14, Captain Hines and Commissioner Thompson met with Clement Vallandigham, the former Ohio congressman who had been arrested for speaking against the war. He had been exiled to the Confederacy but was unhappy in the South and had moved to Canada, settling in Windsor, Ontario, across the river from Detroit. Vallandigham was the primary spokesman for the Copperhead movement and was considered by many to be its unofficial leader.

Vallandigham offered his estimate of the strength of the Copperhead movement. Hines was stunned. Overall membership stood at 300,000, with 80,000 in Illinois, 50,000 in Indiana, and 40,000 in Ohio! Many were trained soldiers who had completed their enlistment in the Union army and were eager to fight in order to end the war. Hines explained his conspiracy plans while Vallandigham listened patiently, but initially the congressman refused to commit the Copperheads to the operation.

A few days later they met again in St. Catherine's, Ontario, not far from Niagara Falls. This time, Vallandigham seemed more encouraging. He had all the national leaders of the Copperhead movement in attendance and agreed that a general popular uprising was the likely result. Thompson was so excited that he spontaneously offered Vallandigham twenty-five thousand dollars, which the congressman personally disdained. However, Thompson was energetically urged to turn the money over to one of Vallandigham's Copperhead associates.

Greatly encouraged, Hines dispatched an enthusiastic report to Confederate Secretary of War Seddon. He noted that all Federal government leaders in Ohio, Indiana, and Illinois were to be assassinated in retribution for what Dahlgren—Ulric the Hun—had planned to do to Richmond.

Commissioner Thompson sent a similarly bloodthirsty message to Secretary of State Benjamin, in which he also requested a cavalry raid into Kentucky and Missouri, timed to coincide with the uprising. He concluded: "*nothing but violence can terminate the war.*"

As the reports of the numbers of men willing to bear arms increased, Hines realized that more weapons and ammunition would be needed. The commissioners sent their secretary, William Cleary, an old friend of Hines, to New York City. At a small violin shop near Washington Square, Cleary purchased thirty thousand dollars' worth of armaments and arranged for their shipment to Canada. Then the goods were smuggled back over the border in boxes labeled Prayer Books and School Books, to lie hidden in haystacks, barns, and cellars throughout Ohio and Indiana.

Nothing came of Commissioner Thompson's recommended cavalry thrust into Kentucky and Missouri to support the Fourth of July uprising. However, in early June, Hines was more successful in arranging for John Hunt Morgan to make a foray into Kentucky. Hines was convinced the Kentucky Copperheads would eagerly join Morgan's attack. To counter this expected uprising, the Union would be forced to move troops south—out of Indiana, Illinois, and Ohio—leaving fewer soldiers to fight the major battle.

It was a good plan, but in a chilling replay of the failed raid the year before, Morgan and his men were not equal to the task. His command had been reduced to twenty-five hundred troopers, a worn, tattered lot with weary horses. They rode one hundred fifty miles over the mountains, only to be caught at night by a larger Union force that sent them fleeing. Their desire to fight evaporated; their discipline, never a strong point, was shattered. They had become a drunken, demoralized mob.

Morgan's men swept down the roads and across the fields, pursued by Union troops at nearly every crossing. It might have helped if the thousands of Kentucky Copperheads had unearthed their arms caches and come to their aid, but they, too, were fleeing. Making good use of informers and spies among the Copperheads, the Yankees had learned of the anticipated uprising and set out to arrest every known dissident. Northern troops ripped up floorboards of barns and demolished haystacks to find the Copperheads' weapons. Only the luckier Kentuckians got away.

As July 4 approached, Copperhead leaders began to lose their nerve. They stopped bragging about how quickly they would bring down the government and end the war and started whining about the dangers in Hines's plan. Morgan's rout in Kentucky and the arrest of the Copperheads there made the leaders much less confident. If Kentucky Copperheads were on Union lists, then most likely the rest of them were also. They were scared.

In addition, the leadership of the Democratic party had postponed the nominating convention's opening day. Instead of July 4, they would not gather until August 29, delaying because of their belief that the war was going so badly for the Union that antiwar sentiment would surely peak by the end of summer.

General Grant had lost more than sixty thousand men in seven weeks in his spring campaign, and another thirty thousand casualties had been reported by Sherman and other generals in the West. Now Grant was locked in a siege with Lee's army at Petersburg. The Army of the Potomac had not moved in a month, and there was no sign of an end to the stalemate in the trenches.

Northern newspapers called Grant a butcher; editorial writers charged him with providing a cripple or a corpse for half the homes in the Union. The Democrats knew that the longer they waited, the greater would be the dissension, accompanied by calls for Lincoln's defeat.

Hines urged the Copperhead leaders not to wait until August 29 to make their move. Meeting with them at Chicago's Richmond House, a hotel at Lake Street and Michigan Avenue, he presented such a strong case that they agreed to begin the uprising July 20. But no sooner had they consented to that date than they rescheduled the attack for August 16. And after Hines reluctantly accepted that change, the Copperhead leaders insisted on August 29 again. Hines began to wonder how reliable they would prove.

Hines was joined by two friends who had served with him under John Hunt Morgan. One was John Castleman, a Kentuckian who had sworn Hines in as a private in Morgan's outfit. At twenty-three, Castleman was two years younger than Hines but also held the rank of captain. Hines was grateful to have someone he could trust working with him. He designated Castleman second in command.

The second new member of Hines's organization, Colonel George St. Leger Grenfell, seemed not unlike a character from a novel by Sir Walter Scott, then all the rage across the South. A larger-than-life adventurer who had fought in more wars than anyone else would see in a lifetime, Grenfell was an extraordinary sixty-two-year-old swashbuckler who looked twenty years younger. Almost six feet tall, he was a striking figure with white shoulder-length hair framing a deeply tanned face and piercing, bright blue eyes.

The misfit in a family of aristocrats, Grenfell had run away from his home in England at age seventeen to North Africa, where he joined a French lancer regiment. For five years his outfit fought the desert tribes. Settling in Tangiers, he found the life there pleasant but boring, so he switched sides and fought the French for nearly five years, serving under Abd-el-Kadar, the Moroccan tribal chief.

After that war ended, Grenfell managed to find another one.

With a commission from the governor of Gibraltar, he outfitted a private yacht and ridded the western Mediterranean Sea of the Riff pirates. Traveling east, he enlisted in a Turkish brigade, fighting as a major in the Crimean War. Then he joined the British Army and fought in India during the Sepoy Rebellion.

His adventurous spirit took him next to South America, where he served with Garibaldi's South American Legion. Then he settled down to raise sheep, but this quiet period lasted only until he read about a civil war in America, and he was on the next boat for Charleston. In Richmond he offered his services to Robert E. Lee and ended up with John Hunt Morgan's wild Kentuckians. "I never encountered such men," Grenfell said, "who would fight like the devil, but would do as they pleased, like these damned rebel cavalrymen."

Morgan set Grenfell to work teaching his unschooled, undisciplined troops British cavalry tactics. He did the job well. The Kentucky boys, one-third Grenfell's age, learned what he had to teach them, but on raid after raid, they failed to keep up with the old man. The Englishman was always out in front, daring an enemy bullet to find him.

Restless, Grenfell moved on to join Braxton Bragg and Jeb Stuart. When he got wind of Tom Hines's operation for the Northwest, he had to go to Toronto to see what it was all about. He stopped in New York, then Washington, to call on Union Secretary of War Stanton. Stanton had heard of Grenfell and questioned him in detail about the strength of General Lee's army. Grenfell answered with the boldest lies he thought Stanton would believe and requested a pass to travel through the United States to Canada.

Stanton issued the pass in return for Grenfell's promise not to fight anymore against the Union. Grenfell agreed, well aware of his own nature. He knew that he would fight whenever he had the opportunity. Stanton never forgave him for breaking that promise.

Grenfell joined Hines in Toronto and figured prominently in the Northwest conspiracy. He later wrote:

> I know nothing of my future movements, but leave them all to fate. . . . But it does not much matter; we have all got to live a

certain time, and when the end comes, what difference will it make whether . . . I died in a four-poster bedstead with a nurse and phials on the bed table or whether I died in a ditch?

Neither would be his fate.

By mid-August, Hines and Castleman had selected sixty men for the Chicago uprising, which was scheduled for August 29. Each man was given a pistol, one hundred dollars, and a round-trip ticket between Toronto and Chicago. Hines instructed them to travel in pairs. He provided each man with the number of a reserved room at Chicago's Richmond House hotel, the headquarters of those Democrats most determined to end the war.

On the night of August 24, the day before the men were to depart for Chicago, Hines assembled them in a farmhouse just outside the Toronto city limits to review the plan. Glancing around the room, Hines was shocked to see twenty unfamiliar faces. Colonel Thompson, the head of Jefferson Davis's commission nominally overseeing the operation, had, on his own, invited twenty strangers to join the group because, as Thompson explained it, he had been impressed with their connections.

Hines was furious. He and Castleman, his second in command, had taken such care in choosing their sixty participants; he knew they could rely on their absolute trustworthiness and loyalty to the Confederacy. Hines knew nothing about these new men. Having them present for the briefing was a huge risk, but it was too late to do more than hope none would turn out to be an informer.

The next day, the rebels boarded the Chicago-bound train. Grenfell, clothed in a gray uniform, traveled in grand style, accompanied by his hunting dog. Someone teased him about his attire.

"Colonel, if you go in those clothes to Chicago, they will arrest you; you will not live there five hours."

"No," Grenfell said confidently, "this is an old uniform that was worn in an English battalion I once belonged to. . . . I have my English papers, and my gun and my dog, and if they ask me what I am doing, I will say I am going hunting."

The men checked into the Richmond House hotel. Following Hines's instructions, they hung signs over the doors of their rooms proclaiming them to be members of the Missouri Democratic delegation. Grenfell wrote to a friend: "We are now on the eve of great events. The Northwest is ready for revolt."

A VERY RISKY
VENTURE

Colonel Benjamin Sweet was a troubled man. He was worried that the five thousand Confederate prisoners in his charge might escape. As commandant of Camp Douglas on the outskirts of Chicago, Sweet had the job of making sure that not a single man slipped past the twelve-foot plank wall that surrounded the seventy-acre compound. He had heard the rumors that some damned rebels hiding out in Canada planned to attack the prison and free the captives.

The consequences for Sweet's career were too horrendous to contemplate, but they had been preying on his mind for more than two months, since the day last June when his clerk noticed something peculiar about the rebel prisoners' letters. The men were writing many more letters than usual, but they filled only about five lines on each sheet of lined paper and left the rest of the page blank.

The commandant chose two letters at random from the pile on the clerk's desk. Why were the prisoners writing so many letters but saying so little? He was puzzled. He carried one of the letters over to the cast-iron stove in the center of the room and held it close to the heat. It took only a few seconds for the invisible writing to become clear.

"The 4th of July is going up like a rocket and an all-fired sight of powder is going to burn."

Sweet grabbed a second letter and held the sheet of paper near the fire.

"The 4th of July will be a grand day for us. Old Sweet won't like it."

The messages were clear: The prisoners were planning a mass escape for Independence Day.

Sweet immediately notified his superiors and pleaded for additional troops to reinforce his contingent of nine hundred guards, but the request was refused; there were no troops to spare. As July 4 approached, Sweet placed his guards on alert and bunked in his office to remain close to the action. When the holiday passed without incident, Sweet assumed his extra security precautions had foiled the prison break.

On August 12, seventeen days before the rescheduled Democratic convention, Sweet received a letter from an army friend in Michigan. The friend referred to a letter he had received from someone in Toronto, Canada, who identified himself as a Confederate army major. The rebel officer proposed a deal: He would reveal the details of a plot to raid Camp Douglas and free the prisoners in return for a reward and a pardon.

Sweet's correspondent in Michigan threw the letter away, but a few days later the major called on him and described Hines's plans for disrupting the Democratic convention. He gave the names of several participants in the plot. In due course, this information was passed up the chain of command.

Once again Colonel Sweet had reason to be worried. Something was stirring up the prisoners, and, if his informant was correct, it could only be a raid on the prison. The rebels knew for certain what Sweet only suspected; they knew they would soon be free.

Captain Thomas Hines was also troubled as the time for the uprising neared. On the surface, all was in order. Hines, Castleman, Grenfell, and the others had arrived in Chicago. The city was jammed with conventioneers. Some one hundred thousand men roamed the streets, sleeping four to a bed in hotels and boardinghouses, drinking whiskey as fast as bartenders could pour it. Several thousand of the visitors were Copperheads, armed and ready to strike.

Hines had paved the road to revolution liberally with money: $2,000 for bribes to railroad employees, $3,000 for horses for the prisoners who were cavalry, $2,000 for lodging for four hundred Copperhead leaders from Ohio and Indiana, $3,000 for couriers to deliver daily status reports to Commissioner Thompson in Toronto. He had even paid $2,000 for whiskey to fire the Copperheads' courage.

Yet for all his careful preparations, Hines remained concerned. The attitude of the Copperhead leaders left him with doubts. They had talked confidently enough in the days before the convention, making prideful promises about the number of men they controlled, boasting about how eager they were to bring down the government. But Hines was uneasy. He was not sure he believed them. After all, they had let him down once before.

On Sunday evening, August 28, the day before the convention was to open, Hines met with Copperhead leaders in his Richmond House suite. He sensed immediately something was wrong. According to Hines's recollection, Walsh and the others acted evasive, even afraid. They said they had not yet notified the rank-and-file Copperhead membership in Indiana, Ohio, and downstate Illinois. (If they offered an explanation for this failure, Hines did not report it.) The Copperheads were supposed to be in Chicago—sober, organized, ready for revolt—but they had not arrived because no one had told them the date of the uprising!

Most of the thousands of men already there had arrived on their own. They lacked training, leadership, equipment, and organization, all of which Hines had assumed was in readiness, because he had so ordered it. The men in Chicago were indeed Copperheads, but they were an unprepared, worthless mob.

The Copperhead leaders meeting in Hines's hotel suite showed their agitation, shifting uncomfortably in their chairs. What they had seen on the streets of Chicago had shaken them badly. Because of the unknown rebel informer, Colonel Ben Sweet knew that Hines and his men were in town, and he knew that their plans depended on the active support of the Copperheads. Further, he knew that however boastful they might be in some bar or secret meeting, the Copperheads remained civilians. When confronted by the cold steel of bayonets, they were likely to lose their ardor.

Sweet's garrison of nine hundred, to guard five thousand rebel prisoners, was not nearly enough to defend the compound against the planned attack by thousands of armed Copperheads. He had continued to hound his department commander, General Samuel Heintzelman, headquartered in Columbus, Ohio, pleading for additional troops, ever since he discovered the messages in invisible ink in the prisoners' letters.

Finally, in the week before the convention, General Heintzelman sent twelve hundred soldiers. These were new recruits, untrained and untested, but at least they could police the walls of the prison compound while Sweet took bolder action with his regulars.

He dispatched his men on highly visible patrols, marching through Chicago's busiest streets with fixed bayonets. Sweet hoped this show of force would intimidate any would-be revolutionaries.

It worked. Walsh and the other Copperhead leaders were intimidated by the sight of the Union troops marching smartly and confidently through the city. The action persuaded them that an uprising at that time would be too dangerous.

And that was precisely what Walsh told Hines. It would be too risky a venture, especially since he had failed to inform most of the Copperhead groups about the operation. Hines was furious. Walsh and the other rabble-rousers had led him on, had bragged about the zeal of their followers, right up to the moment for action. Now they said there would be no uprising in the Northwest. All Hines's planning and stealth and money had been for nothing.

In the hope of salvaging what he could, Hines asked Walsh and his cronies if they could provide a mere thousand men to assault Camp Douglas and free the Confederate prisoners. Once liberated, the five thousand rebel soldiers held there could be armed and loosed on a path of destruction, even without a general Copperhead uprising to support them. Surely, out of all the men in town, Walsh could round up a thousand who were willing to fight.

At first, Walsh agreed, but after talking it over with his colleagues, he informed Hines that such an assault could not be made. Before Hines could argue, Walsh, in a move typical of his boastful, erratic nature, proposed an alternative: to lead thousands of armed Copperheads in revolt throughout Indiana, Illinois, and Ohio, to free rebel prisoners. All Hines had to do was coordinate a large-scale invasion of Kentucky and Missouri, to draw Union troops away from the Northwest. Once again, Walsh and his cronies were sending conflicting signals to Hines.

The plan was impossible, of course. The Confederacy was barely alive. There were no spare troops Hines could call on. And even if there were, arranging an invasion would take weeks. It seemed clear to Hines that his Northwest conspiracy was doomed.

But then another possibility occurred to him. John Castleman had recently returned from Rock Island and had told Hines that the prison camp there was lightly defended. It would be much easier to take than Camp Douglas. He asked Walsh to recruit five hundred men to help him attack Rock Island. Walsh and the others were evasive. They did not think they could possibly get so many men armed and organized by the next day. Hines was willing to settle for two hundred.

Growing angrier and more desperate by the minute, Hines pounded on the table as he outlined his hastily conceived plan for an attack on the Rock Island prison and arsenal. By midnight, he assured Walsh, the freed prisoners, equipped with weapons from the arsenal, would take over the state capital at Springfield. Surely when the Copperheads heard about the rebels' success, they would rise up spontaneously and set the Northwest ablaze. The revolution could still be saved. With two hundred men, Captain Hines could end the war.

Walsh was aroused by Hines's enthusiasm. He quickly promised to gather not two hundred men, but five hundred. All he needed was a few hours to spread the word among his followers. Among the thousands of Copperheads wandering the city streets, he was positive he could find a few hundred with the courage to fight for their beliefs.

While Walsh went off on his recruiting mission, Hines waited in his hotel suite, pacing back and forth, wondering if his plan would work. He saw his answer on Walsh's face the instant the man returned. The Copperhead leader had found only twenty-five men willing to fight. There would be no revolution the following day.

Hines assembled the men who had accompanied him from Toronto and gave them a choice: They could leave, or they could stay with him and pursue the plan to undermine the Union government. Most were too disenchanted with the Copperheads to remain. Some returned to Canada, whereas others opted to head south to the dying Confederacy. Hines, Castleman, and twenty-two others vowed to continue with the Northwest conspiracy.

After bidding farewell to Grenfell, who was going to Carlyle, Illinois, to visit an English friend for the shooting season, Hines and his band boarded a train heading downstate, intent on sabotage. Hines's agents had informed him of two tempting targets: army warehouses at Mattoon and transports loaded with supplies tied up to the city wharf at St. Louis.

Hines took ten men to Mattoon, where they burned some warehouses. Castleman and the others went after the transports, seventy-three ships in all, laden with goods and, to their surprise, lightly guarded. Castleman gave each man a list of three to five ships as their targets and supplied them with "Greek fire," bottles filled with sulfuric acid and other chemicals that ignite when the bottles break and the liquid is exposed to air.

Although some of the bottles turned out to be defective, ten ships were set ablaze before Federal troops poured into the dock area to prevent further attacks. Castleman was disappointed to have done so little damage, but before he could launch another raid, Hines sent word ordering him to proceed to Sullivan, Indiana.

Castleman told his men to leave St. Louis one at a time; he would be the last to depart. Before he arrived in Sullivan, however, John Maughan, one of Hines's men in Mattoon, got drunk in a bar there and bragged too much about his exploits burning down the warehouses. He was easily captured by the Yankees. Maughan was a twenty-one-year-old bank clerk from Toronto who was longing for adventure, but he had a weakness for the bottle. Hines did not trust him. He had come along because he was one of the extra recruits foisted on the operation at the last minute by Commissioner Thompson.

Maughan confessed everything and gave the Union authorities all the names he could think of, as well as the time of their rendezvous in Sullivan, Indiana. Hines and his men barely got out of Mattoon ahead of the Federal troops, but Castleman was not so fortunate. He was arrested the instant he stepped off the train in Sullivan.

When Hines learned of Castleman's arrest, he was determined to rescue his friend. He caught up with Castleman and his escort of Union guards at the railroad station platform at Terre Haute. Hines ordered his men to spread out and approach them slowly. When Hines gave the signal, they were to shoot the guards.

Castleman saw them coming, and he saw something else Hines could not—one hundred Union troops assembling around a corner of the platform. He knew Hines and the others would be killed as soon as they opened fire. He had to get word to his friend to call off the rescue attempt.

He scanned the faces of the civilians on the platform, hoping to find someone who looked trustworthy. But the guards had spread the word that Castleman was a dangerous rebel spy, and most people glared at him with hatred. Suddenly, a middle-aged man spoke to Castleman, saying how sorry he was to see such a young man placed under arrest.

Castleman made up his mind. Speaking softly so his captors would not overhear, he asked the stranger to take a message to his friends. The man agreed, and Castleman nodded toward Hines, who was coming closer. The man was to tell Hines to leave the platform at once. Hines did as he was told, saving his life and the lives of his accomplices.

Hines followed Castleman to the Federal prison at Indianapolis and bribed a guard to smuggle in a small saw blade, but Castleman was caught using it on the bars of his cell.

Hines bought a Bible and paid a bookbinder to take apart the binding and hide thirteen small saws and three thousand dollars inside the cover before rebinding it. He sent the book to Castleman's mother in Kentucky, along with a note asking her to visit Castleman and give him the Bible, saying it came from Hines. She did so, and the unsuspecting commandant handed it to Castleman while recommending its contents highly.

Castleman disassembled the Bible and found the saws and the cash, but decided the prison was too heavily guarded to attempt to escape. When his mother visited the next day, he asked her to tell Hines not to risk any more lives trying to rescue him.

Before he was due to be tried as a spy, Castleman was made part of a prisoner exchange and ordered to leave the country. His health shattered by the months of confinement, he was put aboard a ferry from Detroit to Windsor, Ontario. As the boat approached the Canadian side, he saw a man on shore waving to him. It was Tom Hines.

Despite these setbacks, Hines stubbornly refused to abandon his plans for a Copperhead uprising in the Northwest and the freeing of the Confederate prisoners of war. In the first week of November, he returned to Chicago, undaunted by the Copperheads' past failures. Determined to try again, he chose November 8, election day in the Union.

The key part of the new uprising was a nighttime storming of Camp Douglas by four Copperhead units simultaneously attacking from all sides. The prisoners would be alerted to the time of the assault and were expected to overpower the guards when they saw a skyrocket at the appointed hour. At the same time, other Copperhead groups would cut the telegraph lines from Chicago and set fire to the train stations. As soon as the prisoners were freed, one group would go west to Rock Island to strike at that prison compound; another would head southeast to free the prisoners at Camp Morton, Indiana. They would lay waste Federal supply depots and bases in the Northwest and murder state and city officials. Hines planned the operation with care. It should have been successful, but Federal authorities learned of it in advance.

Colonel Sweet, the commandant of Camp Douglas, near Chicago, learned the details of the plan by November 5, three days before the election. And he knew that Hines, Grenfell, and other Confederates were back in Chicago. On November 7, Sweet found out where they were staying. Some of his information came from James Shanks, one of John Hunt Morgan's men, a Camp Douglas prisoner Sweet bribed with an offer of a rigged prison break. Hines knew Shanks when they rode with Morgan and had never trusted him.

Sweet obtained additional details of Hines's plot from another Confederate informer, Maurice Langhorne, a former sergeant in Morgan's raiders who had deserted to Canada. He walked into Sweet's office one day and told his story. Hines later described him as "the infamous traitor who sold his comrades for 'blood money.'"

At midnight on November 7, Colonel Sweet began arresting the conspirators. Colonel Grenfell was the first to be taken. He had been ill and was lying awake, shivering from a bout of recurring malaria. When the Union patrol burst into his room at the Richmond House, he was sitting by the fireplace, a glass of brandy in his hand, his hunting dog asleep at his feet. On the table beside him was a slip of paper bearing a message from one of Hines's men, warning him to leave the hotel immediately.

Why Grenfell ignored the warning and remained in his hotel room is a mystery. Perhaps he felt too sick to leave or believed his British citizenship would protect him. Maybe he thought nothing serious could ever happen to him; his luck had protected him through all the wars in which he had fought. The Yankees shackled his legs and led him away, hobbling and shaking with fever.

The next to be arrested was Charles Walsh, the ranking Copperhead leader and political boss of Cook County, Illinois. The Union raiding party also captured three of Hines's men who were hiding on the roof of Walsh's house, within sight of Camp Douglas. A huge weapons cache was found, including 142 double-barreled shotguns, 349 revolvers, 13,412 rounds of ammunition, and two kegs of powder, plus assorted knives, hooks, and lances.

A score or more other Copperhead leaders were arrested, but Tom Hines—the man Sweet wanted most—remained at large. Hines was spending the night at the home of Dr. Edward W. Edwards, at 70 Adams Street. With him was Colonel Vincent Marmaduke. A handsome, well-born Southerner whose brother was a general in the Confederate army, Marmaduke had been one of the twenty men chosen by Thompson to accompany Hines and Castleman on the August 29 expedition. Thompson was impressed with Marmaduke's connections, but Hines did not care much for him.

Hines later recalled that when he went to bed that night at Dr. Edwards's house, he sensed that he was in danger. He stuffed his Colt revolver and a knife under his pillow. Fortunately for Hines, Dr. Edwards stayed up late, tending to his wife, who was suffering from diphtheria. Still at his wife's bedside at one-thirty in the morning, Edwards heard horses. He glanced outside in time to see a Union patrol dismounting at his door and rushed to awaken Hines.

Hines knew there were no secure hiding places in the house, so he asked Edwards if he had a large box mattress. Yes, said the doctor, but Mrs. Edwards was sleeping on it. With the Yankees pounding on the door downstairs, Hines ran into her bedroom, slit the mattress, and squirmed his way inside.

The soldiers arrested Marmaduke in his bed and searched the house, including Mrs. Edwards's bedroom. Hines was nowhere to be found. Colonel Sweet was furious. Believing the rebel leader to be holed up in a secret hiding place inside the house, he posted guards outside. Hines was safe for the moment, but he was trapped. He would have to get out before Sweet decided to search the house again.

Hines instructed Dr. Edwards to spread the word among his family and friends that Mrs. Edwards was dying and that it was time to pay their last respects. Many people called at the house the next day. It was raining heavily and most of the visitors who walked up to the front door had their faces hidden by umbrellas. The bored guards, their uniforms soaked through, paid no attention to them. Tom Hines walked out into the rain in the company of Charles

Walsh's daughter. Free again, an hour later he boarded a train for Cincinnati.

Hines had managed to save himself but he had to accept the fact that there would be no Copperhead uprising to topple the Union government. Lincoln had been re-elected with 55 percent of the popular vote. Even a majority of the Yankee soldiers—those who were doing the fighting and the dying—had voted for him. Clearly, most people in the North desired the war to be prosecuted to the finish. If enough of them had desired an end to the fighting, they would have voted for the Democrats' peace candidate, General George B. McClellan.

Lee's Army of Northern Virginia, caught in an ever-tightening siege at Petersburg, was growing weaker from casualties, malnutrition, and disease. Worse, it was suffering a high rate of desertions. Confederates were in retreat on almost all fronts, and in Georgia, outside the ruined city of Atlanta, Sherman was beginning what would be a sixty-mile-wide path of destruction, all the way to the Atlantic Ocean.

The Confederacy was being cut and ground to pieces, and there was no longer anything Captain Hines, or anyone else, could do to stop it. Hines decided it was time for him to do what he had been putting off, marry Miss Nancy Sproule.

He planned the wedding with all the attention to detail that had gone into his missions, but this time, nothing went wrong. Using a ruse, he spirited Nancy out of her convent school in Ohio and brought her, two witnesses, and a clergyman to a farmhouse near Covington, Kentucky. On November 10, they were married.

A month later, Hines returned to Richmond, reporting to Benjamin and Seddon on the failure of the Northwest conspiracy. Commissioner Thompson had asked to be relieved of his duties and allowed to return home, but Benjamin denied the request. He sent a message to Thompson via the personals column of the *New York News*, requesting that he continue his mission. Benjamin told Hines the same thing. He was to go back to Toronto and carry on as best he could.

BITTER, BITTER DEFEAT

Hines's Northwest conspiracy was not the only legacy of terror spawned by the Dahlgren papers. In the months following the attempted raid on Richmond, other Toronto-based Confederate agents staged anti-Union operations. Most worked independently of Hines, but all shared his goal: to overthrow the U.S. government.

Like Hines's planned campaigns, these additional rebel actions were under the control of the Confederate commissioners in Canada, funded by Richmond, and sanctioned by Jefferson Davis and his cabinet officers Benjamin and Seddon. As such, they were an attempt to carry the war to Union cities and a direct result of the Dahlgren papers. Davis and his advisors felt justified in launching these efforts because they believed the Union's plans for a pre-emptive terror campaign had been clearly revealed in Dahlgren's notes. And so while Hines was directing his efforts toward northwestern cities, other Confederate agents were focusing on the Northeast.

The first of these missions was planned for Maine. An ambitious expedition, it involved an invasion by five thousand regular Confederate army troops, with artillery, to be transported to Canada aboard eight blockade runners. They were to land on the Maine coast at night and fan out in five columns, devastate all public and private property, and murder government officials.

So thorough was the planning for the Maine operation that an advance contingent of fifty engineers and topographers set out to map the coastline. For three months they posed as artists, visiting coastal sites to sketch and paint. But some spent too much time bragging in the saloons of St. John's, Quebec, and before long the talk reached the American consul, who informed the secretary of war. Stanton alerted civilian and military leaders in Maine to be prepared for Confederate raids.

On July 16, 1864, three rebel agents rode into the town of Calais, Maine, to rob the bank as a means of funding the operation. They were met by an armed posse. They surrendered rather than be killed on the spot, and one disclosed the details of the five-thousand-man raid. In a fifteen-page statement, he revealed the location of weapons and ammunition stores in New York, St. Louis, and other Union cities. He boasted that in one Brooklyn warehouse the Confederates had a cache of seventeen thousand rifles. The capture of the would-be bank robbers ended the invasion and sacking of Maine, but one rebel agent, George Sanders, liked the idea of robbing Yankee banks so much that he planned another attempt a few months later.

However, Sanders was forced to wait until Hines was preoccupied before he could carry out his plan. Hines opposed bank robbery as a means of obtaining funds for the Confederacy's operations in the North, and he was even more opposed to George Sanders. He disliked and distrusted the suave, handsome *ex officio* member of the Confederate mission who lacked any visible means of support but always managed to have plenty of money and beautiful women.

A mysterious and controversial figure, Sanders sometimes seemed to be harming rather than helping the Confederate effort in Toronto. Some speculated that he was a Union spy. Sanders had spotted the weakest link in the Confederacy's three-man commission in Canada—the lonely, sickly Clement Clay—and made it his business to cultivate and flatter the old man. He hosted lavish dinner parties with Clay as the guest of honor, and it did not take long for Clay to confide his grievances about Hines and the other commissioners, whom Clay felt ignored him.

When Hines left Toronto for Chicago and points south, Sanders approached Clay, seeking approval for his scheme to rob banks. Clay temporized, but finally gave permission for Sanders to proceed, though his response was tentative at best. Sanders was not about to accept anything less than full authorization, however, so he forged Clay's signature to the orders.

Sanders was not the sort to risk his own life in any such venture. From among the many willing firebrands and southern patriots in Toronto, he selected nearly a dozen to carry out the mission. Lieutenant Bennett Young, a handsome ex-divinity student, and Lieutenant William Hutchinson would lead the raid. St. Albans, Vermont, with three banks, was the target. There was no Union garrison nearby, and the town was only fourteen miles from the Canadian border.

Young and Hutchinson arrived in St. Albans on October 15, followed over the next two days by the others in their group, who traveled singly or in pairs. They took rooms in hotels and boarding houses and made themselves familiar with the layout of the town, especially the location of the banks.

Lieutenant Young even found time for a romantic interlude, squiring a pretty woman about town, engaging her in lively discussions about the Bible. She was fascinated by his good looks, his gentle and elegant manners, and his spiritual knowledge. She would never have guessed that he had stashed forty bottles of Greek fire in his hotel room and expected to use them to burn the town after relieving the banks of their money.

The rebels struck St. Albans at three o'clock on the afternoon of October 17. Young strode out to the steps of his hotel, brandished his Navy Colt revolver, and loudly proclaimed St. Albans to be in the possession of the Confederacy. Passersby stared at him as if he were a lunatic. Some burst out laughing.

But the laughter stopped dead a moment later. Four Confederate raiders on horseback raced down the main street, loosing their terrifying rebel yell and firing their Colts in all directions. The townspeople scattered. The rest of the raiders charged the banks, quickly cleaning out the vaults of $175,000 in gold, securities, and cash.

The loot was heavy, and it took time to drag the sacks outside and load up the horses. A few citizens went for their guns. One man fired at Lieutenant Young from a second-story window, but missed. Young whirled around in his saddle and returned fire. He did not miss. The man slumped across the window sill, the first Union civilian residing so far north to be shot by the rebels.

Lieutenant Hutchinson returned fire against another resident, striking him in the chest. Telling a friend he was badly wounded and would go to the pharmacy for help, the man walked out into the middle of the street and into a cross fire, but made it safely to the pharmacy. Once inside, however, he collapsed and died.

The livery stable owner, irate that the Confederates had stolen some of his horses, raised his revolver and drew a bead on Lieutenant Young. He pulled the trigger several times, but the gun kept misfiring. The man reloaded, and the same thing happened again. He reloaded a second time and saw he still had a clear shot, but the gun refused to fire. In disgust, he threw the revolver to the ground and returned to the stable.

Young formed up his men and led them in a charge down the main street, yelling as loudly as they could. They hurled bottles of Greek fire into doorways and through windows. The lieutenant could see a citizens' posse lining up, so he headed his men out of town, directing them to split up into small groups to confuse their pursuers.

They rode north. Young reached the safety of the Canadian border at nine o'clock that night, but seven of his men were caught by the St. Albans posse. The Vermont men illegally had crossed the border in pursuit and captured the raiders on Canadian soil.

Young rode to their rescue but was taken, and placed in a wagon with a noose around his neck. Figuring he had nothing to lose, he grabbed the horses' reins and sped off. When he was recaptured, the Northerners took revenge for the damage to their town. They beat and kicked him with fists, boots, and pistol butts. They might have killed him had a British army major not stopped them. He escorted Young to the nearest post, where the Vermont posse had unwillingly turned over the seven other captured rebels.

The British soldiers, who resented the Yankee invasion of their territory, treated the Confederates decently, and their government resisted demands by Union Secretary of War Stanton to extradite the rebels to the United States for trial. George Sanders showed up at the formal hearing for the Confederates and took charge, issuing orders to court officials. His presence cowed everyone. Sanders also continued his habit of hosting parties at his hotel for local society, with champagne, music, and female companionship. To the prisoners he sent chilled wine and cold chicken every day. After a lengthy hearing, a Canadian judge ruled that the rebels could not be extradited.

Lieutenant Colonel Robert Martin, who had ridden with John Hunt Morgan, was a reckless daredevil. Martin's response to the Dahlgren papers, sanctioned by the Confederate government, was to conceive a mission to set parts of New York ablaze and to take over the city. The date he chose for the assault was November 8, Union election day, the same day Hines and his Copperheads were supposed to begin their uprising in the Northwest. In Richmond, Martin outlined his plan to Secretary of State Judah P. Benjamin, who gave his approval and sent Martin on to Toronto.

Martin chose another of Morgan's raiders, Lieutenant John Headley, to join the expedition, along with several rebel expatriates he recruited in Toronto. Martin planned to firebomb simultaneously New York's leading hotels, to create chaos in the streets on election day. Once the fires were set, twenty thousand men of the Sons of Liberty, a Copperhead group holding a convention in town, would attack City Hall and military installations and occupy police headquarters. Martin's liaison with the Sons of Liberty was Captain Emile Longuemare, who had first proposed a Northwest conspiracy to Jefferson Davis back in 1862.

Martin, Headley, and the others arrived in New York a few days prior to November 8. Longuemare assured them the Sons of Liberty were armed, trained, and dedicated. They would do whatever was necessary to bring down the Lincoln government. They were prepared to tear New York City apart.

The next morning, Headley glanced out the window of his room at the Fifth Avenue Hotel and saw large numbers of Union troops marching up Broadway. The sight shook his confidence. Why were so many Federal soldiers pouring into the city? Before nightfall they learned the reason. Newspapers reported that the troops had been sent to New York because of rumors that there was about to be a raid on the city by rebel guerrillas!

Where was the leak? Who had informed on them? Martin did not know, but he could see that Union authorities were taking no chances. Fully ten thousand northern soldiers were now in New York under the command of General Ben Butler, known to Southerners as Beast Butler for the harsh measures he took against anyone attempting acts of aggression against his Union troops. If Martin and his men were caught, Butler would hang them. And Butler had taken up residence in the Fifth Avenue Hotel, one floor below the rooms of Martin and Headley.

The sudden, massive presence of the Yankee soldiers dampened the martial ardor of the Sons of Liberty. Martin and Headley learned the night before the scheduled assault that, indeed, the group's enthusiasm and bravado had been squelched completely. The Copperheads canceled their convention. Captain Longuemare, Martin's contact with the Sons of Liberty, argued with their leaders, passionately making a case for continuing with the plan. The Sons of Liberty agreed to persevere, if they could postpone any action until Thanksgiving Day, but when that time neared, they canceled again, as did their counterparts in Chicago. At the last minute, they notified Martin that they would have no further connection with any attempt to create chaos in New York. Even Longuemare begged off and left town, telling Martin he would not return until after Martin and Headley had finished their deadly business.

However, Longuemare had given Martin the name of the chemist who had bottled the Greek fire. His laboratory was located in a basement off Washington Square. Headley picked up 144 four-ounce bottles. He and Martin were determined to use them and press on with their original plan, even without the Copperheads. They knew that even a few men with well-placed bottles of Greek fire could do a lot of damage.

At six o'clock on the evening of November 25, the rebels met in a small cottage in Central Park that Martin had rented for their headquarters. Two men failed to show up, which was not a good sign. If they had been arrested, they could at that instant be disclosing to Union authorities everything they knew about the plan. Martin considered his options and decided to go ahead with the mission.

The men in Martin's group had each registered, under false names, at three hotels. Each man was provided with ten bottles of Greek fire and told to set these hotels ablaze. If the men were captured, they were to give their real names, ranks, and commands. Their story was to be that they had started the fires in New York in retaliation for Sherman's destruction of Georgia and South Carolina and the havoc Sheridan was wreaking in the Shenandoah Valley. The hour for the commencement of Martin's operation was eight o'clock that night.

Lieutenant Headley chose his room at the Astor House as the site of his first fire.

> After lighting the gas jet I hung the bedclothes loosely on the headboard and piled the chairs, drawers of the bureaus and [wooden] washstand on the bed. Then stuffed some newspapers about among the mass and poured a bottle of turpentine over it all. I concluded to unlock my door and fix the key on the outside, as I might have to get out in a hurry, for I did not know whether the Greek fire would make a noise or not. I opened a bottle carefully and quickly spilled it on the pile of rubbish. It blazed up instantly and the whole bed seemed to be in flames before I could get out.

By 8:45, the city was in pandemonium. "As I came back to Broadway," Headley recalled, "it seemed that a hundred bells were ringing, great crowds were gathering on the street, and there was general consternation."

By then, nineteen hotels were burning, along with P. T. Barnum's Museum opposite the Astor House. People stampeded from the museum, screaming. Others climbed down ladders from the second and third floors. The manager waved and shouted for help to get his animals out to safety. Headley was surprised; the museum had not been on the list of targets. He learned later that one of his men had started the fire for a lark.

Headley continued down Broadway to the North River wharf, where he tossed incendiary bottles aboard several ships and barges. He mingled with the crowds, returning to watch the firemen battle the blaze at the Barnum Museum. Smaller fires had flared up at Niblo's Garden Theatre and the Winter Garden. Only quick thinking on the part of Niblo's stage manager and one of the actors at the Winter Garden prevented panics, for both theaters were full.

The actor who calmed the Winter Garden audience was Edwin Booth, who was giving his highly acclaimed performance of *Julius Caesar*, along with his brothers, Junius Booth and John Wilkes Booth. The actors' mother was in the audience. She later reported a premonition: "For the first time she felt that some danger was hovering over Wilkes."

Firemen remained on duty until six o'clock the following morning. The damage was estimated at $422,000. No one had been killed or seriously injured; the destruction was slight compared to what might have occurred. Headley concluded that the episode had been a failure. He blamed it on the Greek fire.

Some of the bottles had malfunctioned, failing to explode, and others did not generate sufficiently intense conflagrations, blazes so hot they would be difficult to extinguish. Headley suspected that Longuemare, under pressure from the Sons of Liberty after they declined to participate in the raid, had ordered the chemist to dilute the Greek fire mixture, perhaps hoping that if the damage from the attack was slight, Union authorities might not institute harsh retaliatory measures. How ironic that the man who first proposed the Confederacy's terror campaign in the North may have been responsible for the collapse of the mission in which he was directly involved.

The day after the firebombing, the rebels went to retrieve their baggage, which they had boarded at a piano store owned by a prominent member of the Sons of Liberty. They found the man being arrested.

Only a last-minute warning from the man's daughter as Headley neared the shop saved them all from capture.

The men retired to a saloon at Madison Square and ordered whiskeys to calm their nerves. Martin picked up a newspaper and almost choked on his drink. The lead story on the front page gave the names and descriptions of the Confederate raiders, plus details of their operation. There was also an announcement of the arrests of the two men who had failed to appear—but they were not the ones who had talked.

It was later learned that Federal authorities had known about Martin's raid on New York for a month. Godfrey Hyams had turned informer, for a price. Hyams was from Arkansas and had spread the word around Toronto that he had escaped from a Yankee prison the year before. But Hines had not trusted him anymore than he trusted George Sanders.

Thanks to Hyams's information, Martin, Headley, and the others had been followed by Federal detectives from the moment they left the train in New York City. After two days, however, the detectives lost interest and halted their surveillance. As Headley put it, "they had finally abandoned us as a lot of well-behaved young men who seemed to be simply enjoying ourselves."

Why the detectives arrested two of the rebels just before the fire setting is not known, but it was because of Hyams that Butler and his ten thousand troops were sent to the city. He had also identified twenty-six Copperhead leaders who were later arrested. Once again, a rebel plot was undermined by one of their own.

Martin and his conspirators left New York on November 27 and crossed the border into Canada two days later.

John Yates Beall, acting master in the Confederate navy, hoped to launch a terror campaign by sea against the people of the Union in retaliation for the revelations of the Dahlgren papers. His plan involved the capture of the USS *Michigan*, the only Union warship serving on the Great Lakes. Her home port was Sandusky, Ohio, on Lake Erie. Using the warship, Beall could bombard every U.S. city along the Lake Erie coastline, from Michigan to New York. And he intended to free the twenty-five hundred Confederate officers held on Johnson's Island, just off Sandusky.

It was an ambitious plan for the tubercular twenty-eight-year-old, who had already been invalided out of the army. A graduate of the University of Virginia, Beall began his army career serving under Stonewall Jackson. Severely wounded and with one lung already infected, Beall was given a medical discharge. Annoyed at being officially judged too ill to fight for his country, Beall submitted his plan to free the Johnson's Island prisoners directly to Jefferson Davis, who declined to give his sanction. But that was in 1862, two years before the Dahlgren papers provided Davis with justification for waging war on northern cities. However, Davis did approve another of Beall's ideas: to conduct privateering raids in the Potomac River and Chesapeake Bay.

Beall amassed a band of ten irregulars. They captured a large number of fishing vessels, schooners, and small supply boats. The losses were an expensive nuisance to the Union forces. Beall's men blew up a lighthouse and severed the telegraph cable between Washington, D.C., and Maryland's eastern shore.

On November 11, 1863, Beall and his men were captured. Instead of being treated as prisoners of war, they were charged with piracy; the penalty was death. After the Confederacy placed fifteen Union officers in chains and declared them hostages to Beall's fate, Beall and his men avoided the noose and were exchanged in May of 1864.

In Richmond, Beall was hailed as a hero. What he desired was not praise, however, but a chance to get back into the war. When he heard about the Northwest conspiracy, he made his way to Toronto and proposed his plan directly to Commissioner Thompson. The plan was approved. Early that September Beall met Captain Charles Cole, another former Morgan raider, and together they worked out the details. (Another man was present at their meeting—Godfrey Hyams. He later claimed to have been paid seventy thousand dollars by Union intelligence agents for his information.)

Cole—dashing, jovial, and convivial—enjoyed an active social life, entertaining with the best foods and wines. Posing as a wealthy businessman, he had already become acquainted with the captain and crew of the USS *Michigan* and with Union officers at the Johnson's Island prison camp.

Beall's plan called for Cole to throw a party aboard ship for the *Michigan's* personnel on September 19. Once the captain and crew were sufficiently drunk on drugged champagne, Cole would fire a signal rocket. Beall and a raiding party of twenty would easily commandeer the ship. They would sail the *Michigan* close to Johnson's Island and fire a shot. At that signal, the prisoners would break out of the compound using weapons smuggled in to them by the guards Cole had bribed.

On the night of September 18, Bennett Burley, who had served with John Yates Beall in his pirate days on Chesapeake Bay, embarked on the steamship *Philo Parsons* at Detroit. Boarding from several stops throughout the night and into the next morning, Beall and the rest of his men joined Burley on the ship. At four o'clock in the afternoon, Beall and a few other men crowded into the wheelhouse and announced that they were taking possession of the ship in the name of the Confederate States of America. The rest of Beall's men herded the crew and the surprised passengers into the hold.

They had several hours to pass before they expected Cole's signal from the *Michigan*, so Beall steered the *Philo Parsons* to Middle Bass Island to take on fuel. While the rebels loaded wood aboard the ship, another civilian steamer, the *Island Queen*, anchored alongside. The Confederates swarmed aboard the steamer to capture its crew and passengers, including twenty-five soldiers from an Ohio regiment on furlough. No other Union soldiers had ever been captured so far north.

Beall issued pardons to the soldiers, put the captives from both boats ashore, and scuttled the *Island Queen*. The *Philo Parsons* set sail for Sandusky. At nine o'clock, Beall sighted the *Michigan*. Examining the warship through his spyglass, Beall immediately saw that something was wrong. There was no signal rocket from Cole, and the ship appeared to be in a high state of readiness. The decks had been cleared for action, and it was apparent there was no raucous party on board.

Something, indeed, was wrong. Charles Cole was under arrest and being interrogated. Godfrey Hyams had earned his informer's money.

Beall continued to study the warship and decided to proceed with his mission, even in the absence of Cole's signal. He intended to attack the *Michigan*. He ordered full speed ahead, only to find that everyone but his old friend Burley and one other man refused to proceed. Beall's crew had mutinied, although they took the action formally and politely: They handed Beall a note.

> We, the undersigned, take pleasure in expressing our admiration of the gentlemanly bearing, skill and courage of Captain John Y. Beall as commanding officer and gentleman, but believing and being convinced that the enemy is already apprised of our approach, and so well prepared that we cannot by possibility make it a success, and already captured two boats, we respectfully decline to prosecute it any further.

Beall had no choice but to steer the *Philo Parsons* toward Canada, where the rebels scuttled the ship and went into hiding. Beall later expressed his feelings about the failed raid with the words, "Bitter, bitter defeat."

The Northwest conspiracy wasn't finished yet. Other plots and plans were brewing. One—a pet project of Judah P. Benjamin—involved an attempt to upset the U.S. gold market and cause a financial collapse. Commissioner Thompson chose a Nashville banker by the name of Porterfield to buy gold in New York and export it to England. Porterfield took the British currency he received for the gold and converted it into dollars, using the dollars to buy more gold.

Porterfield exported some five million dollars' worth of gold and persuaded other businessmen to do the same, before Federal banking officials caught on to their scheme. When one of the traders was arrested, Porterfield decided he had done his patriotic duty and left for Canada.

In the winter of 1864, an attempt was made to kidnap Andrew Johnson, the U.S. vice president–elect. This was another project of

Robert Martin and John Headley, an accidental outgrowth of the apparatus set in place in Toronto by the Confederate government in response to the Dahlgren affair.

Commissioner Thompson had ordered Martin and Headley back to Richmond to present to the Confederate government Thompson's latest grandiose scheme to end the war. Thompson proposed having some Confederate forces retreat to a point west of the Mississippi River and then turn north into Iowa, while others threatened Washington, D.C., and moved on to capture Pittsburgh. Martin and Headley realized the plan was ridiculous and impossible to execute, but Thompson was their superior, and so they left for Richmond.

The trip was difficult and dangerous. Both were wanted men. They passed safely through Detroit, Toledo, and Cincinnati. When they reached Louisville, they decided to rest for a few days. On their third day there, they read in the newspaper that Andrew Johnson would be stopping at the Louisville Hotel on his way to Washington for the inaugural. Here was their golden opportunity. Headley recalled:

> We became enthusiastic over the adventure, upon the idea that if we could land Johnson in Richmond as a prisoner of war, it would result at least in a general exchange of prisoners and through him arrangements might be made to end the struggle.

While Headley contacted a local southern sympathizer in Louisville, which was under Union control, Martin visited the Louisville Hotel to observe the vice president–elect's daily routine. Headley found three Confederate officers, all recent escapees from Johnson's Island, who were willing to help with the kidnapping.

They hired a closed carriage in which to transport their victim. The three Confederate officers would wait with the carriage at the ladies' entrance at the rear of the hotel, while Headley and Martin took Johnson from his room and hustled him down the back stairs.

Everyone was in place at six o'clock on the appointed day. Headley went inside to case the lobby and dining room, while Martin checked the reading room and the gentleman's parlor. Neither man saw the vice president–elect. When Johnson had not appeared by 8:30, Headley went upstairs to his room. He knocked on the door. There was no answer.

Headley returned to the lobby and told Martin that Johnson was not in his room. Martin questioned the desk clerk. For reasons that remain a mystery, Johnson had checked out early and left town. As Headley recalled, it was

> an hour and a night of bitter disappointment. The opportunity had been ours, perhaps, to perform a service which might have affected the destiny of our country.

They would have no other opportunities.

In their increasing desperation, the Confederates tried biological warfare. The key figure in that operation was Luke Blackburn, a Kentucky physician who was an authority on yellow fever. When the war started, Blackburn became an aide to General Sterling Price and then somehow turned up in Toronto, where he sought someone to assist with his germ warfare project. He found Godfrey Hyams.

In 1864, Blackburn had spent several months in Bermuda, the main base for southern blockade runners, helping British doctors deal with the yellow fever epidemic. Surreptitiously he had collected the clothing belonging to men who had died of the disease—hundreds of shirts, pants, coats, and blankets he believed to be impregnated with the germs.

He arranged for trunkloads of these items to be shipped via Halifax, Nova Scotia, to Philadelphia, where Hyams claimed the trunks and took them to Washington. There he delivered them to an auctioneer who routinely sold used clothing on the corner of Ninth Street and Pennsylvania Avenue, only a few blocks from the White House. Blackburn hoped the infected garments would start a yellow fever epidemic in the capital. The disease could claim hundreds, including Abraham Lincoln and his entire Cabinet.

Godfrey Hyams later testified that Dr. Blackburn also sent him a separate shipment of elegant shirts, also worn by yellow fever victims, which Hyams was to present to Lincoln personally as a gift. Hyams said he refused to do so, though he did not explain why. Hyams also testified that Commissioner Thompson had approved Blackburn's scheme and appropriated money to pay for it. This vicious plan, clearly the most evil operation of all, indicated "the intensity of hatred for the enemy that pervaded the Confederate government at this stage of the war."

In unleashing these operations under the banner of the Northwest conspiracy, the Dahlgren papers had spawned a vindictive whirlwind. But the conspiracy never accomplished its purpose. It failed to create terror and revolution in Union cities. It did not bring the war into more than a handful of northern homes. It did not release Confederate prisoners of war or force General Grant to transfer troops home, thus easing the pressures on Robert E. Lee. Nor did it lead to a Confederate victory or shorten the war by a single day.

The so-called Northwest conspiracy was no more effective than Dahlgren's raid had been. But people had died, destruction had been caused—and the Confederacy was still doomed.

Chapter 22

DESPERATE MEASURES: WHO WROTE THE DAHLGREN PAPERS?

In January 1865, during the last winter of the war, Francis Preston Blair, of Maryland's politically and socially prominent Blair family, traveled to Richmond to hold unofficial discussions of peace terms with Jefferson Davis, an old friend. Nothing came of the meeting, but while in the Confederate capital, Blair called on the president's wife, Varina.

When the sensitive topic of the Dahlgren papers arose in conversation, Blair said he did not believe the papers could be genuine, whereupon Varina offered to send for Dahlgren's memorandum book. Blair laughed and shook his head. "Now, the fact is," he said, "I do not want to believe it, and if you could convince me I would rather not look at it."

Varina Davis later wrote:

> [She] had felt much the same unwillingness, having been intimate with [Dahlgren's] parents. Once Commodore Dahlgren had brought the little fair-haired boy to show me how pretty he looked in his black velvet suit and Vandyke collar, and I could not reconcile the two Ulrics.

Francis Blair was not alone in being reluctant to accept that Ulric Dahlgren had turned into Ulric the Hun. Virtually no Northerner who had known young Dahlgren believed he had written the papers that now bore his name. Indeed, public opinion in the North was unwilling to accept the fact that *any* Union officer could have contemplated so reprehensible an act as the assassination of Jefferson Davis and the members of his Cabinet. And even if some officer secretly harbored such a repugnant desire, he would never have put it in writing or left proof of it behind.

The Dahlgren papers had to be forgeries; so held the people of the Union. Admiral Dahlgren had testified to that, and if he did not recognize his own son's handwriting, who would? As far as the Union was concerned, the Dahlgren papers were obviously lies and forgeries designed to discredit the reputation of a fine young man and, by extension, the whole of the United States.

The people of the South believed just as fervently that the Dahlgren papers were genuine: The barbaric Yankees would stop at nothing to win the war, even planning to murder Confederate leaders in their beds. Admiral Dahlgren was not being honest when he denounced the papers as fraudulent. What father would not lie to protect the honor of his son? Not that Yankees knew anything about true honor.

Besides, what reason would Confederate leaders have for forging such documents, Southerners asked—unaware of the plans for the Northwest conspiracy. Why would they claim that the Yankees were out to kill them? The South had nothing to gain. Therefore, the Dahlgren papers had to be genuine, not fabricated or tampered with in any way.

Arguments raged between North and South and continue to the present day. Long after Appomattox, long after the monuments and memorials grew stained and pitted with age, long after the last old soldier died, the disagreement endures.

One problem facing contemporary researchers is that the Dahlgren papers available for examination are copies. The original papers allegedly removed from Dahlgren's corpse have been missing since 1865. The historian James Hall has provided a detailed account of the custody of the papers.

When Confederate leaders evacuated Richmond on April 2, 1865, the original Dahlgren papers went with them, part of eighty-one boxes of records from the adjutant general's and inspector general's offices.

The boxes were deposited in Charlotte, North Carolina, when Davis and the other government leaders fled farther south. The Confederate adjutant general Sam Cooper, to whom the papers had been entrusted after Jefferson Davis saw them following the Dahlgren raid, hoped to preserve all the records. He realized that they would provide historians with invaluable documentation.

Cooper advised the Confederate general Joe Johnson, the ranking military officer in North Carolina, of the records' whereabouts. After surrendering, Johnson notified the Union general John Schofield, who arranged for the eighty-one cartons to be shipped to Washington, D.C.

At first, Union leaders showed no interest in the Dahlgren papers. They were searching the Confederate documents for anything that might link Jefferson Davis and other rebel leaders to Lincoln's assassination. Control of the records had been assigned to Dr. Francis Lieber, in the office of the Union adjutant general.

In November 1865, seven months after the Confederate material arrived in Washington, Secretary of War Stanton directed Lieber to locate and turn over the Dahlgren papers to him. This was done on December 1, 1865—and there the visible trail of the Dahlgren papers ends. No record of them exists beyond that day.

Fourteen years later, in 1879, Dr. Lieber began the task of compiling Union and Confederate records for the multivolume war history published by the Government Printing Office as *War of the Rebellion: Official Records of the Union and Confederate Armies*. When Lieber's office could not find the Dahlgren papers, the War Department was asked to return them. The following day, a War Department spokesman said there was no record of the papers in their files. In the early 1980s, James Hall made an extensive search of War Department files but could not find any of the Dahlgren documents. "They were missing in 1879," he wrote, "they are still missing. No record of them has been found."

Whatever the reason for their disappearance—whether some sinister design or an accidental misplacing of a file—we are left with only copies of the Dahlgren papers to evaluate. The disappearance of the originals adds to the mystery surrounding the affair. However, the copies that do exist, plus material from a variety of other sources, permit historians to pursue the question of the authorship and authenticity of the Dahlgren papers.

Let us read the papers taken from Dahlgren's body. They include Dahlgren's orders to Captain Mitchell, a set of general instructions, and notes in a memorandum book. (Dahlgren's alleged address to his men was quoted earlier; see pages 156–157.)

The following are Dahlgren's orders to Captain Mitchell:

> Guides,—pioneers (with oakum, turpentine, and torpedoes), signal officer, quartermaster, commissary, scouts and picked men in Rebel uniform. Men will remain on the north bank and move down with the force on the south bank, not getting ahead of them, and if the communication can be kept up without giving an alarm it must be done; but everything depends upon a surprise, and no one must be allowed to pass ahead of the column. Information must be gathered in regard to the crossings of the river, so that should we be repulsed on the south side we will know where to recross at the nearest point. All mills must be burned and the canal destroyed; and also everything which can be used by the rebels must be destroyed, including the boats on the river. Should a ferry-boat be seized and can be worked, have it moved down. Keep the force on the south side posted of any important movement of the enemy, and in case of danger some of the scouts must swim the river and bring us information. As we approach the city the party must take great care that they do not get ahead of the other party on the south side, and must conceal themselves and watch our movements. We will try and secure the bridge to the city, one mile below Belle Island, and release the prisoners at the same time. If we do not succeed they must then dash down, and we will try and carry the bridge from each side. When necessary, the men must be filed through the woods and along the river bank. The bridges once secured, and the prisoners loose and over the river, the bridges will be burned and the city destroyed. The men must keep together and well in hand, and once in the city it must be destroyed and Jeff. Davis and cabinet

killed. Pioneers will go along with combustible material. The officer must use his discretion about the time of assisting us. Horses and cattle which we do not need immediately must be shot rather than left. Everything on the canal and elsewhere of service to the rebels must be destroyed. As General Custer may follow me, be careful not to give a false alarm.

The following are Dahlgren's general instructions:

The Signal Officer must be prepared to communicate at night by rockets, and in other things pertaining to his department.

The quartermasters and commissaries must be on the lookout for their departments, and see that there are no delays on their account.

The engineering officer will follow to survey the road as we pass over it, etc.

The pioneers must be prepared to construct a bridge or destroy one. They must have plenty of oakum and turpentine for burning, which will be rolled in soaked balls and given to the men to burn when we get in the city. Torpedoes will only be used by the pioneers for destroying the main bridges, etc. They must be prepared to destroy railroads. Men will branch off to the right with a few pioneers and destroy the bridges and railroads south of Richmond, and then join us at the city. They must be well prepared with torpedoes, etc. The line of Falling Creek is probably the best to work along, or as they approach the city Goode's Creek, so that no reinforcements can come up on any cars. No one must be allowed to pass ahead for fear of communicating news. Rejoin the command with all haste, and if cut off cross the river above Richmond and rejoin us. Men will stop at Bellona Arsenal and totally destroy it, and anything else but hospitals; then follow on and rejoin the command at Richmond with all haste, and if cut off cross the river and rejoin us. As General Custer may follow me, be careful not to give a false alarm.

These two sets of papers, along with the address to the troops, were brought to Richmond immediately after they were discovered, carried by Colonel R. L. T. Beale, commanding the Ninth Virginia Cavalry. The memorandum book took a longer route to the capital.

There is no recorded explanation of why Beale kept the memorandum book until March 31, almost a month after Dahlgren was killed, instead of including it with the other papers. However, in due course, the book was sent to Richmond, and on April 1 was published in the *Richmond Examiner*.

Pleasonton will govern details.
    Will have details from other commands, (four thousand).
    Michigan men [Custer's command] have started.
    Colonel J. H. Devereux has torpedoes.
    Hanover Junction (B. T. Johnson). Maryland line.
    Chapin's Farm—Seven miles below Richmond.
    One brigade (Hunton's relieved, Wise sent to Charleston).
    River can be forded half a mile above the city. No works on south side. Hospital near them. River fordable. Canal can be crossed.
    Fifty men to remain on north bank, and keep in communication if possible. To destroy mills, canal, and burn everything of value to the Rebels. Seize any large ferry boats, and note all crossings, in case we have to return that way. Keep us posted of any important movement of the Rebels, and as we approach the city, communicate with us, and to not give the alarm before they see us in possession of Belle Isle and the bridge. If engaged there or unsuccessful, they must assist in securing the bridges until we cross. If the ferry-boat can be taken and worked, bring it down. Everything that cannot be secured or made use of must be destroyed. Great care must be taken not to be seen or any alarm given. The men must be filed along off the road or along the main bank.
    When we enter the city the officer must use his discretion as to when to assist in crossing the bridges.
    The prisoners once loosed and the bridges crossed, the city must be destroyed, burning the public buildings, etc.
    Prisoners to go with party.
    Spike the heavy guns outside.
    Pioneers must be ready to repair, destroy, etc. Turpentine will be provided. The pioneers must be ready to destroy the Richmond bridges, after we have all crossed, and to destroy the railroad near Frederick's Hall (station, artillery, etc.).

Fifteen men to halt at Bellona Arsenal, while the column goes on, and destroy it. Have some prisoners. Then rejoin us at Richmond, leaving a portion to watch if anything follows, under a good officer.

Will be notified that Custer may come.

Main column, four hundred.

One hundred men will take the bridge after the scouts, and dash through the streets and open the way to the front, or if it is open destroy everything in the way.

While they are on the big bridges, one hundred men will take Belle Isle, after the scouts, instructing the prisoners to gut the city. The reserve (two hundred) will see this fairly done and everything over, and then follow, destroying the bridges after them, but not scattering too much, and always having a part well in hand.

Jeff. Davis and Cabinet must be killed on the spot.

Let us consider the evidence supporting the authenticity of these papers. Several witnesses testified that the papers as published in the Richmond newspapers were the same ones removed from Dahlgren's body. These witnesses include the soldiers who first saw the papers, as well as the others in the chain of command who forwarded the documents to Jefferson Davis.

Edward W. Halbach was apparently the first man to read the papers. He wrote that the papers contained

> *every line and every word* as afterwards copied into the Richmond newspapers. Dahlgren's name was signed to one or more of the papers, and also written on the inside of the front cover of his memorandum-book. There the date of purchase, I suppose, was added. The book had been written with a degree of haste clearly indicated by the frequent interlineations and corrections, but the orders referred to had also been re-written on a separate sheet of paper; and, as thus copied, were published to the world. Some of the papers were found loose in Dahlgren's pockets, others were between the leaves of the memorandum-book.
>
> The papers thus brought to light were reserved by myself in the continual presence of witnesses of unquestionable veracity, until about two o'clock in the afternoon of the day after their capture; at which time myself and party met Lieut. Pollard, who,

up to this time, knew nothing in the world of the existence of the Dahlgren Papers. At his request, I let him read the papers; after doing which he requested me to let him carry them to Richmond. At first, I refused, for I thought that I knew what to do with them quite as well as any one else. But I was finally induced, by my friends, against my will, to surrender the papers to Lieut. Pollard, mainly in the consideration of the fact that they would reach Richmond much sooner through him than through a semi-weekly mail. The papers which were thus handed over to the Confederate Government—I state it again—*were correctly copied by the Richmond newspapers....*

If Lieut. Pollard had made any alterations in the papers, these would have been detected by every one who read the papers before they were given to him, and afterwards read them in the newspapers. But all agree that they were correctly copied. In short, human testimony cannot establish any fact more fully than the fact that Col. Ulric Dahlgren was the author of the "Dahlgren Papers."

Colonel Beale, to whom the papers were delivered, later wrote that they specified the killing of government leaders and the burning of the city of Richmond.

Some years later, General Fitzhugh Lee noted that:

what appeared in the Richmond papers of that period as the "Dahlgren papers," was correctly taken from the papers I carried in person to Mr. Davis; and that those papers were not added to or changed in the minutest particular, before they came into my possession, as far as I know and believe; and that, from all the facts in my possession, I have every reason to believe they were taken from the body of Colonel Ulric Dahlgren, and came to me without alteration of any kind.

Secretary of State Judah P. Benjamin told of receiving the papers while he was in conference with Jefferson Davis. Benjamin read the papers with Davis:

of which exact copies were furnished to the Richmond journals for publication. I am, therefore, able to vouch personally for the fact that the passage as to the killing of the President and Cabinet existed in the original, and the photographic copy leaves no room for doubt upon the point.

Later, when Colonel Beale forwarded the memorandum book to Richmond, it was received by Fitzhugh Lee. He sent it to the adjutant general's office with this comment:

> The book, amongst other memoranda, contains a rough pencil sketch of his address to his troops, differing somewhat from his pen-and-ink copy. I embrace this occasion to add, the original papers bore no marks of alteration, nor could they possibly have been changed except by the courier who brought them to me, which is in the highest degree improbable, and the publication of them in the Richmond papers were exact copies in every respect of the originals.

General Josiah Gorgas, the Confederate ordnance chief, also saw the memorandum book. He wrote in his diary:

> I saw today in the hands of General F. H. Lee the pocket memo book of Dahlgren, in which is a rough draft in pencil of his published address to his troops, differing a little here and there; and among other memoranda on another page; "Jeff Davis and his Cabinet must be killed on the spot."

By then even a few people in the North supported the belief that the Dahlgren papers were genuine. General Marsena Patrick, the Union provost marshal, described in his diary a visit from Captain John McEntee, who had ridden on the Dahlgren raid. According to Patrick, Captain McEntee

> had the same opinion of Kilpatrick that I have, and says he managed as all cowards do—He further says that he thinks the papers are correct that were found upon Dahlgren, as they correspond with what D[ahlgren] told *him*.

Of the hundreds of officers and men who rode with Dahlgren on this raid, McEntee is the only one who publicly suggested the papers were factual. However, his evidence is secondhand; we must rely on General Patrick's account. Also, Patrick notes that McEntee "thinks" the papers were correct; there is nothing on record directly from McEntee himself.

In researching his 1996 book *Ashes of Glory: Richmond at War*, the author Ernest Furgurson found two obscure and seemingly incriminating documents never before published. The first is an undated, anonymous paper entitled "Memoranda of the War Commenced Too Late," which Furgurson located in the files of the Virginia Historical Society. The unknown author quoted General George Custer as

> denying Federal claims that the Dahlgren papers were forged or altered. Custer allegedly said that the night before he and Dahlgren parted Dahlgren told him "that he would not take Pres. Davis & his cabinet, but would put them to death, and that he would himself set fire to the first house in Richmond & burn the city." He, Custer did not think this purpose right.

When was this note written, and by whom? A Southerner or a Northerner? Was it written shortly after the raid or many years later? And why was it in the collection of a southern historical archive? Dahlgren and Custer may have known one another, but there is no evidence they had contact prior to the raid. Thus, it is difficult to explain why Dahlgren would have told Custer about the purpose of the mission when he did not even tell his second in command.

The other document Furgurson cited was from the papers of John C. Babcock, held by the Library of Congress. Babcock was a Union intelligence agent whose duties frequently took him to Richmond during the war. Among his papers is this note: "Letters found on Dahlgren's body published in Richmond papers. Authentic report of contents." In this case, as with the alleged report by Custer, there is no evidence that Babcock and Dahlgren knew each other, when or why Dahlgren would have revealed to him any details of the raid, or how Babcock would have seen the papers prior to the raid.

Further, those who insist the papers are genuine have offered intriguing, even ingenious, explanations for the incorrect spelling of Dahlgren's name: DALHGREN instead of DAHLGREN. James

Hall argues that the error appeared during the process of making the photographic facsimiles of the Dahlgren papers, leading to the appearance of a misspelling. Dahlgren's address to his men, Hall noted, was handwritten on paper so thin that the ink stained through to the reverse side. Hall suggested that, to obtain a clean, unsmudged copy, the lithographic technician touched up the stains.

> To complicate this, it was decided to move the last six lines with the signature and designation of rank, to the bottom of the second page of the lithographic copy. This simplified things greatly as the whole text could then be reproduced on a wide sheet containing two pages, side by side. But the signature undoubtedly puzzled the technician who did the work. It did look like D-A-L-H-G-R-E-N. When he touched it up, that is the way it came out.

Hall also reported that, after the war ended, the Confederate general Jubal Early became fascinated with the growing controversy over Dahlgren's signature. In 1879, he sent his set of photographic copies of the papers to the Reverend John Jones of the Southern Historical Society, along with a letter supporting his claim that the papers were genuine.

Early noted that the paper was so thin that the writing on one side of the signature page could be seen from the reverse side. Using a mirror, he told Jones, he could easily read the reverse wording.

> [Early] saw that the tail of the "y" in the word "destroying" on the first page came through precisely at the right point and at the right angle to make it appear that the letter "l" came before the letter "h" in the signature on the reverse side.

This kind of convoluted conjecture, allegedly proving that the surname had not been misspelled and that therefore the papers had not been forged, was also proposed by the author Virgil C. Jones. In his 1957 book on the Dahlgren raid, *Eight Hours Before Richmond*, Jones reported that by enlarging the signature and exposing it to bright lights, he could confirm the explanation offered by General Early. The tail of the letter "y" had soaked through the paper at precisely the right spot to cause the "h" in Dahlgren's name to look like an "l." Thus, what appeared to be a transposition of letters was simply a fortuitous ink stain.

The reasoning and the demonstrations made by Early and Jones may explain why the "h" looks like an "l," but they fail to explain why the "l" looks like an "h." Thus, we are left with a transposition of letters causing the misspelling of a name written by the person himself. Is it likely that Dahlgren, even if he were writing hurriedly, would sign his own name incorrectly?

Were the papers forged by the Confederates? We have seen some credible evidence for the accusation that Dahlgren wrote the infamous papers. However, this evidence has been countered by testimony from those who claim to have seen Dahlgren's orders and instructions to his men prior to his death, and who insist that these documents differ from those printed in the Richmond newspapers.

General Kilpatrick, Captain Mitchell, and the *New York Times* correspondent E. A. Paul all testified that Dahlgren neither possessed nor issued instructions to kill Jefferson Davis and his cabinet or to sack and burn Richmond. We cited their statements earlier in this book. The declaration of Captain Mitchell warrants repeating, since he was Dahlgren's second in command. As such, he would have been informed of the details and purpose of the raid to be able to continue the expedition if Dahlgren was incapacitated or killed. Here is Mitchell's account:

> With regard to the address and memoranda of plans alleged by rebel papers to have been found on Colonel Dahlgren's person, I would state that no address of any kind was ever published to either officers or men . . . and that I know it was not Colonel Dahlgren's intention to kill Jeff. Davis, in case he could be captured.

A few months after Dahlgren's death, Lieutenant Reuben Bartley, Dahlgren's signal officer, was released from a Confederate prison. Commenting on the Dahlgren papers, he wrote:

I pronounce these papers a *base forgery*. . . . I was with the expedition in the capacity of signal officer, and was the only staff-officer with him. I had charge of all the material for destroying bridges, blowing up locks, aqueducts, etc. I knew all his plans, what he intended to do and how he intended doing it, and I know that I never received any such instructions as those papers are said to contain. I also heard all the orders and instructions given to the balance of the officers of the command. Men cannot carry out orders they know nothing of. The colonel's instructions were, that if we were successful in entering the city, to *take no life except in combat*; to keep all prisoners safely guarded, but to *treat them with respect*; liberate all Union prisoners, destroy the public buildings and government stores, and leave the city by way of the Peninsula.

Two Confederate officers who had been taken prisoner by Dahlgren—Lieutenant Henry Blair and Captain William Dement—had nothing but praise for their captor. "He was most agreeable and charming," one said. In Richmond following Dahlgren's death, the men reported that he had treated them well and shared his food with them. Both testified that "they had heard nothing during the four days from Dahlgren, his officers or men, of the 'hellish design' later attributed to him."

If Dahlgren's men had known they were out to kill Jefferson Davis, the president of the Confederacy, it seems surprising that not a one boasted of it to their rebel prisoners. No one taunted the Southerners with the precious knowledge of the history the Yankees were about to make or predicted the demise of the southern cause once Dahlgren's men had done their job. Soldiers on the battlefield tend to be talkative, bragging easily about daring exploits undertaken or about to be, if only to bolster their courage. Yet not one man of several hundred mentioned a thing to Blair or Dement.

Strong evidence indicates, then, that if there was a plan to murder Confederate leaders, Dahlgren's men had not been told about it. Also, even if they all (except, supposedly, Captain McEntee) were lying to protect themselves and their slain leader—if they really had been told their mission included assassination—then Dahlgren omitted one vital piece of information from his address, instructions, and memorandum book.

How were the troopers supposed to find Jefferson Davis and the other targets of the plot? Dahlgren was familiar with Richmond, but most of the men were not. How were the soldiers, fighting through the streets of the rebel capital, expected to locate the homes and offices of the various officials? There is no indication that Captain Mitchell or the other officers were briefed on the location of these alleged targets.

Another unanswered question involves the retaining of the Dahlgren papers. If the papers were genuine—if Dahlgren intended to kill the Confederacy's civilian leaders in Richmond—why would he, an experienced military officer, keep such incriminating evidence on his person for two days and forty miles after he knew the raid had failed? There was no possibility of accomplishing the mission by then. Surely Dahlgren would have foreseen the damage any such papers would have done to his good name, and the embarrassment to his country if he were captured or killed. He had demonstrated in his career coolness under fire and the ability to think and plan ahead. It seems unlikely he would have kept such damning documents during the retreat.

Another inconsistency involves a phrase in the instructions to Captain Mitchell and the set of general instructions. Both documents say, "as General Custer may follow me, be careful not to give a false alarm." A similar line is found in the memorandum book: "will be notified that Custer may come."

Those would be strange comments for Dahlgren to have written, because there is no truth to them. In all the records of the expedition as included in the *War of the Rebellion: Official Records of the Union and Confederate Armies*, there is no indication that Custer would ever attempt to join either Kilpatrick's or Dahlgren's columns.

Custer's orders were clear: His movement was planned as a diversion, a feint, to draw attention away from the main columns. Custer's troops were to approach Charlottesville as closely as they could, try to burn a railroad bridge, and return to camp—nothing more.

Dahlgren had no reason to hope that "Custer may come." It was never part of the plan. Because he would not have considered Custer's arrival a possibility, it seems unlikely he would have written such remarks.

On the other hand, the Confederates had reason to suspect that Custer's column *was* part of the attack. A scout reported to Wade Hampton on February 29, the day after the raid began, that the entire Union army was "prepared to leave . . . whole army seems in motion. Sutlers and women ordered to rear." Lee knew that Union cavalry was moving on his right and left flanks, one unit toward Charlottesville and the other toward Frederick's Hall. It would be natural for him to assume he was facing a two-pronged attack. The Confederates knew exactly when Custer left camp, and they were aware that a large-scale expedition was developing. Hampton's scout also reported that Kilpatrick had received marching orders and that his men were to carry three days' rations.

It would be logical for Confederate military leaders to assume that Custer's men would head south from Charlottesville to join Kilpatrick and his forces approaching from the Rapidan. Whereas Dahlgren had no basis for making any pronouncement about Custer's move to join the attack, the Confederates did.

In the days following Dahlgren's death and the capture of the majority of his troops, there was confusion in rebel headquarters about who should receive credit for the ambush. Had Captain Fox been in command, or Lieutenant Pollard?

Both men prepared reports on the facts of the ambush and forwarded them to General Fitzhugh Lee. Captain Fox wrote on March 9, seven days after Dahlgren's death. Lieutenant Pollard wrote on March 7, five days after the ambush, and again on April 9. The reports are highly detailed in describing the specifics of the ambush, but neither man made any written reference to papers found on Dahlgren's body, even though, by that time, the papers had been publicized by the Richmond press.

How strange for the officers to have omitted from their reports what was publicly being acknowledged as the most important result of their action. Captain Fox and Lieutenant Pollard ignored the fact that their unit had discovered some of the most important and incriminating documents of the war.

On March 9, Colonel Beale sent a report of his part in the operation to Fitzhugh Lee. Along with details of troop movements, casualties, and the like, there appeared this brief paragraph:

> I received at Old Church a dispatch from Lieutenant Pollard, with a note-book and sundry papers taken from the body of Colonel Dahlgren. I forwarded the papers and reported the captures to you at Richmond. The note-book I still have.

Sundry papers? Is that all Beale can say about a heinous plan for murder and arson, as it had been described in the newspapers by that time? Perhaps those sundry papers were merely the plans of yet another Yankee cavalry raid—times, places, bridges, towns, troop concentrations—routine documents to be forwarded up the chain of command. That is what they sound like from Beale's report. And if they were so ordinary, that would account for the failure of Pollard and Fox even to mention them.

After the war, Colonel Beale wrote in the Southern Historical Society's *Papers* that the Dahlgren papers ordered the killing of the leaders of the Confederate government. But a few days after he had read those same papers, he had described them only as "sundry papers." Perhaps that is all they were.

Let us deal with the timing of the Northwest conspiracy. Tom Hines had presented his plan to Jefferson Davis in January, but the president could not bring himself to implement it. He was sensitive to public opinion both in Europe and in the South. The Confederacy could not be seen as the first party to carry a war of terror to civilians.

Was it coincidence that Hines was recalled to Richmond within days of Dahlgren's death? Or had Confederate leaders planned the event ever since learning that the Union was preparing to mount a raid on Richmond? In January, the raid was known throughout the social circles of Washington—"all Willards [Hotel] talks of it"—and Dahlgren heard of it then.

With the efficient Confederate spy network in place in

Washington, the fact that a raid of some kind was in the offing had to be known in Richmond long before any Yankees departed Brandy Station. Dahlgren's death and the securing of his general orders, along with blank sheets of "Headquarters Third Division" stationery, provided the opportunity for the South to fabricate a set of orders that would demonstrate that the North had been the first side to resort to a new, barbaric style of warfare.

With a discreet clerk to handwrite a new set of orders and instructions, the so-called Dahlgren papers could easily have been based on Dahlgren's actual orders. It had to be made to appear that the plan was dastardly—release the vengeful Union prisoners on Richmond's helpless civilians, torch the hateful city, kill the president and his Cabinet—to justify the launching of the Northwest conspiracy. And, in an effort to be thorough, the line about Custer was added, for the rebels believed his troop movement was part of the overall expedition.

Also among the puzzling circumstances is the misspelling of Dahlgren's name. As mentioned on page 200, the signature on the Dahlgren papers does not seem to match Dahlgren's known signature. As Admiral Dahlgren wrote, and as Ulric's letters on file in the Library of Congress show, Ulric Dahlgren always signed his full name, never only his first initial and surname.

Examination of the two signatures has suggested that they were not written by the same hand. The author Virgil C. Jones postulates that a Union clerk could have written the instructions at Dahlgren's command and signed them for the colonel. But there remains the question of Lieutenant Bartley. As a signal officer, he would have seen or heard of the orders, no matter who had actually penned them or how Dahlgren's name was spelled. And Kilpatrick, too, would have seen the orders, along with Captain Mitchell and perhaps Dahlgren's friend E. A. Paul.

What of Kilpatrick's claim to have endorsed Dahlgren's address to his men an hour before departing on the raid? The word "approved" and Kilpatrick's signed endorsement do not appear on the photographic copy of Dahlgren's address that General Lee sent to General Meade.

There is the question of the disposition of Dahlgren's remains. Why was the body brought to Richmond to be identified? If papers bearing Dahlgren's name were taken from the body of a one-legged Union colonel, was that not sufficient identification? Particularly since two Confederate officers had ridden with Dahlgren, knew his name, and shared his food? Certainly they could have identified the body where it fell.

Why would Jefferson Davis concern himself with the burial? Such a routine matter was normally handled by lower-ranking officers. Why should it matter whether the location of Dahlgren's grave site was known? Why later attempt to have the body exhumed? And why deviate from the usual practice of returning the body to the family? Indeed, one could suggest that Davis would want to do so as quickly as possible, since the Davis and Dahlgren families had been friends in Washington before the war.

Did Davis want to personalize the supposed evil represented by the Dahlgren papers, to give it a human face, especially a face wearing "an expression of agony?" Did he believe the southern people needed to personify the plot against him with a corpse they could see, rather than reading about it in the newspapers? Once the body was in the grave, it had served its purpose. Was that why Colonel Atkinson was ordered to remove it and return it to Admiral Dahlgren?

Thus there remain unexplained happenings, coincidences, and questions that challenge the Confederate contention that the papers were genuine. That Ulric Dahlgren, perhaps in some mad bid for glory, risked infamy and opprobrium from friend and foe alike by deciding to assassinate the leaders of the Confederacy. That he did not inform his officers or men or indicate where their targets might be found. That he misspelled his own name and told his men that Custer would be coming when he knew that was an impossibility. That he left evidence of his intentions for all the world to see, when there was no longer any hope of success.

Whoever wrote the Dahlgren papers, the compelling coincidence of timing between their appearance and the onset of the Northwest conspiracy suggests that the papers were deliberately used as moral justification for a terror campaign against northern civilians. Desperate times had called for desperate measures. Many of the secrets bearing on the authenticity of the Dahlgren papers and the activities of the Northwest conspiracy were taken to the grave by the perpetrators. The truth may have died with Ulric Dahlgren and all the others involved, leaving us with a mystery that may never be resolved.

Chapter 23

THE DAHLGREN
AFFAIR: AFTERMATH

When the war ended, Ulric Dahlgren—Ulric the Hun—came home, a year and four months after his death. Admiral Dahlgren had waited a long time to give his son a proper burial.

Throughout the war, the admiral had remained obsessed with the disposition of his son's remains. The subject was on his mind constantly, and periodically he received letters from Virginians that provided additional reminders. These people claimed to have in their possession articles taken from his son's body or to know where such items could be found, generously offering to send them—in return for certain sums of money, of course.

Admiral Dahlgren kept the letters but never replied. He knew that as soon as the countryside around Richmond was secured by Union troops, General LaFayette Baker's detectives would ferret out any such items. The general had assured him that the recovery of Ulric's corpse and his effects had the highest priority. The mistreatment of the body and the stain on the Dahlgren honor spread by the forged papers had sparked outrage in the North, a feeling that remained strong.

Baker's detectives were thorough in tracking down Ulric

Dahlgren's possessions, beginning with his artificial leg. After being displayed in a Richmond shop window, it was returned to Lieutenant James Pollard, who had organized the ambush in which Dahlgren was killed.

A few months later, Pollard himself lost a leg. He tried to have Dahlgren's leg, which was of exceptional quality, fitted for his own use, but it was too short. For the last ten months of the war it was used by John Ballard of Mosby's Rangers.

One of the detectives employed by LaFayette Baker to track Dahlgren's effects after the war was F. W. E. Lohmann. He had been one of Elizabeth Van Lew's agents in Richmond and had been involved in the secret reburial of Dahlgren's body. In October 1865, Lohmann learned that Dahlgren's ring had been taken by Cornelius Martin, formerly of Company H, Ninth Virginia Cavalry. Lohmann and another detective traced Martin to a house in Caroline County, Virginia. At first, Martin denied his identity, pretending to be someone else. He also denied any knowledge of the ring, as well he might, since he had cut off Dahlgren's finger to get it.

After persistent questioning, he admitted to being Martin and stealing the ring, but claimed to have given it to a Dr. Saunders. With Martin in custody, the detectives found Saunders and "after some difficulty caused him to produce the ring which Martin vouched was the one he took from Col. Dahlgren's fingers."

Eventually, Lohmann and other detectives also recovered Dahlgren's pocket watch and coat, the latter a melancholy memento pierced by four bullet holes in the left side.

Dahlgren's body reached Washington in June 1865, two months after Lee's surrender and several months before all Dahlgren's possessions were recovered. A few weeks later, Admiral Dahlgren arrived in Washington to identify the remains. Satisfied that Ulric had finally returned, he hoped to proceed with the elaborate memorial and burial services he had planned, but the weather was too hot. He noted: "The intense heat of the weather rendered it inadvisable to attempt their transference to the burial lot of the family." The family was forced to wait four more months until October 30, when the weather had turned suitably cool.

The memorial service was held in Washington. The body, in a metal casket, was transported in a solemn procession to City Hall, led by a military honor guard. It lay in state in the council chamber until the next day. The casket was draped with an American flag on which rested the letter from Secretary of War Stanton giving Dahlgren his colonel's commission.

At noon, with the pageantry associated with full military honors, the casket was carried to a nearby church. Two generals and six colonels served as pallbearers. The church was crowded with civilian and military dignitaries, including President Andrew Johnson (who never knew how close he had come to being kidnapped) and most of his Cabinet members. The eulogy was delivered by the fiery Henry Ward Beecher, the famous preacher and abolitionist.

"Dahlgren!" he exclaimed. "As long as our history lasts, Dahlgren shall mean truth, honor, bravery and heroic sacrifice."

The casket was sent by train to Philadelphia, where it lay in state for a day at Independence Hall, an exceptional honor. Admiral Dahlgren wrote: "Few dead are honored by resting there. The last who preceded was the body of . . . President Lincoln, Ully's friend."

Generals Meade and Humphreys, neither of whom had favored the Dahlgren raid, were among the distinguished mourners at the North Hill Cemetery grave site. After the final blessing there was a moment of silence, broken "by the quick, clear click of muskets, and then comes the loud volley from a thousand muskets, repeated again and again." Admiral Dahlgren continued: "[R]emembered among those the nation mourns, will be the name of Ulric Dahlgren."

Absent from the prominent people paying homage to young Ulric Dahlgren at his memorial service in Washington and his burial in Philadelphia was Major General Hugh Judson Kilpatrick, even though he was on leave. Perhaps he did not wish to be reminded of his failed attempt to take Richmond.

That failure cost him dearly at the time, for he "lost the confidence of both his superiors and the men in the ranks." When General Grant assumed command of all the Union armies, shortly after the Dahlgren raid, the cavalry service was reorganized and Kilpatrick relieved of his command. He no longer had a place in the Army of the Potomac; his only options were to leave the service or apply for a transfer.

Kilpatrick elected to try his luck with Sherman's army in the West. Sherman knew Kilpatrick—he had called him "a hell of a damn fool"—but he was aware that Kilpatrick could be a fearless fighter. Sherman gave Kilpatrick command of the Third Cavalry Division, six thousand troopers strong, and Kill-Cavalry quickly proved his worth.

On May 13, 1864, Kilpatrick's division led General Sherman's attack against a rebel railroad junction at the town of Resaca, Georgia. Kilpatrick was out in front of his troopers, leading the charge with saber drawn. A rebel bullet tore through his left thigh, ending the battle for him. He returned to West Point in order to recuperate, and by the end of July was able to rejoin his outfit.

Kilpatrick continued to impress Sherman and the other commanders with his aggressive leadership in the field, but he also displayed less desirable characteristics. Whenever he lost a battle or made an error in judgment, he could never admit the unpleasant truth. And as earlier in his career, his reports tended to exaggerate his accomplishments. "Repeated evasions, misrepresentations and distortions of the actual situation made the general appear even more preposterous and susceptible to grave accusations."

He continued to be known as a womanizer. A young Chinese girl called Molly joined Kilpatrick's entourage, ostensibly as a laundress. Before long she was pregnant. Kilpatrick found another woman, whom he called Charley, and dressed her in a soldier's uniform. No one was deceived. A soldier recalled seeing Kilpatrick and Charley kissing passionately. "That first excited [my] suspicion as to [her] sex," the man recalled.

In other ways, Kilpatrick was still capable of acting like a hell of a damn fool. Once again he was surprised by a rebel attack. As had happened outside Richmond when Wade Hampton's men roared through, Kilpatrick had placed only a few pickets on duty when he made camp at Monroe's Cross Roads in North Carolina one night in early March 1865. His sleeping men had no warning of the assault.

Kilpatrick was caught entertaining a young woman, Marie, who had been traveling with him for several days. They were in bed in a small cabin when the rebels attacked, neatly effecting a complete rout:

> [T]he Confederates galloped into the camp screaming the rebel yell and firing their pistols. Union troopers jumped from their bedrolls, blankets and equipment flying everywhere. Men in nightclothes scurried in all directions, grabbing their carbines and pistols and running for cover in the swamp. The Confederates, firing their pistols, and slashing with their sabers, rode them down.

Two rebel officers reined up in front of Kilpatrick, who had pulled on a nightshirt and gone outside to see what the commotion was.

"Where is General Kilpatrick?" they demanded.

"There he goes on that horse," replied the general, pointing to one of his fleeing troopers.

Kilpatrick escaped, but the rebels took his favorite horse. Marie, whom Kilpatrick had abandoned, was rescued by a gallant Confederate officer. Eventually Kilpatrick rallied his men and beat back the attack, but the episode came to be known as Kilpatrick's Shirttail Skedaddle, and the tale followed him for the rest of the war.

Once again defeat had been inflicted on Kilpatrick by Wade Hampton, the man who had chased him from Richmond. The "crowning indignation" was Hampton's return of Kilpatrick's favorite horse with a "warning to take better care of him in the future."

By the time the war ended, Kilpatrick had received the second star of a major general. Only twenty-nine, he was far too young, aggressive, and ambitious to sit behind a desk in the peacetime army. He took a leave of absence and spent several months campaigning for the Republican candidate for governor of New Jersey. Thanks to Kilpatrick's impressive oratorical skills, the man won the election. Kilpatrick's reward, granted by the grateful Secretary of War Stanton and Secretary of State Seward, was an appointment as Envoy Extraordinary Minister Plenipotentiary to Chile. The post paid a lavish annual salary of ten thousand dollars, plus five hundred dollars in expenses.

Kilpatrick spent three years in Chile, where he married Louisa Valdivoso, the niece of the archbishop of Santiago. On their return, he became a popular public speaker, lecturing about his war experiences throughout the United States.

He tried the life of a gentleman farmer in New Jersey, edited a ladies' magazine, and wrote a play (*Allatoona*) based on the war. It was performed once, for a reunion of thirty thousand Union military veterans. In the 1930s, the work was revised by the playwright Christopher Morley, retitled *The Blue and the Gray, or War Is Hell*, and ran for fifty-two performances at the Rialto Theatre in Hoboken, New Jersey.

Kilpatrick remained restless. Nothing satisfied him for long, so he decided to pursue his old interest in a political career. He ran for congressman, then governor, of New Jersey, and was beaten decisively in both elections. In 1881, he returned to Chile for a second tour as a government minister. In Santiago, on December 4, 1881, Kilpatrick died of Bright's disease. Only forty-six, he never achieved his dreams of glory.

In death Kilpatrick left behind an imposing monument at his West Point grave site, paid for by his men and fellow officers and by his twin granddaughters—the children of his daughter, Laura—who appeared determined to carry on the family tradition of notoriety. One of the twins, Gloria Morgan, married Reginald Vanderbilt in 1922 and gave birth to a daughter, whom the press later dubbed Little Gloria. After Reginald died young, Laura began a campaign to obtain custody of Little Gloria and some of the Vanderbilt fortune as well. Laura attacked her daughter's fitness as a mother and in 1934 legally contested Gloria Morgan Vanderbilt's guardianship of the child. The court ruled against the child's mother and made Little Gloria a ward of the state and a worldwide celebrity.

The other twin, Thelma Morgan, married the wealthy grandson of the founder of Bell Telegraph but divorced him four years later to marry a British aristocrat. Soon after, she began a five-year affair with the Prince of Wales. Thelma was so confident she would marry this future king of England that she divorced her husband in 1932. Two years later, temporarily bored with the Prince of Wales, she had a dalliance with Prince Aly Khan. When the Prince of Wales found out, he turned for solace to Thelma's friend, Wallis Simpson. When Thelma was later asked what she might have done differently in her life, she said, "I would never have introduced Wallis Simpson to the Prince of Wales."

Kilpatrick's grandson, Harry Judson Kilpatrick Morgan, pursued a military career. He joined the U.S. Army and fought in the Argonne campaign in World War I.

How Kilpatrick would have loved it all.

When the war ended, Tom Hines was in Kentucky trying to organize a new command. Lee's surrender was a dreadful personal blow. He wrote to his father: "It is a grief almost too sacred for words." He left immediately for Canada but nearly lost his life in a bar before he could reach Windsor.

This was two days after the assassination of Abraham Lincoln, and the nationwide manhunt for John Wilkes Booth was in full cry. Hines, who resembled Booth, was in a Detroit saloon waiting to board the ferry to Canada. Suddenly, someone pointed at him, yelling that he was Booth. Men lunged at him from all sides. Hines clubbed one with the butt of his Navy Colt revolver and kicked another in the stomach. He ran for the ferry, which had just docked, and commandeered the boat at gunpoint, ordering the startled captain to take him across. When the boat docked on the Canadian side of the lake, Hines apologized to the captain and gave him five dollars for his inconvenience.

Hines traveled to Toronto to become part of the colony of expatriates that included Commissioner Thompson, John Castleman, Bennett Young, and other conspirators wanted by the Federal government. Secretary of War Stanton had issued arrest warrants for them and posted a reward of ten thousand dollars for Hines. Hines's wife, Nancy, journeyed north to be with him. Hines enrolled at the university to study French and literature, and in the evenings he read law.

In May 1865, President Andrew Johnson issued an amnesty

proclamation, granting pardons to most of the men who fought for the Confederacy if they were willing to take an oath of allegiance to the United States. However, pardons would not be granted to certain persons, including Hines. Nevertheless, two months later, Hines took the ferry to Detroit and risked taking the oath of allegiance. To his relief, he was not arrested. Nevertheless, friends in Kentucky warned him not to return. The Federal arrest warrant was still in effect. Back home, Hines remained a wanted man.

In May 1866, a year and a month after Lee's surrender, Tom and Nancy Hines returned to Kentucky, assured by friends that it was safe to do so. Hines passed the bar exam and opened a law office in Bowling Green. In 1875, he was elected chief justice of Kentucky's court of appeals. Nancy passed away suddenly in 1898, and Hines died three weeks later.

Hines never revealed the details of the Northwest conspiracy or his role in it. He did, however, start to write an article about the conspiracy in 1882, intending it for publication in the prestigious *Southern Bivouac* magazine. He wrote to Jefferson Davis to request an interview to discuss the events in which they had played such prominent roles. Davis never replied, and Hines did not pursue the matter. Three years later, Basil Duke, the magazine's editor (and John Hunt Morgan's brother-in-law), asked Hines to write of his wartime experiences. Hines was too involved with his law practice at the time, so he sent his papers to his old friend John Castleman, asking him to tell the story.

While Castleman was preparing the article, the magazine published a teaser, telling its readers that the full story of the Northwest conspiracy would be revealed in forthcoming issues. Jefferson Davis was outraged. He wrote a strong letter of protest to Basil Duke, urging him not to reveal the campaign's details or the names of anyone involved. Shading the truth, Davis also insisted he knew nothing about any terror operations in the North. "As you are doubtless aware, I had no connection with the transactions which this narrative will record, and no personal knowledge of them." Even more than two decades after the fact, Davis did not want the conspiracy, which he had approved, to become known. Such remained his power in southern life that his wishes were respected. No articles were written, and Hines never again attempted to tell his story in print.

None of the other participants in the conspiracy's various activities told their stories. Commissioner Jacob Thompson planned to leave Toronto in grand style. With money from his Northwest conspiracy funds, he purchased a schooner, outfitted it for the long sea voyage to Texas, and hired a captain. He asked Hines and Castleman to join him, but they refused. His plan came to naught when Federal authorities learned of it. The schooner was sold and Thompson elected to go abroad. Castleman went with him, and together they toured England, Scotland, and Ireland. They called on Judah P. Benjamin, who had settled in London.

Thompson remained in Europe for four years. In 1869 he moved to Oxford, Mississippi. He maintained his friendship with Jefferson Davis, and the two men often visited. Thompson faced "years of controversy regarding the alleged misuse of funds during the Canadian cloak-and-dagger operations." More than two million dollars was never adequately accounted for. No charges were filed against Thompson, nor was he publicly accused of misappropriation of funds. He died in 1885, leaving a sizable estate.

Commissioner Clement Clay was less fortunate and less farsighted. He left Toronto in December 1865, and surrendered to Federal authorities in Georgia, convinced that they would not persecute or prosecute a man in failing health. He was arrested and confined at Fortress Monroe for almost a year. Clay's wife appealed in person to President Johnson and to Edwin Stanton for her husband's release. They both refused, although General Grant recommended that Clay be set free. Finally, in April 1866, Clay was released without trial. He returned home to Huntsville, Alabama, and died in 1882.

Jefferson Davis was confined at Fortress Monroe following his capture in Georgia by Union troops on May 10, 1865. He was placed in irons, but his physical suffering was considered so great that he was moved to more comfortable quarters. Mrs. Davis was permitted to join him. Davis was charged with treason but never brought to trial. On

May 13, 1867, he was released on bond, after two years of imprisonment.

He spent his remaining years on an estate in Mississippi, where he wrote a two-volume account of his career, *The Rise and Fall of the Confederate Government*. State officials in Mississippi pleaded with him to return to Washington as their senator, but he declined. If he were to stand for election, he would have to request a pardon from the Federal government. That he vowed never to do. Jefferson Davis died in 1880.

Judah P. Benjamin remained with Davis until the collapse of the Confederacy. Before fleeing Richmond, he burned all the records dealing with Hines and the conspiracy. Determined to begin a new life and career, he evaded the Union patrols searching for him and made his way to Florida, the West Indies, and then London. He became a prominent and successful lawyer and legal scholar. He died in 1884 and was buried in Paris.

James Seddon retired as the Confederacy's secretary of war in February 1865, for health reasons. He lived until 1880.

Most of the Confederates who fought the clandestine war in the North lived many years after the war, with the exceptions of John Yates Beall and George St. Leger Grenfell. On February 14, 1865, Beall, who had tried to capture the USS *Michigan* on Lake Erie, wrote a last letter to his brother:

> Ere this reaches you, you will most probably have heard of my death through the newspapers; that I was tried by a military commission and hung by the enemy; and hung, I assert, unjustly. . . .
>
> Remember me kindly to my friends. Say to them, I am not aware of committing any crime against society. I die for my country.

Ten days later, on February 24, Beall was transported from his dungeon at Fort Lafayette in New York Harbor to Fort Columbus on Governor's Island, and marched to the gallows.

The band struck up the death-march, and the solemn procession moved forward. Beall caught the step of the regulars, and moved with them; he was a soldier, and knew how to keep step even to the music of his own death-dirge.

He walked up the five steps to the gallows and stood still while the officer in charge began to read the specifications of the court martial. The officer droned on for a full nine minutes while the crowd of five hundred spectators grew impatient, then angry, at the cruelty of drawing out this punishment. Even the hangman was upset at the delay. "Cut it short, cut it short!" he yelled. "The captain wishes to be swung off quick!" But the officer continued until the complete document had been read. Beall was asked if he had anything to say.

"I protest against the execution of this sentence," he replied calmly. "It is a murder! I die in the service and defense of my country. I have nothing more to say."

Colonel George St. Leger Grenfell was sentenced to death after a trial that lasted four months. President Johnson later commuted the sentence to life imprisonment. It was, however, a sentence of living death; Grenfell was transported to that hellhole of a prison, Fort Jefferson in the Dry Tortugas.

Located sixty-eight miles west of Key West, the Tortugas are seven small islands, each nothing more than a spit of barren, hot, humid, hurricane-swept sand. The three-story fort, built on Gordon Key, was constructed of yellow brick, which appeared blinding in the constant bright sun. The fort was ringed by a moat inhabited by an ever-circling shark.

At first, Grenfell was treated abominably but was eventually allowed to work in the garden. A fellow prisoner was Dr. Samuel Mudd, who had set John Wilkes Booth's broken leg after the Lincoln assassination. When a yellow fever epidemic broke out in the prison, Grenfell volunteered to help Mudd nurse the sick and dying. For three months, the two men worked day and night in a gun room turned into a makeshift hospital. They treated three hundred fever victims, losing only forty—an extremely low number of casualties, given the conditions under which the men labored.

The prison commandant was so impressed with Grenfell's dedication amid such extreme personal peril that he praised the Englishman in letters to the president and the secretary of war. Representatives of the British government petitioned for Grenfell's release, as did Tom Hines and other prominent Confederates. Grenfell himself wrote to President Johnson requesting clemency. Everyone connected with the case believed clemency would be granted, given Grenfell's heroism in the yellow fever epidemic, but Andrew Johnson turned down all such requests. Apparently, he was influenced by Stanton, who had never forgiven Grenfell for violating his promise to Stanton not to fight against the United States. (Dr. Mudd was pardoned in 1868 for his part in combating the yellow fever epidemic.)

On the night of March 7, 1868, Grenfell and three other prisoners did what had been deemed impossible. They escaped from Fort Jefferson in a small open boat, rowing out beyond the raging surf into the path of a violent storm. None of the men was ever seen again. A search of the area found no signs of wreckage. They were presumed drowned.

Clement Vallandigham, who bore more responsibility than anyone else for the failure of Tom Hines's planned uprising in Chicago, was never reelected to public office. He returned to work as a trial lawyer in Dayton, Ohio. In 1871, while demonstrating how a murder victim had been shot by his client, he accidentally shot himself. He died the next day.

Frank Stringfellow of Mosby's Iron Scouts, who had danced at the Army of the Potomac's George Washington's Birthday Ball, continued to lead a charmed life. In 1864, John Yates Beall asked Stringfellow to accompany him to Canada to take part in a daring raid against the Yankees. Stringfellow declined, judging the expedition to be ill conceived. The mission was the attack on the USS *Michigan*. Stringfellow spent the rest of the war as a spy and courier in Alexandria, Virginia, and Washington, D.C., frequently staying at Willard's Hotel and at Mrs. Surratt's boarding house, the latter long considered "a way station for Confederate secret agents." (Mrs. Surratt was hanged for her apparent role in the assassination of President Lincoln.)

At the war's end, Stringfellow was suspected of being an accomplice of John Wilkes Booth because of his association with Mrs. Surratt. He fled to Canada with a price of ten thousand dollars on his head. In 1865 he accepted the Union's amnesty offer and returned to Virginia. After enrolling in a theological seminary, he became an ordained Episcopal minister and served as a U.S. army chaplain during the Spanish-American War. He died peacefully in 1913.

Colonel Thomas Rose, who led the escape from Libby Prison, was exchanged for a Confederate colonel on April 21, 1864. "Many who knew him prior to his capture said later that he suffered from a personality change as a result of his imprisonment, becoming uncharacteristically irritable, emotional, and suspicious." Rose was wounded at Kenesaw Mountain in Georgia and was later promoted to the brevet rank of brigadier general. He stayed in the army after the war, reverting to the rank of captain and retiring in 1894 as a colonel. He died in 1907 and was buried on the grounds of Robert E. Lee's former home, which had become Arlington National Cemetery.

Mary Bowser, recruited by Elizabeth Van Lew to serve as a spy in Jefferson Davis's house, was recognized officially for her work and on June 30, 1995 was posthumously inducted into the U.S. Army's Intelligence Hall of Fame at Fort Huachuca, Arizona.

Libby Prison was emptied of its last Union captives in May 1864, three months after the Dahlgren raid. Before the Yankees left, they destroyed their homemade furniture and anything else they thought the enemy might find useful. Before the war ended, the old warehouse briefly housed some rebel prisoners and then was reconverted to a storage facility.

In 1887, a group of Chicago businessmen bought the Libby Prison building and had it shipped in pieces to Chicago, where it was reassembled as a Civil War museum. Opening in 1889, the attraction became popular, particularly during the 1893 World's Fair. It was razed in 1895 and parts of it were used in the construction of the Chicago Coliseum and the Chicago Historical Society's Civil War room. The remainder of its bricks and timbers were bought by a state senator who used them to build a barn that stood until 1960.

On the day Richmond surrendered to the Yankees, an angry mob assembled in front of Elizabeth Van Lew's home on Church Hill. The crowd threatened to torch her house, and they were mad enough to do it. The Yankees were not even inside the city yet, and that damned fool woman— everyone had said she was a spy and this proved it—had placed a huge American flag atop her roof, the first Yankee flag anywhere in the city.

Miss Van Lew stepped out on her wide front porch and faced down the mob. Some in the crowd were her neighbors, and she pointed a finger at those she recognized.

"I know you and you," she said. "General Grant will be in town in an hour. You do anything to my home, and all of yours will be burned before noon."

That did it. People backed away, grumbling among themselves, but they left her alone after that.

When the Union army entered Richmond later that day, one of their first duties, under orders from General Grant, was to post a guard at her door. When the guard detail arrived, Miss Van Lew was not at home. Although it was dangerous to be out on the streets, she had gone downtown, determined to search through the abandoned War Department offices for any papers that might be valuable to the Union. The center of Richmond was in chaos as the rebels destroyed everything of value, setting off explosions and fires. Drunken deserters and civilians looted everything else.

When General Grant toured Richmond briefly that fall, he visited few local officials, but he did call on Miss Van Lew. The two sat on her front porch, sipping tea and chatting, in full view of the neighbors. She was immensely proud that Grant had come to see her, and she kept the general's calling card as long as she lived. To her, it was as precious as a medal.

Elizabeth Van Lew may have been a hero to the North, but her years as a Union spy consumed most of her family fortune, leaving her nearly destitute. When Grant became president in 1869, he appointed her postmaster of Richmond to provide her with a steady income, in gratitude for her wartime services. The appointment was not well received by the local citizens. A newspaperman wrote: "We regard the selection of a Federal spy to manage our post-office as a deliberate insult to our people."

Miss Van Lew donated much of her postmaster's salary to various charities, particularly those dedicated to the well-being of the newly freed Negroes. She remained in the position eight years. The next U.S. president, Rutherford B. Hayes, refused to renew her appointment, despite a plea from Grant. Grant had also tried to get Congress to award her the sum of fifteen thousand dollars as compensation for money she had lost during the war, but the federal legislators never took any action on the measure.

She lived in virtual poverty and isolation until her death in 1900. Except for an invalid niece who lived with her and her loyal but aging servants, she saw no one. She wrote in her diary:

> I live here in the most perfect isolation. No one will walk with us on the streets, no one will go with us anywhere; and it grows worse and worse as the years roll on and those I love go to their long rest.
>
> I live—and have lived for years—as entirely distinct from the citizens as if I were plague-stricken. Rarely, very rarely, is our door-bell ever rung by any but a pauper. . . .
>
> September, 1875, my mother was taken from me by death. We had not friends enough to be pall-bearers.

In 1891, twenty-six years after the war ended, she wrote: "We are held so utterly as outcasts here. Social outcasts." Two Episcopal ministers who lived across the street refused to return her calls, and even a friendly neighbor told her that "We can never forget . . . nor ever forgive you."

When Elizabeth Van Lew died thirty-five years after the war ended, the feelings against her were still so strong that not a single person from Richmond, other than her servants, attended the funeral. The only other mourners were relatives of Colonel Paul Revere of Massachusetts, whom she had helped in Libby Prison. Revere's family was so grateful for her aid that they ordered a huge slab of Massachusetts granite as a headstone. They commissioned a bronze plaque with these words:

> She risked everything that is dear to men—friends, fortune, comfort, health, life itself, all for the one absorbing desire of her heart—that slavery might be abolished and the Union preserved.

Not long after that, the headstone was vandalized.

Chapter Notes

Note: Complete information for works cited in the chapter notes can be found in the Bibliography (pp. 283–288).

EPIGRAPHS

"The war had changed": Catton, *The Army of the Potomac*, vol. III, p. 16. "The blood boils": R. E. Lee, *The Wartime Papers of R. E. Lee*, p. 678.

1. MANY ARE DEAD AND GONE

"Who would have dreamed": Favill, *The Diary of a Young Officer*, p. 273. "God help my country": Chesnut, *Mary Chesnut's Civil War*, p. 519. "Unless there is a change": Lee, quoted in Anderson and Anderson, *The Generals*, p. 436. "Imbecile President": Foote, *The Civil War*, vol. II, p. 648. "Our bleeding": Greeley, quoted in McPherson, *Battle Cry of Freedom*, p. 762. "Must I shoot": Lincoln, quoted in Morris, "It Can't Happen Here," *America's Civil War*, March 1991, p. 6. "A War of Extermination": *Richmond Examiner*, quoted in Catton, *The Army of the Potomac*, vol. III, p. 118. "In both North and South": Catton, p. 118.

2. IT IS A PERILOUS TIME

"Beef was held at $2.50": J. B. Jones, *A Rebel War Clerk's Diary*, pp. 324,

325, 353. "As fast as they got": quoted in Sears, *Chancellorsville*, p. 108. "Chided them for crying": William Davis, *Jefferson Davis*, p. 497. "We do not desire": Jefferson Davis, quoted in William Davis, p. 198. "Wild turkey, wild ducks": Chesnut, *Mary Chesnut's Civil War*, p. 550. "Gumbo, ducks, and olives": Chesnut, p. 551. "My daughter's cat": Jones, p. 539. "It is a perilous time": Jones, p. 329.

3. IT IS A GREAT PLAN

"Modest, courteous, and imperturbable": Castleman, quoted in Starr, *Colonel Grenfell's War*, p. 93. "Dear Col."; quoted in Horan, *Confederate Agent*, p. 36. "Castle Merion, cell no. 20": Hines, quoted in Swiggett, *The Rebel Raider*, p. 173. "He passed his good right eye": William Davis, *Jefferson Davis*, p. 389. "Meals at the Executive Mansion": Davis, p. 540. "It is a great plan": Davis, quoted in Swiggett, p. 95. "Yesterday, we rode": Gorgas, quoted in McPherson, *Battle Cry of Freedom*, p. 665. "We should neglect no honorable": R. E. Lee, *The Wartime Papers of R. E. Lee*, p. 508.

4. THE TIME TO STRIKE

"For years the great of America": Kane, *Spies For The Blue and Gray*, p. 233. "Uncompromising, ready to resent": Van Lew, quoted in Kane, p. 235. "Southern swains": Furgurson, *Ashes of Glory*, p. 76. "We had threats": Van Lew, quoted in Furgurson, p. 76. "Two ladies, mother and daughter": quoted in Kane, p. 236. "My dear Miss": Butler, quoted in West, *Lincoln's Scapegoat General*, p. 227. "Mrs. Babcock": Markle, *Spies and Spymasters of the Civil War*, p. 182. "Glide toward the attic": Kane, pp. 241–242. "I always went to bed": Van Lew, quoted in Beymer, "Miss Van Lew," *Harper's Magazine*, June 1911, pp. 91, 89. "I have turned to speak": Van Lew, quoted in Beymer, p. 85. "It is intended to remove": *War of the Rebellion: Official Records*, series 1, volume 33, p. 520. "He said to say": *War of the Rebellion*, p. 520. "Now or never": Butler, quoted in Kane, pp. 243–244.

5. WHOLESALE MISERY AND DEATH

"Beans are very wormy": Ransom, quoted in Denney, *Civil War Prisons and Escapes*, p. 146. "Seems pretty rough": Ransom, quoted in Denney, p. 143. "A good deal of fighting": Ransom, quoted in Denney, p. 152. "Hair, beard, and clothing": Gindlesperger, *Escape From Libby Prison*, p. 222. "It never would do": Lincoln, quoted in Donald, *Lincoln*, pp. 547–548. "The gloomiest": Libby Custer, quoted in Wert, *Custer*, p. 149. "I observe that the President": John Dahlgren, quoted in Donald, p. 426. "Fifty victims every day": *New York Times*, November 28, 1863. "The first demand": *New York Times*, November 28, 1863. "In these grim months": Donald, p. 489.

6. THE CHANCES ARE PRETTY HAZARDOUS

"He had begun to be a terror": Kidd, *A Cavalryman With Custer*, pp. 93, 95. "Pyrrhic victories": Pierce, "General Hugh Judson Kilpatrick in the American Civil War," p. 8. "A little man": Howard, *Civil War Echoes*, p. 214. "Stories about his multifarious affairs": Pierce, p. 264. "Could not escape": Pierce, p. 174. "It sounds like a big thing": Wainwright, *A Diary of Battle*, p. 265. "Consistently demonstrated": Pierce, pp. 272–273. "Is a frothy braggart": Lyman, *Meade's Headquarters, 1863–1864*, p. 79. "I know Kilpatrick": Sherman, quoted in Lewis, *Sherman: The Fighting Prophet*, p. 405. "In after years": Kilpatrick, quoted in Pierce, pp. 265, 267. "That savage, little rooster": Lewis, *It Takes All Kinds*, p. 47. "Kill is going to the field": quoted in Martin, *Kill-Cavalry*, p. 19. "Are we going to stay here": Kilpatrick, quoted in Pierce, p. 25. "Alice" and "Kilpatrick": Martin, p. 26. "He has just lost his wife": Wainwright, p. 324. "Angered by the slur": Martin, p. 144. "The same rude colony": Adams, quoted in Leach, *Reveille In Washington*, p. 5. "Vast practical joke": quoted in Leach, p. 278. "One of the worst pestholes": Lee, "Ordnance: The Humble Undertaker Performed a Distasteful but All Too Necessary Role During the Civil War," *America's Civil War*, November 1996, p. 20. "If the people": Leach, p. 232. "In the new year": Leach, p. 283. "The whole place": Donald, *Lincoln*, p. 312. "From the information": *War of the Rebellion*, series 1, volume 33, p. 173. "Not feasible at this time": *War of the Rebellion*, series 1, volume 33, p. 171. "I will most willingly": *War of the Rebellion*, series 1, volume 33, p. 172. "I have been a good deal": Meade, *The Life and Letters of George Gordon Meade*, pp. 167–168. "With this force": *War of the Rebellion*, series 1, volume 33, pp. 173–174. "For some days": Lyman, pp. 76–78.

7. THE PALACE OF PLEASURE

"The army is overrun": Meade, *The Life and Letters of George Gordon Meade*, p. 167. "The girls thought": Favill, *The Diary of a Young Officer*, p. 279. "Such glorious breakfasts": Favill, p. 279. "Kilpatrick was happy": Howard, *Civil War Echoes*, p. 214. "A beardless youth": quoted in Bakeless, *Spies of the Confederacy*, p. 119. "Other feminine fripperies": Bakeless, p. 118. "Why, Frank": Marsten, quoted in Brown, *Stringfellow of the Fourth*, p. 247. "My God": quoted in Brown, p. 255. "Yes, madam": quoted in

Catton, *The Army of the Potomac*, vol. III, p. 2. "We have had": Meade, p. 167. "Gayly sped the feet": Favill, p. 280. "With sabers all drawn": Howard, p. 221.

8. HOW LITTLE WE KNOW WHO WILL GO NEXT

"It seemed as if": John Dahlgren, *Memoir of Ulric Dahlgren*, p. 17. "When I have nothing": Ulric Dahlgren, quoted in John Dahlgren, p. 23. "The whole of it is": Ulric Dahlgren, quoted in John Dahlgren, p. 25. "As you know": Ulric Dahlgren, quoted in John Dahlgren, p. 25. "The American flag": Ulric Dahlgren, quoted in John Dahlgren, p. 30. "I am in the midst": Ulric Dahlgren, quoted in John Dahlgren, p. 48. "Sometimes Lincoln drove": Schneller, *A Quest For Glory*, p. 186. "Captain Dahlgren": quoted in John Dahlgren, p. 149. "I cannot too highly": Hooker, quoted in John Dahlgren, p. 155. "Paul, I have got it": Ulric Dahlgren, quoted in *New York Times*, March 9, 1864. "Wounded": Ulric Dahlgren diary, March 6, 1864, John Dahlgren Personal Papers. "4 or 5 pieces bone": Ulric Dahlgren diary, March 7, 1864, John Dahlgren Papers. "Had better come off": Ulric Dahlgren diary, March 8, 1864, John Dahlgren Papers. "I have been concerned": John Dahlgren to Ulric Dahlgren, July 20, 1863, John Dahlgren Papers. "Often while lying down": Ulric Dahlgren, quoted in V. C. Jones, *Eight Hours Before Richmond*, p. 82. "It is not so much": John Dahlgren letter, August 19, 1863, John Dahlgren Papers. "I called at the White House": Ulric Dahlgren to John Dahlgren, January 31, 1864, John Dahlgren Papers. "We will start soon": letter of Ulric Dahlgren, February 26, 1864, John Dahlgren Papers. "I have not returned": Ulric Dahlgren to John Dahlgren, February 26, 1864, John Dahlgren Papers.

9. DON'T KNOW YET WHERE WE ARE TO GO

"Confidential": *War of the Rebellion*, series 1, volume 33, p. 183. "He'll come back": Brown, quoted in Wert, *Custer*, p. 140. "Don't know yet": quoted in Starr, *The Union Cavalry In the Civil War*, vol. II, p. 57. "The Major-General": *War of the Rebellion*, series 1, volume 33, p. 175. "The largest camp": Bakeless, *Spies of the Confederacy*, pp. 343–344.

10. A DARKNESS THAT COULD BE FELT

"Myriads of stars": *War of the Rebellion*, series 1, volume 33, p. 189. "It was a complete surprise": *War of the Rebellion*, series 1, volume 33, pp. 181–182. "Madam, these Yankees": Kurtz, quoted in V. C. Jones, *Eight Hours Before Richmond*, p. 49. "My cavalry expedition": Meade, *The Life and Letters of George Gordon Meade*, p. 168. "A cavalry expedition": *War of the Rebellion*, series 1, volume 33, p. 615. "Gave general satisfaction": quoted in John Dahlgren, *Memoir of Ulric Dahlgren*, p. 212. "The dark forms": *War of the Rebellion*, series 1, volume 33, p. 189. "Now it stormed": *War of the Rebellion*, series 1, volume 33, p. 189. "A darkness that could be felt": Kidd, *A Cavalryman With Custer*, p. 158. "Who could complain": quoted in John Dahlgren, p. 213. "We'll have some supper": Ulric Dahlgren, quoted in John Dahlgren, p. 213.

11. WE ARE GOING ON

"Then I knew you": Mrs. Seddon, quoted in V. C. Jones, *Eight Hours Before Richmond*, pp. 72–73. "Mrs. Seddon": quoted in K. Jones, *Ladies of Richmond*, p. 204. "He was most agreeable": quoted in Swiggett, *The Rebel Raider*, p. 208. "At the last moment": *War of the Rebellion*, series 1, volume 33, p. 221. "The colonel then told": quoted in V. C. Jones, p. 163. "Cheerful intelligence": Kidd, *A Cavalryman With Custer*, p. 162. "We are going on": Ulric Dahlgren, quoted in John Dahlgren, *Memoir of Ulric Dahlgren*, p. 216. "The colonel's coolness": quoted in John Dahlgren, p. 216. "Of course you can imagine": Meade, *The Life and Letters of George Gordon Meade*, p. 169.

12. THE CHASE WAS A NIGHTMARE

"Bad humor": William Davis, *Jefferson Davis*, p. 543. "Every reliable man": Van Lew, quoted in Kane, *Spies for the Blue and Gray*, p. 245. "The enemy's cavalry": J. B. Jones, *A Rebel War Clerk's Diary*, p. 344. "Last night a hole was dug": Dow, quoted in Hesseltine, *Civil War Prisons*, p. 74. "Assured him that": quoted in Hesseltine, p. 75. "I do not expect": Turner, quoted in Furgurson, *Ashes of Glory*, p. 251. "A more dreary": quoted in Pierce, "General Hugh Judson Kilpatrick in the American Civil War," p. 214. "It was a wild": quoted in V. C. Jones, *Eight Hours Before Richmond*, p. 67. "I was for the time": Kidd, *A Cavalryman With Custer*, p. 165. "Making all tight": Kidd, p. 167. "Large force of mounted infantry": *War of the Rebellion*, series 1, volume 33, p. 186.

13. RETURN THEIR FIRE!

"Daring Raid of The Enemy": *Richmond Daily Dispatch*, March 2, 1864. "Every few minutes": *War of the Rebellion*, series 1, volume 33, p. 196. "Who are you?": Dahlgren, quoted in Beaudrye, *Fifth New York Cavalry*, p. 109.

14. LIKE A PARCEL OF OLD WOMEN

"We were just getting": Halbach, quoted in Pollard, *The Lost Cause*, p.

505. "Arrived all safe": *War of the Rebellion*, series 1, volume 33, p. 197. "I have reached": *War of the Rebellion*, series 1, volume 33, p. 182. "Great Cavalry Raids": *New York Times*, March 4, 1864. "Thus ends the great raid": *Richmond Daily Dispatch*, March 4, 1864. "His highest exploit": *Richmond Daily Dispatch*, March 4, 1864. "It is impossible": *War of the Rebellion*, series 1, volume 33, p. 186. "If Colonel Dahlgren": *War of the Rebellion*, series 1, volume 33, p. 187. "Behold my prophecy": Lyman, *Meade's Headquarters, 1863–1865*, p. 79.

15. ULRIC THE HUN

"Kill Jeff Davis": Dahlgren, quoted in Hall, "The Dahlgren Papers," *Civil War Times Illustrated*, November 23, 1983, p. 33. "This means you": Davis, quoted in Hall, p. 33. "General, I have the honor": *War of the Rebellion*, series 1, volume 33, p. 217. "Some extraordinary memoranda": J. B. Jones, *A Rebel War Clerk's Diary*, p. 346. "Noted for calm judgment": Hall, p. 33. "Dear Sir": *War of the Rebellion*, series 1, volume 33, pp. 217–218. "The Last Raid": *Richmond Daily Dispatch*, March 5, 1864. "The reader will be": *Richmond Daily Dispatch*, March 5, 1864. "Are these men": *The Whig*, March 5, 1864. "Headquarters Third Division": *War of the Rebellion*, series 1, volume 33, pp. 219–220. "Soldiers, read these papers": *Richmond Inquirer*, March 5, 1864. "The papers taken from": Furgurson, *Ashes of Glory*, p. 255. "To play a dangerous game": Hines, quoted in Horan, *Confederate Agent*, p. 71. "Our soldiers should": *Daily Examiner*, March 5, 1864. "Hereafter those": Gorgas, *The Civil War Diary of General Josiah Gorgas*, p. 85. "I have reason": Jones, p. 346. "I enclose to you": *War of the Rebellion*, series 1, volume 33, p. 218.

16. AN EXPRESSION OF AGONY

"You have doubtless seen": Meade, *The Life and Letters of George Gordon Meade*, p. 170. "Poor Dahlgren is killed": Wainwright, *A Diary of Battle*, p. 334. "The Cavalry Raid": *New York Times*, March 6, 1864. "It would seem something": *Richmond Examiner*, March 8, 1864. "A small man": *The Whig*, March 7, 1864. "With a detail": Atkinson, quoted in Stuart, "Colonel Ulric Dahlgren and Richmond's Union Underground," *Virginia Magazine of History*, 1964, vol. 72, p. 155. "What would have been": *Richmond Inquirer*, March 7, 1864. "Henceforth the name": *The Whig*, March 7, 1864. "That our people and the world": *War of the Rebellion*, series 1, volume 33, p. 222. "And dropped down": Furgurson, *Ashes of Glory*, p. 254. "Go, I authorize it": Lincoln, quoted in Schneller, *A Quest For Glory*, p. 283. "May an avenging God": John Dahlgren, quoted in Schneller, p. 283. "The outrageous treatment": *War of the Rebellion*, series

1, volume 33, p. 186. "My cavalry has returned": *War of the Rebellion*, series 1, volume 33, p. 245. "Important from Richmond": *New York Times*, March 9, 1864. "Brave almost to rashness": *New York Times*, March 9, 1864. "General Kill": *New York World*, March 15, 1864. "The chief criminals": *Richmond Daily Dispatch*, March 14, 1864.

17. A PRETTY UGLY PIECE OF BUSINESS

"To travel to Toronto": Seddon, quoted in Horan, *Confederate Agent*, p. 71. "Confederate States of America": Swiggett, *The Rebel Raider*, pp. 216–217. "Exposing of its women": Benjamin, quoted in Swiggett, p. 216. "They speak for themselves": Benjamin, quoted in V. C. Jones, *Eight Hours Before Richmond*, pp. 125–126. "Careful inquiry be made": *War of the Rebellion*, series 1, volume 33, p. 175. "General": *War of the Rebellion*, series 1, volume 33. p. 175. "Testify that he published": *War of the Rebellion*, series 1, volume 33, p. 176. "Colonel Dahlgren": *War of the Rebellion*, series 1, volume 33, p. 176. "With regard to the address": *War of the Rebellion*, series 1, volume 33, p. 197. "The simple fact": *New York Times*, March 14, 1864. "The Rebel Calumny": *New York Times*, March 15, 1864. "No officer of the American": *New York Times*, March 15, 1864. "The government is in": *War of the Rebellion*, series 1, volume 33, p. 178. "General: I am instructed": *War of the Rebellion*, series 1, volume 33, p. 178. "Colonel Dahlgren received": *War of the Rebellion*, series 1, volume 33, p. 180. "In reply": *War of the Rebellion*, series 1, volume 33, p. 180. "Everybody's reputation": George, "Black Flag Warfare: Lincoln and the Raids Against Richmond and Jefferson Davis," *The Pennsylvania Magazine*, July 1991, p. 311. "This was a pretty": Meade, *The Life and Letters of George Gordon Meade*, pp. 190–191.

18. FULL AND BITTER TEARS

"Sir: I have the honor": *War of the Rebellion*, series 2, volume 6, pp. 1034–1035. "Dear Sir: I have received": *War of the Rebellion*, series 1, volume 33, p. 177. "Northern papers hint": *Richmond Examiner*, April 5, 1864. "That he knew": Atkinson, quoted in Stuart, "Colonel Ulric Dahlgren and Richmond's Union Underground," p. 157. "Would be of": Atkinson, quoted in Stuart, p. 158. "I received a sharp": Atkinson, quoted in Stuart, p. 158. "Upon going to the grave": *War of the Rebellion*, series 1, volume 33, pp. 180–181. "I have reliable information": *War of the Rebellion*, series 1, volume 33, p. 181. "The remains are not so far": *War of the Rebellion*, series 1, volume 33, p. 181. "The heart of every": Van Lew, quoted in Stuart, p. 162. "Pickling pork": Lipscomb, quoted in Stuart, p.

191. "Dahlgren's hair was very short": Van Lew, quoted in Stuart, pp. 173–174. "Wary and vigilant": Van Lew, quoted in Stuart, p. 174. "Whose peach trees": quoted in Stuart, p. 174. "It would be a pity": quoted in Stuart, p. 175. "Full and bitter tears": John Dahlgren, quoted in Schneller, *A Quest For Glory*, p. 299. "He has given limb": John Dahlgren, quoted in Schneller, p. 284. "To get abroad": Weller, quoted in Schneller, p. 286. "Had Ulric's amputated leg": Schneller, p. 284. "Occupied in collecting": John Dahlgren, quoted in Schneller, p. 286. "Dahlgren a spy": *Richmond Examiner*, June 16, 1864. "I have patiently": *New York Times*, July 28, 1864. "The document alleged": John Dahlgren, *Memoir of Ulric Dahlgren*, p. 233. "Evidence almost as positive": John Dahlgren, pp. 233, 235. "My son, my son": John Dahlgren, quoted in Schneller, p. 324. "May God scourge": John Dahlgren, quoted in Schneller, p. 324.

19. ON THE EVE OF GREAT EVENTS

"Political counterpart": Starr, *Colonel Grenfell's Wars*, p. 149. "Sir: Confiding special trust": quoted in Mancini, "Confederate Cloak and Dagger," *America's Civil War*, July 1995, p. 45. "Inclined to believe": Mancini, p. 45. "Nothing but violence": Thompson, quoted in Horan, *Confederate Agent*, p. 93. "I never encountered": Grenfell, quoted in Brown, *The Bold Cavaliers*, p. 72. "I know nothing": Grenfell, quoted in Starr, p. 41. "Colonel, if you go": quoted in Starr, p. 172.

20. A VERY RISKY VENTURE

"The 4th of July": quoted in Horan, *Confederate Agent*, p. 126.

21. BITTER, BITTER DEFEAT

"After lighting the gas jet": Headley, *Confederate Operations in Canada and New York*, pp. 274–275. "As I came back": Headley, p. 275. "For the first time": quoted in Kimmel, *The Mad Booths of Maryland*, p. 193. "They had finally": Headley, p. 279. "We, the undersigned": quoted in Headley, p. 48. "Bitter, bitter, defeat": Beall, quoted in Horan, *Confederate Agent*, p. 162. "We became enthusiastic": Headley, p. 402. "An hour and a night": Headley, p. 410. "Indicative of the intensity": Tidwell, *Come Retribution*, p. 187.

22. DESPERATE MEASURES: WHO WROTE THE DAHLGREN PAPERS?

"Now, the fact is": Blair, quoted in Varina Davis, *Jefferson Davis*, p. 472. "Had felt much the same": Varina Davis, p. 472. "They were missing": Hall, "Fact or Fabrication: The Dahlgren Papers," *Civil War Times*

Illustrated, November 22, 1983, p. 39. "Guides—pioneers": *War of the Rebellion*, series 1, volume 33, p. 179. "Pleasonton will govern": *Richmond Examiner*, April 1, 1864. "Every line and every word": Halbach, quoted in Pollard, *The Lost Cause*, pp. 505–506. "What appeared in": Fitzhugh Lee, quoted in Varina Davis, p. 471. "In conference with the": Benjamin, quoted in Richardson, *Messages and Papers of the Confederacy*, vol. II, p. 639. "The book, amongst other": *War of the Rebellion*, series 1, volume 33, p. 224. "I saw today": Gorgas, *The Civil War Diary of General Josiah Gorgas*, p. 89. "Had the same opinion": Patrick, quoted in Hall, p. 37. "Memoranda of the War": quoted in Furgurson, *Ashes of Glory*, p. 255. "Letters found on": Babcock, quoted in Furgurson, p. 255. "To complicate this": Hall, pp. 37–38. "He saw that the tail": Hall, p. 38. "With regard to the": *War of the Rebellion*, series 1, volume 33, p. 197. "I pronounce these papers": Bartley, quoted in John Dahlgren, *Memoir of Ulric Dahlgren*, p. 235. "He was most agreeable": quoted in Swiggett, *The Rebel Raider*, p. 208. "That they had heard nothing": Swiggett, p. 210. "Prepared to leave": *War of the Rebellion*, series 1, volume 33, p. 210. "I received at Old Church": *War of the Rebellion*, series 1, volume 33, p. 208. "In these grim months": Donald, *Lincoln*, p. 489.

23. THE DAHLGREN AFFAIR: AFTERMATH

"After some difficulty": quoted in Stuart, "Colonel Ulric Dahlgren and Richmond's Union Underground," p. 169. "The intense heat": John Dahlgren, *Memoir of Ulric Dahlgren*, p. 275. "Dahlgren!": Beecher, quoted in John Dahlgren, p. 285. "Few dead are honored": John Dahlgren, quoted in Schneller, *A Quest For Glory*, p. 235. "By the quick, clear click": John Dahlgren, pp. 288, 289. "That first excited": quoted in Martin, *Kill-Cavalry*, p. 233. "The Confederates galloped": Mangum, "Kill Cavalry's Nasty Surprise," *America's Civil War*, November 1996, p. 46. "Where is General Kilpatrick?": quoted in Mangum, p. 46. "Kilpatrick's shirttail": quoted in Pierce, "General Hugh Judson Kilpatrick in the American Civil War," p. 285. "Crowning indignation": Pierce, p. 286. "Envoy extraordinary": Martin, p. 238. "The Blue and the Gray": V. C. Jones, *Eight Hours Before Richmond*, pp. 142, 174. "Little Gloria": quoted in Martin, p. 267. "I would never": Thelma Morgan, quoted in Martin, p. 267. "As you are doubtless": Jefferson Davis, quoted in Horan, *Confederate Agent*, p. 28. "Years of controversy": Mancini, "Confederate Cloak and Dagger," *America's Civil War*, July 1995, p. 82. "Ere this reaches you": Beall, quoted in Headley, *Confederate Operations in Canada and New York*, p. 359. "The band struck up": Headley, p. 363. "Cut it short": quoted in Headley, p.

365. "I protest against": Beall, quoted in Headley, p. 366. "Oh, come on along": Beall, quoted in Brown, *Stringfellow of the Fourth*, p. 269. "A way station": Bakeless, *Spies of the Confederacy*, p. 122. "Many who knew him": Gindlesperger, *Escape From Libby Prison*, p. 241. "I know you": Van Lew, quoted in Kane, *Spies For the Blue and Gray*, p. 185. "We regard the selection": quoted in Ryan, p. 19. "I live here": Van Lew, quoted in Markle, *Spies and Spymasters of the Civil War*, p. 185. "I live—and have lived for years": Van Lew, quoted in Beymer, "Miss Van Lew," *Harper's Magazine*, June 1911, p. 98. "We are held": Van Lew, quoted in Ryan, p. 131. "She risked everything": quoted in Markle, *Spies and Spymasters of the Civil War*, p. 186.

Anderson, Nancy. "'Crazy Bet' Van Lew Was General Grant's Eyes and Ears in Richmond." *America's Civil War*, July 1991, pp. 8, 54–57.

Anderson, Nancy Scott, and Anderson, Dwight. *The Generals: Ulysses S. Grant and Robert E. Lee.* New York: Vintage Books, 1989.

Bakeless, John. *Spies of the Confederacy.* Philadelphia: J. B. Lippincott, 1970.

Beale, R. L. T. "Ninth Virginia Cavalry and the Dahlgren Raid." *Southern Historical Society's Papers (Richmond)*, vol. 3 (1864–1881), pp. 219–221.

Beaudrye, Louis N. *Historical Records of the Fifth New York Cavalry.* Albany, N.Y.: J. Munsell, 1868.

Beymer, William G. "Miss Van Lew." *Harper's Magazine*, June 1911, pp. 86–99.

Brockett, L. P. "Brevet Major-General Hugh Judson Kilpatrick." *United States Service Magazine*, vol. 4 (November 1865), pp. 419–430.

Brooks, Noah. *Washington in Lincoln's Time.* New York: Rinehart, 1958.

Brown, Dee A. *The Bold Cavaliers: Morgan's 2nd Kentucky Cavalry Raiders*. Philadelphia: J. B. Lippincott, 1959.

Brown, R. Shepard. *Stringfellow of the Fourth*. New York: Crown, 1960.

Catton, Bruce. *The Army of the Potomac*, Vol. III: *A Stillness at Appomattox*. Garden City, N.Y.: Doubleday, 1953.

Chesnut, Mary. *Mary Chesnut's Civil War*. New Haven: Yale University Press, 1981.

Dahlgren, Rear Admiral John A. *Memoir of Ulric Dahlgren*. Philadelphia: J. B. Lippincott, 1872.

————. Personal papers. Washington, D.C.: Library of Congress, #41824.

Davis, Varina. *Jefferson Davis: Ex-President of the Confederate States of America*. New York: Belford Company, Publishers, 1890.

Davis, William C. *Jefferson Davis: The Man and His Hour*. New York: HarperCollins, 1991.

Dawson, Gladys. "Northern 'Copperhead' Clement Vallandigham Paid a Heavy Price for Speaking Out Against the War." *America's Civil War*, March 1991, pp. 8, 69, 71–72, 74.

Denney, Robert E. *Civil War Prisons and Escapes: A Day-by-Day Chronicle*. New York: Sterling, 1993.

Donald, David Herbert. *Lincoln*. New York: Simon & Schuster, 1995.

Favill, Josiah Marshall. *The Diary of a Young Officer*. Chicago: R. R. Donnelley, 1909.

Foote, Shelby. *The Civil War*, Vol. II: *Fredericksburg to Meridan*. New York: Vintage Books, 1986.

Furgurson, Ernest B. *Ashes of Glory: Richmond at War*. New York: Alfred A. Knopf, 1996.

George, Joseph, Jr. "'Black Flag Warfare': Lincoln and the Raids Against Richmond and Jefferson Davis." *Pennsylvania Magazine of History and Biography*, vol. 65(3), July 1991, pp. 291–318.

Gindlesperger, James. *Escape from Libby Prison*. Shippensburg, Pa.: Burd Street Press, 1996.

Gorgas, Josiah. *The Civil War Diary of General Josiah Gorgas*, edited by

Frank E. Vandiver. University, Alabama: University of Alabama Press, 1947.

Hall, James O. "The Dahlgren Papers: A Yankee Plot to Kill President Davis." *Civil War Times Illustrated*, November 22, 1983, pp. 30–39.

Headley, John W. *Confederate Operations in Canada and New York*. New York: Neale Publishing Company, 1906.

Hesseltine, William B., ed. *Civil War Prisons*. Kent, Ohio: Kent State University Press, 1972.

Horan, James D. *Confederate Agent: A Discovery in History*. New York: Crown, 1954.

Howard, Hamilton Gay. *Civil War Echoes: Character Sketches and State Secrets*. Washington, D.C.: Howard Publishing Company, 1907.

Isham, Asa B. *An Historical Sketch of the Seventh Regiment, Michigan Volunteer Cavalry, 1862–1865*. New York: Town Topics Publishing Company, 1893.

Jones, John B. *A Rebel War Clerk's Diary*, condensed, edited, and annotated by Earl Schenck Miers. New York: Sagamore Press, 1958.

Jones, Katherine M. *Ladies of Richmond: Confederate Capital*. Indianapolis: Bobbs-Merrill, 1962.

Jones, Virgil C. *Eight Hours Before Richmond*. New York: Holt, 1957.

Kane, Harnett T. *Spies for the Blue and Gray*. Garden City, N.Y.: Hanover House, 1954.

Kidd, James H. *A Cavalryman with Custer: Custer's Michigan Cavalry Brigade in the Civil War*. 1908. Reprint, New York: Bantam Books, 1991.

Kimball, William J. *Richmond in Time of War*. Boston: Houghton Mifflin, 1960.

Kimmel, Stanley. *The Mad Booths of Maryland*. New York: Dover, 1969.

Klein, Frederic S. "The Great Copperhead Conspiracy." *Civil War Times Illustrated*, vol. 4, 1965, pp. 20–26.

Lee, James C. "Ordnance: The Humble Undertaker Performed a Distasteful but All Too Necessary Role During the Civil War." *America's Civil War*, November 1996, pp. 20, 22, 24.

Lee, Robert E. *The Wartime Papers of R. E. Lee*, edited by Clifford Dowdey and Louis H. Manarin. New York: Bramhall House, 1961.

Leech, Margaret. *Reveille in Washington: 1860–1865*. New York: Harper & Brothers, 1941.

Lewis, Lloyd. *It Takes All Kinds*. 1947. Reprint, Freeport, N.Y.: Books For Libraries Press, 1970.

Lewis, Lloyd. *Sherman: Fighting Prophet*. New York: Harcourt, Brace, 1958.

Lyman, Theodore. *Meade's Headquarters 1863–1865: Letters of Colonel Theodore Lyman from Wilderness to Appomattox*, selected and edited by George R. Agassiz. Boston: Atlantic Monthly Press, 1922.

Mancini, John. "Confederate Cloak and Dagger." *America's Civil War*, July 1995, pp. 45–49, 82.

Mangum, William Preston, II. "Kill Cavalry's Nasty Surprise." *America's Civil War*, November 1996, pp. 42–48.

Markle, Donald E. *Spies and Spymasters of the Civil War*. New York: Hippocrene Books, 1994.

Martin, Samuel J. *Kill-Cavalry: Sherman's Merchant of Terror: The Life of Union General Hugh Judson Kilpatrick*. Madison, N.J.: Fairleigh Dickinson University Press, 1996.

McPherson, James M. *Battle Cry of Freedom: The Civil War Era*. New York: Oxford University Press, 1988.

Meade, George. *The Life and Letters of George Gordon Meade*. New York: Charles Scribner's Sons, 1913.

Morris, Roy. "'It Can't Happen Here,' Americans Like to Believe, but During the Lincoln Administration, It Did." *America's Civil War*, March 1991, p. 6.

Moyer, H. P. *History of the Seventeenth Regiment Pennsylvania Volunteer Cavalry*. Lebanon, Pa.: Sower Printing Company, 1911.

Nevins, Allan, ed. *A Diary of Battle: The Personal Journals of Colonel Charles S. Wainwright, 1861–1865*. New York: Harcourt, Brace & World, 1962.

Peterson, C. S. *Admiral John A. Dahlgren*. New York: Hobson Book Press, 1945.

Pierce, John Edward. "General Hugh Judson Kilpatrick in the American Civil War." Ph.D. dissertation, Pennsylvania State University, 1983.

Pollard, Edward A. *The Lost Cause: A New Southern History of the War of the Confederates.* 1866. Reprint, Freeport, N.Y.: Books for Libraries Press, 1970.

Richardson, James, ed. *Messages and Papers of the Confederacy*, Vol. II. Nashville: United States Publishing Company, 1905.

Ryan, D. D., ed. *A Yankee Spy in Richmond: The Civil War Diary of "Crazy Bet" Van Lew.* Mechanicsburg, Pa.: Stackpole Books, 1996.

Schneller, Robert J., Jr. *A Quest For Glory.* Annapolis: Naval Institute Press, 1996.

Sears, Stephen W. *Chancellorsville.* Boston: Houghton Mifflin, 1996.

Sparks, David, S., ed. *Inside Lincoln's Army: The Diary of Marsena Rudolph Patrick, Provost Marshal General, Army of the Potomac.* New York: Thomas Yoseloff, 1964.

Spera, W. H. "Kilpatrick's Richmond Raid." In H. P. Moyer, *History of the Seventeenth Regiment Pennsylvania Volunteer Cavalry.* Lebanon, Pa.: Sowers Printing Company, 1911, pp. 229–260.

Starr, Stephen Z. *Colonel Grenfell's Wars: The Life of a Soldier of Fortune.* Baton Rouge: Louisiana State University Press, 1971.

———. *The Union Cavalry in the Civil War*, Vol. II: *The War in the East From Gettysburg to Appomattox 1863–1865.* Baton Rouge: Louisiana State University Press, 1981.

Stuart, Meriwether. "Colonel Ulric Dahlgren and Richmond's Union Underground, 1864." *Virginia Magazine of History and Biography*, vol. 72, 1964, pp. 152–204.

Swiggett, Howard. *The Rebel Raider: The Life of John Hunt Morgan.* Indianapolis: Bobbs-Merrill, 1934.

Thomas, Emory M. "The Kilpatrick-Dahlgren Raid," Part I. *Civil War Times Illustrated*, vol. 16, February 1978, pp. 4–9, 46–48.

———. "The Kilpatrick-Dahlgren Raid," Part II. *Civil War Times Illustrated*, vol. 17, April 1978, pp. 26–33.

Tidwell, William A. *Come Retribution: The Confederate Secret Service and the Assassination of Lincoln.* Jackson: University Press of Mississippi, 1988.

————. *April '65: Confederate Covert Action in the American Civil War.* Kent, Ohio: Kent State University Press, 1995.

Tower, R. Lockwood, ed. *Lee's Adjutant: The Wartime Letters of Colonel Walter Herron Taylor, 1862–1865.* Columbia: University of South Carolina Press, 1995.

U.S. War Department. *War of the Rebellion: A Compilation of the Official Records of the Union and Confederate Armies.* Washington, D.C.: Government Printing Office, 1880–1901.

Ward, Joseph R. C. *History of the One Hundred and Sixth Regiment Pennsylvania Volunteers, 1861–1865.* Philadelphia: Faires & Rodgers, 1906.

Warnes, Kathy. "Escape From Libby." *America's Civil War,* January 1994, pp. 55–60.

Wert, Jeffry D. *Custer: The Controversial Life of George Armstrong Custer.* New York: Simon & Schuster, 1996.

West, Richard S., Jr. *Lincoln's Scapegoat General: A Life of Benjamin F. Butler, 1818–1893.* Boston: Houghton Mifflin, 1965.

Wilson, James Harrison. *Under the Old Flag,* Vol. I. New York: Appleton, 1912.

Wright, Mike. "Humble But Observant War Department Clerk J. B. Jones Left Behind an Invaluable Account of Wartime Richmond." *America's Civil War,* January 1993, pp. 18, 20, 22, 24.

Younger, Edward, ed. *Inside the Confederate Government: The Diary of Robert Garlick Hill Kean.* Baton Rouge: Louisiana State University Press, 1985.

Index

Abolitionism, 49

Adams, Henry, 74

Allatoona (Kilpatrick), 263

Amnesty proclamation, 77, 79

Anderson, L. B., 115

Antiwar movements, 18–20, 33–35, 37–40, 42–47, 205–9, 215–18, 220–23,
   228–32

Ashes of Glory: Richmond at War (Furgurson), 248

Astor House hotel, 230

Atkinson, John Wilder, 173–74, 192–93, 256

Atlee Station, 137

Aylett's Landing, 139

Babcock, John C., 248

Bagby, Richard Hugh, 147–48

Baker, LaFayette, 76, 106, 258–59

Ballard, John, 259

Ballard House, 24, 27

Banking schemes, 235

Bank robberies, 225–27

Barnum, P. T., 230

Barnum Museum, 230–31
Bartley, Reuben, 146–48, 250, 255
Beale, R. L. T., 148, 153, 243–44, 246–47, 254
Beall, John Yates, 232–35, 267–69
Beaudrye, Louis, 142–43, 146–48
Beauregard, P. G. T., 203
Beaver Dam, 113–14
Beecher, Henry Ward, 260
Belle Isle prison camp, 32, 59–60, 65–66, 130
Bellona arsenal, 78
Benjamin, Judah P., 46, 153, 158, 180, 183, 207, 223, 224, 228, 235, 246, 266, 267
Biological warfare, 237–38
Birney, David, 80, 104, 107, 112
Blackburn, Luke, 237–38
Blacks, 38, 39, 75
Blair, Francis Preston, 239–40
Blair, Henry, 251
Booth, Edwin, 231
Booth, John Wilkes, 33, 183, 231, 264, 268, 269
Booth, Junius, 231
Bowser, Mary Elizabeth, 53, 270
Bragg, Braxton, 153, 159, 160, 210
Brandy Station, 68, 89, 91, 99, 105, 151
Brook Pike, 121–22
Brothels, 75, 76
Brown, Eliza, 104
Buchanan, James, 203
Bull Run, 50, 94, 95
Burley, Bennett, 234–35
Butler, Benjamin, 52–53, 55–56, 66, 78, 112, 131, 132, 138, 149–51, 177, 182, 190–95, 229, 232

Camp Douglas prison, 205–6, 213–14, 217, 220–21
Camp Morton prison, 220
Castleman, John, 209, 211, 214, 217–220, 222, 264–66
Catton, Bruce, 23
Cavalry charge, 89
Censorship, 30, 38–39
Chancellorsville campaign, 79, 96
Chesnut, Mary, 16, 31
Clay, Clement C., 204–5, 225–26, 266
Cleary, William, 207

Coal bombs, 40–41

Coffee substitutes, 17

Cole, Charles, 233–35

Columbus, Ohio, prison camp, 35–36

Confederate States of America:
  Diplomatic missions to Canada, 181, 203–7, 211, 223–25, 238
  Diplomatic missions to Europe, 28, 47, 183
  Secession, 94

Confederate White House, 41, 53

Conscription, 17, 19, 39

Cooke, Edwin, 142–43, 146–49

Cooper, Sam, 153, 241

Copperhead antiwar organizations, 18–20, 33–35, 39–40, 42–47, 205–9,
        215–18, 220–23, 228–32

Courier mail service, 52, 53

Custer, George Armstrong, 69, 73, 80, 104, 107, 112, 116, 125, 243–45, 248,
        252–53, 255, 256

Custer, Libby, 65, 104

Dahlgren, John, 65, 91, 94, 95, 97–99, 118, 176–77, 190–91, 193–94, 197–201,
        239–40, 255–56, 258–60

Dahlgren, Ulric, 91–104, 143, 148–51, 183–202, 207, 224, 228, 232, 233, 236
  Corpse, return and treatment of, 145–46, 160, 172–77, 190–99, 258–60

Dahlgren papers, 23, 144–45, 148, 152–60, 174, 177, 238
  Authenticity, 184–89, 199–201, 239–57

Dahlgren raid, 92, 108–9, 112–14, 117–21, 124–25, 128–30, 134–35, 137–43,
        146–48, 171–72
  See also Kilpatrick-Dahlgren raid

Danville & Richmond Railroad, 78

Davis, Henry, 123

Davis, Jefferson, 17–18, 28–30, 36, 37, 40–47, 66, 105, 116, 127, 148, 158–60,
        173–74, 179, 180, 192–93, 203–4, 224, 233, 254, 256, 265–67
  Alleged plot against, 152, 154, 156, 157, 185–89, 240–42, 245–48, 250–52

Davis, Mrs. Jefferson (Varina Howell), 31, 41, 239, 266

Dement, William, 142, 251

Democratic party, nominating convention, 205, 208, 211–12, 214
  See also Peace Democrats

Devereux, J. H., 244

Devin, Thomas, 102

Diversionary forces, 80–81, 103–4, 107, 112, 115–16, 125

Dover Mill ford, 120

Dow, Neal, 130

Draft opposition, 19, 39

Duke, Basil, 265

Early, Jubal, 249–50
Edwards, Edward W., 222
Eight Hours Before Richmond (V. Jones), 249
Ellery, Albert, 137
Ely's Ford, 105, 108
Emancipation Proclamation, 39

Food shortages, 17, 28–32, 41–42, 58, 59
Fort Sumter, 94
Fortress Monroe, 176, 190
Fox, Edward C., 141, 144, 243, 254
Fredericksburg Railroad, 78
Frederick's Hall Station, 78, 113, 116
Furgurson, Ernest, 248

George Washington's Birthday Ball, 83–90
    Confederate spy at, 87–88, 106
Gettysburg campaign, 45
Gibbs, George, 51
Gloskoski, Joseph, 109, 113, 114
Gold market, 235
Goochland Court House, 78
Gorgas, Josiah, 45, 159, 247
Grant, Ulysses S., 17, 55, 205, 208–9, 238, 261, 266, 271–72
Greek fire, 218, 226, 229–31
Greeley, Horace, 19
Green, Emma, 87
Grenfell, George St. Leger, 209–12, 214, 218, 221, 267–69
Gurney's Station, 78

Habeas corpus, 18, 19, 30, 38
Hagerstown, Maryland, battle, 96–97
Halbach, Edward W., 141, 144–45, 148, 149, 245
Hall, James, 240–41, 249
Halleck, Henry W., 112
Hampton, Wade, 27, 87, 105, 112, 113, 132–34, 137, 138, 148, 150, 253, 261–62
Hanovertown Ferry, 138
Harris, Sam, 103
Hayes, R. B., 272
Headley, John, 228–32, 236–37

Heintzelman, Samuel, 216
Henry, Patrick, 49
Hines, Thomas Henry, 33–40, 42–47, 158, 180–83, 202–12, 214–26, 232, 254,
	264–66
Hogan, Martin, 108, 149
Holcombe, James P., 204–5
Home guard troops. *See* Richmond defense forces
Hood, Sam, 31
Hooker, Joseph, 96, 97
Hotels, attacks on, 228–31
Howard, Jacob, 74, 86, 89
Humphreys, A. A., 81, 104, 184, 260
Hungary Station, 134–35, 137
Hutchinson, William, 226–27
Hyams, Godfrey, 232–34, 237–38

Immigrant laborers, 38
Inflation, 28–29, 41
Invisible ink, 52–53, 213, 216
Iron Scouts, 105–6
Island Queen (steamship), 234

Jackson, Stonewall, 233
James River crossing, 118–21
Johnson, Albert Sidney, 34
Johnson, Andrew, 260, 264, 266, 268, 269
	Kidnap attempt, 235–37
Johnson, Bradley, 113, 121, 244
Johnson, Joe, 241
Johnson's Island prison camp, 35, 233–34
Jones, Annie, 69
Jones, John (Reverend), 249
Jones, John B., 29–31, 129, 153
Jones, Virgil C., 249–50, 255
Jude's Ferry crossing, 120

Kidd, James, 68, 114, 123, 132, 133
Kilpatrick, Hugh Judson, 67–82, 86, 89, 117, 128, 138, 150, 153, 171, 176–79,
	183–86, 188–89, 247, 250, 253, 255, 260–64
	On Dahlgren papers, 185
Kilpatrick-Dahlgren raid, 68, 70, 77–79, 92, 99, 101–7, 109–10, 113–15,
	121–24, 131–35, 137, 148–51
	Advance news of, 104–5

Knights of the Golden Circle, 18
Kurtz, L. B., 110

Labor unrest, 38, 75
Langhorne, Maurice, 221
Lee, Fitzhugh H., 148, 152–53, 246–47, 253, 254
Lee, Robert E., 15, 17, 46–47, 78–80, 96, 104–7, 112–16, 152, 159, 174–75,
        187–89, 205, 208, 210, 238, 253, 255, 270
Lee, Rooney, 175
Libby prison camp, 22, 32, 48–52, 54, 57–63, 67, 119, 130–31, 175–76, 270
        Escape attempt, 60–63, 67
Lieber, Francis, 241
Lincoln, Abraham, 19, 20, 38, 64–67, 71, 74, 77–80, 151, 158, 179, 237–238
        And Dahlgren, 95–97, 99, 176, 199, 260
        Assassination, 241, 264, 269
        Reelection, 20–21, 43, 45, 180, 209, 223
Lincoln, Mrs. Abraham (Mary Todd), 64
Lind, Jenny, 49
Lipscomb, Martin Meredith, 194–95
Littlepage, William, 141, 144–45, 148
Lohmann, F. W. E., 194–95, 259
Lohmann, John, 195
Longuemare, Emile, 44, 228–29, 231
Lyman, Theodore, 81, 151, 178

Maine, raid on, 224–25
Mantapike Hill, 141, 148–49
Marmaduke, Vincent, 222
Marshall, John, 49
Marsten, Sally, 87–88
Martin, Cornelius, 145, 259
Martin, Robert, 228–30, 232, 236–37
Mattaponi River crossing, 139–40, 146
Maughan, John, 219
Mayo, Joseph, 29–30
McAnerny, John, 130
McClellan, George B., 223
McDowell, Irvin, 72
McEntee, John, 247–48, 251
Meade, George G., 15, 69, 70, 74, 77, 79–81, 85, 88, 102, 105, 109, 110, 112,
        125–26, 137, 150, 171, 184–90, 255, 260
Memminger, Christopher, 51
Michigan (Union warship), 232, 234–35, 269
Mitchell, John, 117, 120, 125, 134–35, 137–38, 157, 186, 199, 242, 250, 252, 255

Morgan, John Hunt, 24, 31, 33–37, 39, 42, 44–45, 47, 181–82, 206–10
Morse (Union gunboat), 176
Mt. Carmel Church, 78
Mudd, Samuel, 268–69
Murray, Thomas, 25–28, 31–32, 173, 199
   See also Dahlgren, Ulric

Naval blockade, 28
New York City, raid on, 228–32
New York Herald (newspaper), 115
New York Times (newspaper), 65–66, 96, 97, 149–50, 172, 178–79, 186–87, 199
New York Tribune (newspaper), 109
New York World (newspaper), 179
News censorship, 30, 38–39
Niblo's Garden Theatre, 231
Northwest conspiracy, 37–40, 42–47, 158–59, 180–83, 202–24, 238
   Financing of, 182–83, 215

Old Church, 134, 138
Orange & Alexandria Railroad, 105
Order of the American Knights, 18, 39
Orrock, Robert, 197
Ould, Robert, 190–93

Palmer, Charles, 55
Pamunkey River crossing, 138–39
Patrick, Marsena, 247–48
Paul, E. A., 97, 178, 186–87, 250, 255
Peace Democrats, 18–19, 38, 42–46
Peace negotiations, 17, 43, 239
Petersburg & Richmond Railroad, 78
Petersburg siege, 208, 223
Philo Parsons (steamship), 234–35
Pleasonton, Alfred, 74, 77, 79–80, 102, 109, 149, 151, 171, 184, 244
Poe, Edgar Allan, 49
Pollard, James, 139–41, 144, 148, 152, 153, 245–46, 253, 254, 259
Price, Sterling, 237
Prisoners of war:
   Confederate, 17, 35–36, 42, 175, 182, 213–14, 220, 233
   Exchanges and paroles, 17, 26, 176
   Union, 17, 20, 55, 63–67, 77, 136, 147, 175, 233
   See also Belle Isle; Libby prison camp
Privateering raids, 233
Profiteering, 28, 75

Racism, 38

Ransom, John, 59

Rapidan River army camps, 15–16, 24–25, 83

Revere, Paul, 272

Richmond:
   Defense forces, 27–28, 55–56, 107, 115, 128–30, 136–37, 141–42
   Wartime conditions, 24–32, 40

Richmond Daily Dispatch (newspaper), 136, 150, 154–55, 179

Richmond Examiner (newspaper), 23, 156–57, 159, 191, 199

Richmond House hotel, 209, 211, 212, 215

Richmond Inquirer (newspaper), 157, 174

Richmond Sentinel (newspaper), 171

Richmond Whig (newspaper), 155–56, 174

Rise and Fall of the Confederate Government (J. Davis), 267

Robinson, Martin, 118–20

Rock Island prison camp, 217

Rose, Thomas Ellwood, 57–58, 60–63, 176, 270

Rowley, William S., 195–97

Sabot Hill plantation, 117, 120

Sanders, George, 225–26, 228, 232

Schofield, John, 241

Scott, Hugh, 105, 109, 112, 133

Secret Service (Confederate), 27, 42, 53, 55, 63, 76, 105–6, 173, 193

Secret Service (Union), 19–20, 33, 39, 76, 106, 258–59

Seddon, James A., 46–47, 130, 153, 159, 174–75, 180–82, 207, 223, 224, 267

Seddon, Mrs. James A. (Sallie Bruce), 118–20

Sedgwick, John, 80, 103, 107, 112

"Seeing the elephant," 25

Seward, W. H., 179, 262

Shailer, Alice, 71–73

Shanks, James, 221

Sheridan, Philip H., 230

Sherman, William T., 70, 208, 223, 230, 261

Shipping, attacks on, 218, 232–35

Sigel, Franz, 95–96

Slavery, 37–39, 49–50, 75

Slidell, John, 183

Smallpox epidemic, 41

Smith, Channing, 105

Songs, 16

Sons of Liberty, 18, 39, 228–231

Spera, W. H., 102–3

Spies. *See* Secret Service
Spottswood Hotel, 27
Spottsylvania Court House, 110
Sproule, Nancy, 34, 158, 223, 264–65
St. John's Church, 49, 63
Stanton, Edwin M., 56, 77, 80, 95, 149, 158, 182, 198, 210, 225, 228, 241, 262, 264, 266, 269
Starvation parties, 31
Stephens, Alexander, 17
Stevens, Walter, 128
Stringfellow, Frank, 87–88, 106, 269–70
Stuart, J. E. B., 24, 31, 69, 87, 107, 125, 210
Surratt, Mary, 269
Sweeney, John, 137
Sweet, Benjamin, 213–14, 216, 221–22

Tanner, Dan, 105, 109, 112, 133
Telegraph communications, 78, 79, 113, 233
Terrorist activities. *See* Northwest conspiracy
Thompson, Jacob, 203–7, 211, 215, 223, 233, 235, 236, 238, 264, 266
Todd, David, 50–51
Transports, attacks on, 218
Tunstall Station, 138
Turner, Thomas, 131

Ulric the Hun, 156, 173, 191, 207, 240, 258
    See also Dahlgren, Ulric

Vallandigham, Clement, 20, 206–7, 269
Van Lew, Elizabeth, 48–56, 58, 62–63, 66–67, 127, 128, 173, 182, 194–98, 259, 270–72
Vicksburg campaign, 45, 98
Virginia Central Railroad, 78, 113, 136

Wages, 28–29, 41, 75
Wainwright, Charles, 70, 73, 171
Walker, Thaddeus, 24–27, 32, 173, 199
Walsh, Charles, 205–6, 216–18, 221, 223
War of the Rebellion: Official Records, 241, 252
Warehouses, attacks on, 218
Washington, D. C.:
    Navy Yard, 94, 95, 198
    Wartime conditions, 74–76, 94–95

Welles, Sumner, 198
Westham, 117, 121, 129
White House, 64–65, 76–77, 95, 99
White House of the Confederacy, 41, 53
Willard's Hotel, 81–82
Winder, John Henry, 27, 51, 53, 55, 63, 76, 130, 173, 193, 199
Winter Garden Theatre, 231
Wistar, Isaac, 66, 177
Women:
    In food riots, 29–30
    In Southern society, 48–52
    At Washington's Birthday Ball, 85–86

Yellow fever epidemic, 237–38, 268–69
Young, Bennett, 226–27, 264